THE SPACE AND MOT
COMMUNICATING A

The world is increasingly populated with interactive agents distributed in space, real or abstract. These agents can be artificial, as in computing systems that manage and monitor traffic or health; or they can be natural, e.g. communicating humans, or biological cells. It is important to be able to model networks of agents in order to understand and optimise their behaviour. Robin Milner's purpose is to describe in this book just such a model, and he does so by presenting a unified and rigorous structural theory, based on bigraphs, for systems of interacting agents. This theory is a bridge between the existing theories of concurrent processes and the aspirations for ubiquitous systems, whose enormous size challenges our understanding.

The book begins with an assessment of the problems that a structural model for distributed communicating systems must address. Bigraphs are introduced first informally, then rigorously, before being used to describe the configuration of component agents. The static theory of Part I gives way in Part II to examining the dynamics of interactions, leading to the notion of behavioural equivalence and its consequences.

The final Part explores a number of developments, in particular with regard to ubiquitous computing and biological systems. Ideas for future research and applications are presented. The book is reasonably self-contained mathematically, and is designed to be learned from: examples and exercises abound, solutions for the latter are provided.

Like Milner's other work, this is destined to have far-reaching and profound significance.

THE SPACE AND MOTION OF COMMUNICATING AGENTS

ROBIN MILNER

University of Cambridge

CAMBRIDGE
UNIVERSITY PRESS

CAMBRIDGE UNIVERSITY PRESS
Cambridge, New York, Melbourne, Madrid, Cape Town, Singapore, São Paulo, Delhi

Cambridge University Press
The Edinburgh Building, Cambridge CB2 8RU, UK

Published in the United States of America by Cambridge University Press, New York

www.cambridge.org
Information on this title: www.cambridge.org/9780521490306

First published 2009

Printed in the United Kingdom at the University Press, Cambridge

A catalogue record for this publication is available from the British Library

ISBN 978-0-521-49030-6 hardback
ISBN 978-0-521-73833-0 paperback

to My Family:
Lucy, Barney, Chloë,
and in Memory of Gabriel

Contents

Prologue

The informatic challenge

Computing is transforming our environment. Indeed, the term 'computing' describes this transformation too narrowly, because traditionally it means little more than 'calculation'. Nowadays, artifacts that both calculate and communicate pervade our lives. It is better to describe this combination as 'informatics', connoting not only the passive stuff (numbers, documents, ...) with which we compute, but also the activity of informing, or interacting, or communicating.

The stored-program computer, which sowed the seeds of this transformation 60 years ago, is itself a highly organised informatic engine specialised to the task of calculation. Computers work by *internal* communication among their parts; no-one expected that, within half a century, most of their work – bar highly specialised applications – would involve *external* communication. But within 25 years arose networks of interacting computers; the control of interaction then became a prime concern. Interacting systems, such as the worldwide web or networks of people with phones, are now commonplace; software takes part in them, but most prominent is communication, not calculation.

These artifacts will be everywhere. They will control driverless motorway traffic, via communication among sensors and effectors at the roadside and in vehicles; they will monitor and treat our health via communication between devices installed in the human body and software in hospitals. Thus the term 'ubiquitous computing' represents a vision that is being realised.[1] In 1994 Mark Weiser, a pioneer of this vision, wrote[2]

Populations of computing entities will be a significant part of our environment, performing tasks that support us, and we shall be largely unaware of them.

---

[1] The terms 'ubiquitous' and 'pervasive' mean roughly the same when applied to computing. I shall only use 'ubiquitous'.

[2] Citations of related work will be found in Chapter 12.

This suggests that informatic behaviour is just one of the kinds of phenomena that impinge upon us. Other kinds are physical, chemical, meteorological, biological, ..., and we have a good understanding of them, thanks to an evolved culture of scientific concepts and engineering principles. But understanding still has to evolve for the behaviour of a population of informatic entities; we have not the wisdom to dictate the appropriate concepts and principles once and for all, however well we understand the individual artifacts that make up the population.

This understanding is unlikely to evolve in large steps. The qualities we shall attribute to ubiquitous systems are extraordinarily various and complex. Such a system, or its component agents, will be *self-aware*, possess *beliefs* about their environments, possess *goals*, enter *negotiation* to achieve goals, and be able to *adapt* to changing circumstances without human intervention. Here is an incomplete list (in alphabetical order) of concepts or qualities, all of which will be used to specify and analyse the behaviour of ubiquitous systems:

agent, authenticity, belief, connectivity, continuous space, data protection, delegation, duty, encapsulation, failure management, game theory, history, knowledge, intelligence, intention, interaction, latency, locality, motion, negotiation, protocol, provenance, route, security, self-management, specification, transaction, trust, verification, workflow.

Much has been written about principles and methods of system design that can realise these qualities, and much experimental work done in that direction. That body of work is one part of the background for this book, and is discussed in greater detail – with citations – in Chapter 12.

The design task for ubiquitous systems is all the harder because they will be at least an order of magnitude larger than present-day software systems, and even these have often been rendered inscrutable by repeated ad hoc adaptation. Yet ubiquitous systems are expected to *adapt themselves without going offline* (since we shall depend upon their continuous operation). It is therefore a compelling scientific challenge to understand them well enough to gain confidence in their performance. This has been adopted as one of the Grand Challenges for Computing Research by the UK Computing Research Committee.

Looking at our list of system qualities in greater detail, we notice that some are more sophisticated, or 'higher-level', than others. Some, such as trust, are properties normally attributed to humans, not to artifacts. But when an assertion such as 'A trusts B' is made at a high level of modelling, we expect it to be realised at a lower level by A's behaviour; for example, A may grant B's requests on the basis of evidence of B's past behaviour.[3] If a stratification of modelling can be achieved by such realisations, then the task of description and design of ubiquitous systems will become tractable.

---

[3] A behaviourist philosopher might insist that this is the *meaning* of 'A trusts B', even for humans.

To model ubiquitous systems of artifacts will be hard enough. But, as the reader may already be thinking, such systems will also contain natural organisms. They will occur at dramatically different levels; we already mentioned people with phones, and we should also include more elementary biological entities. We should seek to model not only interactive behaviour among artificial agents, but also interaction with and among natural agents. Ultimately our informatic modelling should merge with, and enrich, natural science.

Space

Where can we start, in building a stratified model of ubiquitous systems? The key term here is 'stratified'. The agents of a ubiquitous system stand to it in the same relation as musical instruments stand to an orchestra. Instruments existed long before orchestras; how to combine them in groups and then into the whole would have puzzled the early virtuosi of each instrument. It would have gradually emerged how the physical qualities of each instrument would combine to realise qualities of the group; for example, how the tone-colours of different wind instruments would yield the more abstract quality of tenderness, or of humour, in a wind quartet. Thus gradually emerges the huge spectrum of qualities of a whole orchestra.

Where this analogy becomes strained is in the brute fact of *size*; a ubiquitous system will involve millions of agents, whereas an orchestra has a mere hundred instruments.

Let us return to stratification. In a ubiquitous system, a quality attributed to a larger subsystem must be realised by simpler properties of smaller subsystems or of individual components. This realisation, in turn, surely depends on how the system and its subsystems are constructed. So, to realise system qualities, we must first understand possible structures for ubiquitous systems. We may be grateful for this conclusion; it poses a challenge more accessible than that of realising human-like qualities in a machine. Structure is itself difficult, especially for systems that will reorganise their own structure. But one can at least make proposals about the possible ingredients of structure, without being bewildered by the immense range of behavioural qualities that it will support.

This book works out such a proposal. It starts from the recognition that a notion of *discrete space* is shared by existing informatic science on the one hand and imminent ubiquitous systems on the other. This space involves just three of the concepts listed above: *agent*, *locality* and *connectivity*. When we come to reconfiguration of the space we must consider two more of those concepts: *motion* and *interaction*.

At this point, the reader may object: 'How can you be sure that we can base our understanding of system behaviour on these concepts? You aim to explain systems that have some of the intelligence of humans, and these chosen concepts are at the level of the basic structure of matter! Your proposal is analogous to claiming that we can base our understanding of the brain on chemistry.' The simple answer is: I am *not* sure that these concepts are sufficient; but I do claim they are necessary. Brain researchers are faced with a task harder than ours in many ways; but they are fortunate that much chemistry was known before brain research began. We, on the other hand, have work to do to formulate the analogue of chemistry for ubiquitous systems.

Let us now turn to discussing a space of agents, based upon locality and connectivity. Since these ideas pervade the whole book, we shall denote them by the simpler words *placing* and *linking*. It is instructive to reflect how placing and linking run through existing informatics. Even before the stored-program computer, calculation depended on ways to organise space – not the space of Euclidean geometry, but a discrete space involving properties like adjacency and containment. Arabic numerals use one-dimensional placing to represent the power of digits; this allows two-dimensional placing to be used to arrange data in the basic numerical algorithms – addition, multiplication, and so on. Algorithms for solving differential equations with a manual calculator deployed the use of placing for data and calculation in sophisticated ways.

In stored-program computers the space became more refined. Programs use one storage register to 'point at' another; that is, an integer variable is used to index through a sequence of elements (where previously a human calculator would run his or her finger through the sequence). Thus linking became distinct from simple properties of placing, such as adjacency or containment. Placing and linking became independent; for example, an element *placed* within an array can be *linked* to something else occupying a distant place.

It is striking that wireless networks allow us similarly to think of linking as independent of physical placing in ubiquitous systems. We assume this independence when we describe the internet. Moreover placing and linking can be either physical or virtual; we even mix the two within a single system, using the relationships of physical entities as metaphors for relating the virtual ones. These metaphors abound in our vocabulary for software: flow chart, location, send and fetch, pointer, nesting, tree, etc. Concurrent computing expands the vocabulary further: distributed system, remote procedure call, network, routing, etc.

Motion

Any model of ubiquitous systems based on placing and linking, whether of physical or virtual entities or both, must accommodate motion and interaction. In fact it is unsatisfactory to separate these two concepts, so I tend to conflate them. (In moving into a room, I can be said to interact with the room.) The picture below illustrates a mixture of the physical with the virtual; it also shows how a system may reconfigure itself.

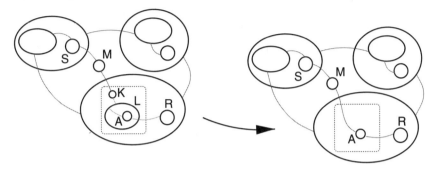

It represents a change of state in which a message M moves one step closer to its destination. The three largest nodes may represent countries, or buildings, or software agents. In each case the sender S of the message is in one, and the receiver R in another. The message is en route; the link from M back to S indicates that the message carries the sender's address. M handles a key K that unlocks a lock L, reaching an agent A that will forward the message to R. This unlocking can be represented by a *reaction rule*; such rules define how a part of the system may change both its placing and its linking. A rule that defines the above reconfiguration is as follows:

Here, both key and lock are virtual; but of course physical reconfiguration can happen in the same system. For example, at any time the (physical) receiver R may move away from her location. Can the message chase R and catch her up? Perhaps some interaction between her and the forwarding agent A makes this possible. Indeed, as she goes, R may construct an informatic record of her (physical) journey, and send it back to assist the forwarding agent. So there is no doubt that a model of space and interaction has to coordinate informatic and physical entities.

I shall show that these diagrams, and their reconfiguration, are a presentation of a rigorous theory. I aim to develop that theory to the point that it can begin to underlie experiments with real systems, and so form the basis for theories that deal with the more subtle notions mentioned above, such as beliefs, self-awareness and adaptability.

The bigraph model

The graphical structures we have just illustrated will be called *bigraphs*. Like an ordinary graph, a bigraph has nodes and edges, and the edges link the nodes. But unlike an ordinary graph, the nodes can be nested inside one another. So a bigraph has *link* structure and *place* structure; hence the prefix 'bi' in bigraph.[4] Bigraphs will be introduced with more detail in Chapter 1, but a few comments will be helpful here:

(i) The two structures – placing and linking – will be treated independently in the basic theory of bigraphs. This accords with our observation that both pointers in computer programs and wireless links in the real world can arbitrarily cross place boundaries. This independence property has another benefit; when first introduced, it was found to simplify the theory of bigraphs dramatically.

(ii) The reader may ask 'What is the space in which bigraphs live and move?' The answer is that bigraphs themselves *are* the space of the model. My proposal is that this notion of space is enough to represent an enormous range of structures. Experiment with this simple space will reveal whether and when a more complex space is required.

(iii) A single bigraph may represent both virtual and physical entities (a country, a message, ...). This may seem surprising, but creates no difficulty; indeed, it is very convenient. To push our example a little further, imagine that the receiver R is a traveller who carries a laptop in which she makes a schematic map of the places she visits. This physical laptop is then represented by a node in the bigraph, and the virtual structure (the map) it contains may be represented by the contents of that node.

Generality

Let us now discuss the degree of generality achieved by bigraphs. Will they serve as a platform for building ubiquitous systems? To answer this we must present the bigraph model as a design tool, to be used not only for analysis but even as a programming language; then experiments can be done to reveal its power and generality.

But to establish the model as a candidate for this long-term role, we must first make sure that it accommodates, or generalises, already existing theories of interactive agents. This shorter-term challenge is more well-defined. We must encode

---

[4] The term 'bigraph', as used here, was introduced in 2001. I recently found that the term was already used then as a synonym for 'bipartite graph', a well-established notion in graph theory. The meanings differ, but the use of the same term is unlikely to cause confusion.

each previous model – including its rules of interaction – into bigraphs. Indeed bigraphs should not only represent the agents and reactions of previous models; they should also provide theory that applies uniformly to those models. In other words, bigraphs should tend to unify theories of processes.

This book gives priority to the latter challenge: to generalise existing process models. Therefore in Chapter 12, the final chapter, I explain how bigraphs have drawn ideas from preceding models, and were developed in order to strengthen and generalise their theory. The result has been positive. To give perspective, I give a brief summary here. (A little familiarity with process models will be helpful in the next paragraph, but it can be skipped.)

Each process model (for example Petri nets, CSP, mobile ambients, π-calculus) defines processes syntactically, and then presents its rules of interaction. Thus each model is represented in bigraphs by two parameters: a *sorting discipline* – which includes a *signature* – that makes the bigraphs represent the model's formal entities, and a set of *reaction rules* to represent their behaviour. These two parameters yield a *bigraphical reactive system* (BRS) that is specific to the model. BRSs for several process models are presented in the book. Often the agreement with the model is exact; in other cases nearly exact. It is worth making specific points:

(i) For the purpose of both analysis and programming, many existing models have a convenient algebraic (i.e. modular) representation of processes. In bigraphs there is a uniform algebraic presentation, and this bears a close relation to that of existing models. Thus bigraphs contribute uniformity of expression.

(ii) Some calculi, including CCS and the π-calculus, define what it means for two processes to behave alike. This is called *behavioural equivalence*. A typical example is bisimilarity. Such an equivalence is usually a congruence – i.e. it is preserved by insertion of the processes into any environment. The proof of congruence has typically been somewhat ad hoc. Bigraphs provide a degree of uniformity here; in bigraphs not only do we treat bisimilarity uniformly across process calculi, but we also provide a uniform proof of congruence.

(iii) For most of the book we retain the full independence of placing and linking; this yields most of the results. However Section 11.3 defines uniformly a way to relax this independence; it defines how to localise a link and thereby to represent the *binding* of a name; this has allowed us to handle (for example) the π-calculus.

Thus the aim to generalise or subsume existing process calculi serves as a focus for developing our model. But these very calculi not only aspire to an engineering role, as a means to express and analyse the design of complex systems;

they also aspire to advance the fundamental science of informatics. They represent a challenge to the models of computation that were dominant in the twentieth century. By exposing computation as an especially disciplined form of informatic behaviour, they have opened the way to a science of such behaviour in which the determinacy and hierarchy found in traditional computing are the exception, not the rule. They replace calculational structure with communicational structure.

This book can therefore be seen as advancing the science of communicational structures. By working in the explicit model of bigraphs, I also attempt to bridge between this science and the engineering of large future informatic systems. My hope is that, with this foundation, models of such future systems can be built in a principled way. To tackle substantial examples of these models in detail would have expanded the present book unreasonably. Furthermore, to submit such models to analysis and experiment will demand a variety of software tools based upon our theory. Such tools are already being developed – see below under 'Deployment' – and their existence will create a strong incentive to build large experimental models; these will, in turn, subject our theory to severe test.

Modelling of the present kind aspires to build a bridge from informatic science not only to the engineering of new artifacts, but to the study of natural systems. In other words, it extends the repertoire of models available to natural scientists. For example, with the help of a stochastic treatment of interaction we are able to apply the bigraphical model to the predictive analysis of biological systems. This application is explained a little more in Section 11.4.

Rigour

Working at a broad frontier of informatics, spanning science and engineering, demands prioritisation; as I have already stated, it lies beyond the scope of a single book both to explore all possible applications (natural and artificial) and to establish a model in full detail. I have chosen to do the latter because, as we saw in the preceding section, there already exist many precise models in the form of process calculi, and they pose an accessible challenge – to recover them as instances of a more impartial study. This challenge, to establish commonality among existing formal models, must itself be addressed formally if we are to make it a firm platform on which to tackle a still wider range of applications. But I have interleaved formal development with discussion, and have not relied on previous knowledge of any particular mathematical theory.

I use the medium of category theory, but the level at which I use it is elementary, and I define every categorical concept that I use. Large informatic systems are complex, and any rigorous model must control this complexity by means of adequate structure. After many years seeking such models, I am convinced that categories provide this structure most convincingly. It is true that they can also express deep mathematical abstractions, many of which at present lie beyond the interest of informatic scientists. But there is a sharp division of motive between pursuing these abstractions per se and using categorical primitives as a means to understand informatic structure. The work in this book is of the latter kind. Readers familiar with categories will follow their use here without difficulty; others who wish to tame informatic structure may find this work a pleasant way to learn some mathematics suited to that purpose.

Models are built to aid people's understanding, and different people seek different levels of understanding. Engineering scientists seek a rigorous model; software designers seek something softer, but with equal intuitions, and this is even more true for their client companies and for end-users. So we would like to know that softer models of communicating agents can arise from our rigorous model. Fortunately, by their very nature these systems involve a concept of space, which is reflected in the idea of bigraphs and lends itself to informal understanding based upon diagrams. Throughout the book I work as much as possible with bigraphical diagrams; they express the rigorous ideas but do not replace them.

Deployment

It is one thing to develop a rigorous model; quite another thing to bring it into use by those concerned mainly with applications. But this usage is a primary goal for our model; moreover, it is only by deploying the model in applications that we can subject it to stringent testing.

Even protypical applications tend to be complex; one need only think of phenomena in ubiquitous computing and in biology. It follows that software tools are essential for exploring the efficacy of the model, both for scientific analysis and for advanced software engineering. Such tools have several roles: in *programming* and *specifying* complex systems; in *simulating them*, with the help of stochastic dynamics; and in *visualising* them at various levels of abstraction, exploiting the graphical presentation inherent in the model.

Work in these directions is under way at the IT University (ITU) in Copenhagen, as outlined in Chapter 12. A strategy exists for modular tool development, which can proceed in collaboration among different institutions. I would be glad to hear from anyone willing to contribute seriously to this development.

Outline of the book

Bigraphs are developing in various ways. All these developments are based upon *pure* bigraphs: those in which the independence of placing and linking is strictly maintained. So most of the book is devoted to pure bigraphs, whose theory is more or less settled. Part I presents their structure; Part II handles their behaviour; and Part III deals with their development, past and future.

In Part I, Chapter 1 introduces bigraphs starting from standard notions in graph theory. The main idea of bigraphs is to treat the placing and the linking of their nodes as independently as possible. Chapter 2 defines bigraphs formally, together with the operations that build them; it then introduces various kinds of category that will help to develop their theory. Chapter 3 develops the algebra of bigraphs, with operations for both placing and linking; it also derives operations familiar from process calculi. Chapter 4 defines relative pushouts, a categorical tool for structural analysis. Chapter 5 applies this tool to bigraphs, preparing for the later derivation of transitions. Chapter 6 develops a sorting discipline for bigraphs that is reminiscent of many-sorted algebra.

In Part II, Chapter 7 defines the notion of a wide reactive system (WRS), more general than bigraphs. For such systems it defines reaction rules and derives (labelled) transition systems; it then obtains important results such as the congruence of bisimilarity. WRSs have an abstract notion of space, enough to allow reaction to be confined to certain places. Chapter 8 specialises this work to bigraphs, yielding the more refined notions of a bigraphical reactive system (BRS) and its transition systems; it also identifies certain well-behaved kinds of BRS. Chapter 9 uses link graphs, a simplified version of the theory, to analyse behaviour in arithmetic nets and Petri nets. Chapter 10 applies bigraphs to CCS, and recovers its original theory.

In Part III, Chapter 11 discusses several developments beyond pure bigraphs. First, it examines how to *track* the identity of agents through interaction; this would allow one to express, and to verify, assertions about a BRS such as 'Each agent receives each message at most once' or 'Mary has visited three rooms since she entered the building'. Second, it proposes a generic way to represent agents with infinite behaviour using finite bigraphs, with the help of rules for structural *growth*. Third, it discusses how to constrain placing and linking so that certain links have *scope*, or are *bound*, in the familiar way that variables in a programming language have scope or are bound as formal parameters of a procedure. Finally, it summarises recent work on the *stochastic* interpretation of bigraphical systems; this is essential for simulating nondeterministic systems, in particular in biological applications, where the more likely of two possible reactions is that which is attributed the higher rate in an exponential distribution.

Chapter 12 outlines how bigraphs have developed, and discusses related work with full citations. These show how much the work of this book owes to my close colleagues, as well as to influences from other research initiatives.

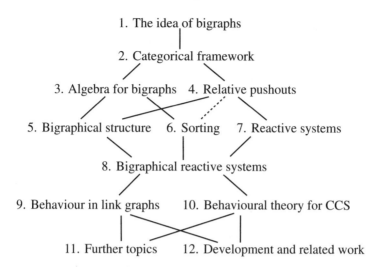

Fig. 0.1. Dependency among the chapters

Using the book

The chapters need not be read in strict sequence. Mostly, later chapters point back to what they need from earlier ones. Figure 0.1 gives a guide to the dependency among chapters. For example if you reach Chapter 8 by going down the left side, you read about bigraphs and then get the theory when you need it; if you reach it down the right side you stay at the general level of reactive systems as long as possible. Leaping ahead may also be useful; for example, those who know something of process calculi may leap from Chapter 1 to Chapter 10, to gain motivation for returning to the intervening chapters.

The book is suitable for teaching yourself; there are many exercises, and solutions to all of them. It can also be used for a Masters' course, where the amount of theory included can be adapted to the students' knowledge. Parts are appropriate for an optional final year Undergraduate course.

The book can also serve as the foundation for a lecture course that concentrates upon the intuition of bigraphs and upon exploring their application. I have designed such a course; from my website, http://www.cl.cam.ac.uk/~rm135, the reader may download a sequence of 70 or more slides that I have used. Accompanying them is (or, at the time of writing, will soon be) a slide-by-slide narrative, linking the slides together and making copious reference to this book – especially for locating the underlying rigorous development. This combination of slides and narrative will evolve in response to my own experience, and to the experience of others who use them. I shall be delighted to receive comments by email (rm135@cam.ac.uk) from anyone, based on such experience; thus I hope to improve the slides, the book and ultimately the theory itself.

Acknowledgements

I owe much to early collaboration on bigraphs with Jamey Leifer and Ole Høgh Jensen. I am most grateful for their creative insights. I thank Philippa Gardner and Peter Sewell for important contributions in work that led from action structures (a previous model) to bigraphs. Several people have generously given time to careful reading, helping me to express things better: Samson Abramsky, Mikkel Bundgaard, Troels Damgaard, Marcelo Fiore, Sam Staton and David Tranah.

I also thank warmly all those I have worked with, or learnt from, in this subject over nearly 30 years, in particular: Martín Abadi, Samson Abramsky, Jos Baeten, Martin Berger, Jan Bergstra, Gérard Berry, Lars Birkedal, Clive Blackwell, Gérard Boudol, Mikkel Bundgaard, Ilaria Castellani, Luca Cardelli, Adriana Compagnoni, Troels Damgaard, Rocco De Nicola, Hartmut Ehrig, Marcelo Fiore, Philippa Gardner, Arne Glenstrup, Andy Gordon, Matthew Hennessy, Thomas Hildebrandt, Jane Hillston, Yoram Hirshfeld, Tony Hoare, Kohei Honda, Alan Jeffrey, Ole Høgh Jensen, Jan-Willem Klop, Jean Krivine, Cosimo Laneve, Kim Larsen, Jamey Leifer, Alex Mifsud, George Milne, Kevin Mitchell, Faron Moller, Ugo Montanari, Uwe Nestmann, Mogens Nielsen, Catuscia Palamidessi, David Park, Joachim Parrow, Carl-Adam Petri, Benjamin Pierce, Gordon Plotkin, John Power, Sylvain Pradalier, K.V.S. Prasad, Corrado Priami, Michael Sanderson, Davide Sangiorgi, Vladi Sassone, Peter Sewell, Mike Shields, Sam Staton, Bernhard Steffen, Colin Stirling, Chris Tofts, Angelo Troina, David Turner, Rob Van Glabbeek, Bjorn Victor, David Walker, Glynn Winskel, Nobuko Yoshida.

I acknowledge the Préfecture of the Île-de-France Region for the award of a Blaise Pascal International Research Chair, which enabled me to advance this work during a recent year in Paris. I warmly thank Jean-Pierre Jouannaud and Catuscia Palamidessi, who were my welcoming hosts at École Polytechique at Saclay during this period.

Part I :   Space

Part 1: Space

1

The idea of bigraphs

In this chapter we develop the notion of a *bigraph* from the simple idea that it consists of two independent structures on the same set of nodes.

To prepare for the formal Definitions 1.1–2.7, we start informally from two well-known concepts: a *forest* is a set of rooted trees; and a *hypergraph* consists of a set of nodes, together with a set of edges each linking any number of nodes.

Idea *A bigraph with nodes V and edges E has a forest whose nodes are V; it also has a hypergraph with nodes V and edges E.*

Let us call an entity with this structure a *bare bigraph*. We shall use $\breve{F}, \breve{G}$ to stand for bare bigraphs. Here is a bare bigraph $\breve{G}$ having nodes $V = \{v_0, \ldots, v_5\}$ and edges $E = \{e_0, e_1, e_2\}$, with its forest and hypergraph:

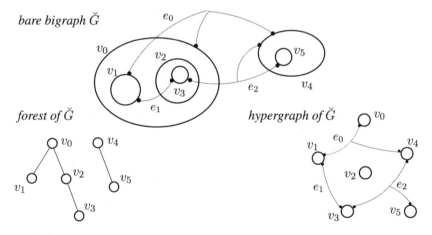

The upper diagram presents both the forest and the hypergraph; it depicts the forest by nesting. The lower two diagrams represent the two structures separately, in a conventional manner. The *children* of each node are the nodes immediately below

3

it in the forest (i.e. immediately within it, in the upper diagram). Thus v_1 and v_2 are children of v_0, which is their *parent*.

An edge is represented by connected thin lines; $\check{G}$ has two edges that each connect three nodes, and one that connects two nodes. The points at which an edge impinges on its nodes are called *ports*, shown as black blobs.[1]

We now add further structure to a bare bigraph. It will allow bigraphs to be composed, and will allow one bigraph to be considered as a component of another. Here is $\check{F}$, informally a 'part' of $\check{G}$, having only some of its nodes and with one hyperlink broken. Can we call it a component of $\check{G}$?

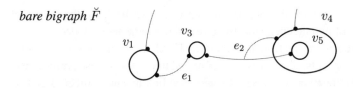

To make it so, we add *interfaces* to bare bigraphs, thus extending $\check{F}$ and $\check{G}$ into bigraphs F and G. This will allow us to represent the occurrence of F as a component of G by an equation $G = H \circ F$, where H is some 'host' or contextual bigraph. We do this extension independently for forests and hypergraphs; a forest with interfaces will be called a *place graph*, and a hypergraph with interfaces will be called a *link graph*.

Let us illustrate with the bare bigraph $\check{F}$. A place graph interface will be a natural number n, which we shall treat as a finite ordinal, the set $n = \{0, 1, \dots, n{-}1\}$ whose members are all preceding ordinals. A place graph's *outer* and *inner* interfaces – or *faces* as we shall call them – index respectively its *roots* and its *sites*. For the forest of $\check{F}$ we choose the outer face $3 = \{0, 1, 2\}$, providing distinct roots as parents for the nodes v_1, v_3 and v_4. For the inner face of $\check{F}$ we choose 0, i.e. it has no sites. This extends the forest to a place graph $F^{\mathsf{P}} : 0 \to 3$, an arrow in a precategory[2] whose objects are natural numbers. It is shown at the left of the diagram below.

---

[1] By making ports explicit we permit distinct roles to be played by the edges impinging on a given node, just as each argument of a given mathematical function plays a distinct role.

[2] We shall define precategories in Chapter 2. For now, it is enough to know that a precategory has two kinds of entity, *objects* and *arrows*; that each arrow goes from a tail to a head, both of which are objects; and that these entities behave nicely together. Both objects and arrows may have all kinds of structure.

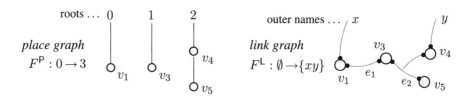

The outer and inner faces of a link graph are *name-sets*: respectively, its *outer* and *inner names*. For the hypergraph of $\check{F}$ we choose outer face $\{xy\}$, thus naming the parts of the broken hyperlink, and inner face $\emptyset$.[3] This extends the hypergraph to a link graph $F^{\mathsf{L}} : \emptyset \to \{xy\}$, an arrow in a precategory whose objects are finite name-sets. Names are drawn from a countably infinite vocabulary $\mathcal{X}$.

Finally, a *bigraph* is a pair $B = \langle B^{\mathsf{P}}, B^{\mathsf{L}} \rangle$ of a place graph and a link graph; these are its *constituents*. Its outer face is a pair $\langle n, Y \rangle$, where n and Y are the outer faces of B^{P} and B^{L} respectively. Similarly for its inner face $\langle m, X \rangle$. For our example $F = \langle F^{\mathsf{P}}, F^{\mathsf{L}} \rangle$ these pairs are $\langle 3, \{xy\} \rangle$ and $\langle 0, \emptyset \rangle$ respectively. We call the trivial interface $\epsilon \stackrel{\text{def}}{=} \langle 0, \emptyset \rangle$ the *origin*. Thus $\check{F}$ is extended to an arrow $F : \epsilon \to \langle 3, \{xy\} \rangle$ in a precategory whose objects are such paired interfaces. F will be drawn as follows:

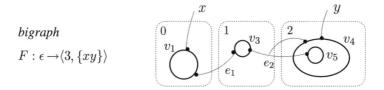

The rectangles in F – sometimes called *regions* – are just a way of drawing its roots, seen also in F^{P}. The link graph F^{L} has four *links*. Two of these are the edges e_1 and e_2, also called *closed* links; the other two are named x and y, and are called *open* links.

Let us now add interfaces to the bare bigraph $\check{G}$, extending it into a bigraph G. It has no open links, i.e. all its links are edges, so the name-set in its outer face will be empty. Let us give it two roots; then, if G is placed in some larger context, v_0 and v_4 may be in distinct places – i.e. may have distinct parents. The diagram below shows G and its constituents. Note that there is no significance in where a link 'crosses' the boundary of a node or region in a bigraph; this is because the forest and hypergraph structures are independent.

---

[3] We use single letters for names, so we shall often write a set $\{x, y, \ldots\}$ of names as $\{xy \cdots\}$, or even as $xy \cdots$, when there is no ambiguity.

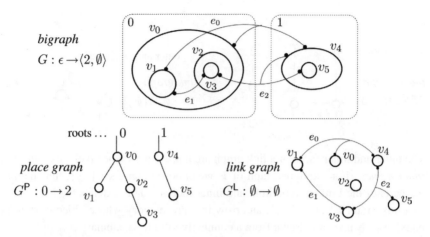

We are now ready to construct a bigraph H such that $G = H \circ F$, illustrating composition, which will later be defined formally. The inner face of H must be $\langle 3, \{xy\} \rangle$, the outer face of F; to achieve this, H must have three *sites* $0, 1$ and 2, and inner names x and y. Here are H and its constituents, with sites shown as shaded rectangles:

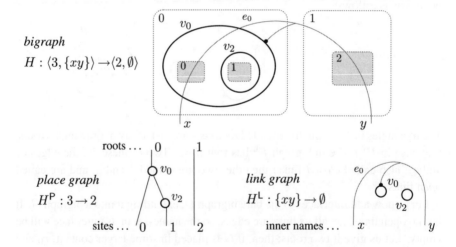

In the place graph, each site and node has a parent, a node or root; in the link graph, each inner name and port belongs to a link, closed or open. Just as it is insignificant where links 'cross' node or root boundaries, so it is insignificant where they 'cross' a site. We draw inner names below the bigraph and outer names above it; this is merely a convention to indicate their status as inner or outer. A name may be both inner and outer, whether or not in the same link.

In general, let $F : I \to J$ and $H : J \to K$ be two bigraphs with disjoint nodes and edges, where $I = \langle k, X \rangle$, $J = \langle m, Y \rangle$ and $K = \langle n, Z \rangle$. Then the composite bigraph $H \circ F : I \to K$ is just the pair of composites $\langle H^P \circ F^P, H^L \circ F^L \rangle$, whose constituents are constructed as follows (informally):

(i) To form the place graph $H^P \circ F^P : k \to n$, for each $i \in m$ join the ith root of F^P with the ith site of H^P;

(ii) To form the link graph $H^L \circ F^L : X \to Z$, for each $y \in Y$ join the link of F^L having the outer name y with the link of H^L having the inner name y.

Thus H and F are joined at every place or link in their common face J, which ceases to exist. The reader may like to check these constructions for H and F as in our example.

In our formal treatment, operations on bigraphs will be defined in terms of their constituent place and link graphs. But it is convenient, and even necessary for practical purposes, to have diagrams not only for the constituents but for the bigraphs themselves, such as for F, G and H in the example above. Such a diagram must be to some extent arbitrary, because we are trying to represent placing and linking, which are independent, in two dimensions! In particular, note that we have drawn outer names above the picture (in F and G for example), and we have drawn inner names below the picture (in H for example). Other conventions are possible.

It will be helpful to look now at Figure 1.2, at the end of this chapter, showing the anatomical elements of bigraphs that will later be defined formally. In the present chapter we give only one formal definition, which determines how to introduce different kinds of node for different applications.

Definition 1.1 (basic signature) A *basic signature* takes the form $(\mathcal{K}, ar)$. It has a set $\mathcal{K}$ whose elements are kinds of node called *controls*, and a map $ar : \mathcal{K} \to \mathbb{N}$ assigning an *arity*, a natural number, to each control. The signature is denoted by $\mathcal{K}$ when the arity is understood. A bigraph over $\mathcal{K}$ assigns to each node a control, whose arity indexes the *ports* of a node, where links may be connected. □

A signature suitable for our example is $\mathcal{K} = \{K : 2, L : 0, M : 1\}$. (Thus arities are made explicit.) Here is our bigraph $G : \epsilon \to \langle 2, \emptyset \rangle$, with controls assigned to the nodes:

bigraph G
with controls

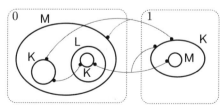

We have omitted node- and edge-identifiers, as we often shall when they are irrelevant. To end this chapter, let us look at a realistic (but simplified) example, which indicates that bigraphs can go beyond the usual topics for process calculi.

Example 1.2 (a built environment) The next diagram shows a bare bigraph $\check{E}$ over the signature $\mathcal{K} = \{\mathsf{A}:2,\ \mathsf{B}:1,\ \mathsf{C}:2,\ \mathsf{R}:0\}$, which classifies nodes as agents, buildings, computers and rooms. The node-shapes are not significant, except to indicate the purpose of each port. The figure represents a state which may change because of the movement of agents, and perhaps other movements. Think of the five agents as conducting a conference call (the long link). An agent in a room may also be logged in (the short links) to a computer in the room, and the computers in a building are linked to form a local area network.   □

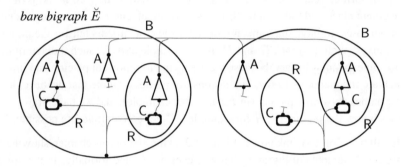

Bearing in mind our earlier example, the following exercise will be instructive.

EXERCISE 1.1

   (1) Draw a bare bigraph $\check{D}$ representing the three agents that are inside rooms. Make this into a bigraph D by defining its outer face.

   (2) Propose an outer face that makes $\check{E}$ into a bigraph E, allowing the possibility that the two buildings may be situated in different cities. Draw the bigraph C, with sites, such that $C \circ D = E$.   □

Although the detailed study of dynamics is deferred to Part II, let us now illustrate how bigraphs can reconfigure themselves. We are free to define different reconfigurations for each application. This is done by *reaction rules* each consisting of a *redex* (the pattern to be changed) and a *reactum* (the changed pattern). Part of the idea of bigraphs is that these changes may involve both placing and linking.

   The redex and reactum of a rule are themselves bigraphs, and may match any part of a larger bigraph. (This remark will be made precise in Part II.) Here are three possible rules for built environments, such as the system E:

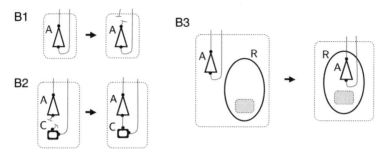

Rule B1 is the simplest: an agent can leave a conference call. The redex – the left-hand pattern – can match any agent; the out-pointing links mean that either of her ports may at first be linked to *zero or more* other ports, in the same place or elsewhere. If she is linked in a conference call to other agents, perhaps in other buildings, the reaction by B1 will unlink her; any link to a computer is retained.

Rule B2 shows a computer connecting to an agent in the same place (presumably a room). The redex insists that at first the agent is linked to no computer and the computer is linked to no agent. Rules B1 and B2 change only the linking – not the placing – in a bigraph, though the redex of B2 does insist on juxtaposition.

Rule B3, by contrast, changes the placing; an agent enters a room. Again, the rule requires the agent and the room to be in the same place (presumably a building). The site (shaded) allows the room to contain other occupants, e.g. a computer and other agents. The matching discipline allows these occupants to be linked anywhere, either to each other or to nodes lying outside the room.

Another feature of B3 is that its redex allows the lower port of the agent to be already linked to a computer somewhere, perhaps in another room. B3 retains any such link. Equally, there may be no such link – the context in which the rule is applied may close it off. Thus B3 can be applied to the system represented by $\breve{E}$, or E, allowing an agent in the right-hand building to enter a room.

Taking this a step further, observe that in E an agent and a computer are linked only when they occupy the same room. Moreover, starting from E, our rules B1–B3 will preserve this property, since only B3 creates such links, and only within a room. We therefore call the property an *invariant* for E in the system with this rule-set. We now briefly discuss invariants.

Given a rule-set, we refer to the configurations that a system may adopt as *states*. The rule-set determines a reaction relation $\longrightarrow$ between states. The diagram below shows the state E_3 adopted by E after three reactions

$$ E \longrightarrow E_1 \longrightarrow E_2 \longrightarrow E_3 \ ; $$

in the first, B1 is applied to the third agent from the left; in the second, B3 is applied to the fourth agent; this enables **B2** to be applied to that agent in the third reaction.

bigraph E_3

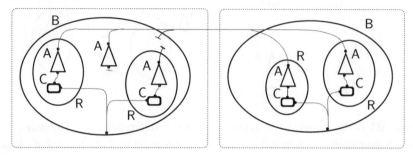

We say that a property of states is (an) *invariant* for E (under a given rule-set) if it holds for all states reachable from E via reactions permitted by the rule-set, i.e. it holds for all E' such that $E \longrightarrow \cdots \longrightarrow E'$. For example, under the rule-set **B1–B3**, the property 'there are exactly five agents' is invariant for E.

Of course, our present rule-set is very limited. The following exercise suggests how to enrich this rule-set a little, and explores what invariants may then hold.

EXERCISE 1.2

    (1) Add a rule **B4** to enable an agent linked with a computer to sever this link, and another rule **B5** to allow an agent unlinked to a computer to leave a room. Give a few examples of invariants for E under the rule-set **B1–B5**.

    (2) Instead of **B4** and **B5**, design a single rule **B6** that allows an agent to leave a room, simultaneously severing any link with the computer. How does this change affect your invariants? □

Our behavioural model of the occupants of a building is crude, of course. But reaction rules of this kind, hardly more complex, are beginning to find realistic application in biological modelling. A crucial refinement is to add stochastic information that determines which reactions are more likely to occur, and therefore to preempt others. In the built environment, an interesting refinement is to allow agents to discover who is where, and record this information via the computers; these stories can then be combined so that the system becomes *reflective*, meaning that it can represent (part of) itself, and answer questions such as 'where is agent X?'.[4]

In another direction, bigraphs can model process calculi. In this case, the controls of a bigraph represent the constructors of the calculus. As an example, we

---

[4] These experimental applications are discussed, with citations, in Chapter 12.

take the calculus of mobile ambients, which partly inspired the bigraph model. In mobile ambients the main constructor is 'amb' with arity 1, representing an *ambient* – a region within which activity may occur; its single port allows an ambient to be named. Other constructors represent commands, or capabilities.

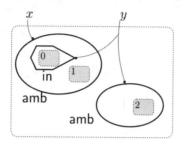

The above diagram shows two ambients, each with arbitrary content represented by the sites; one ambient also contains an 'in' capability, which refers to the other ambient by name. Let us use this example to illustrate the algebraic language for bigraphs, which we shall develop in later chapters. Here is the algebraic term for the above system:

$$\mathsf{amb}_x.(\mathsf{in}_y.d_0 \mid d_1) \mid \mathsf{amb}_y.d_2 \ .$$

The combinator '|' represents juxtaposition, and is commutative and associative; the combinator '.' denotes nesting. We shall see in Chapter 3 that both combinators are derived from the categorical operations of composition and tensor product. The metavariables d_0, d_1 and d_2 stand for parameters, i.e. arbitrary occupants of the sites.

Let us now look at the dynamics of ambients. The above bigraph is, in fact, the redex of one of the reaction rules for mobile ambients, three of which are shown in Figure 1.1. In the first rule, the 'in' command causes its parent ambient named x, together with all its other contents, to move inside the ambient named y. The 'in' command, having done its job, vanishes; this exposes its contents to reactions with the ambient's other occupants. Note that reconfiguration is permitted within an 'amb' node, but not within an 'in' node; the occupant of an 'in' node has a potential for interaction, which becomes actual only when the node itself has vanished.

In the second rule, conversely, the 'out' command causes the exit of its parent ambient from its own parent. These two rules provide our first example of moving sub-bigraphs from one region to another.

Finally, in the third rule the 'open' command causes an ambient node to vanish, exposing its contents to interactions in a wider region.

EXERCISE 1.3 Modify rule A3 to use a 'send' command instead of 'open'. It

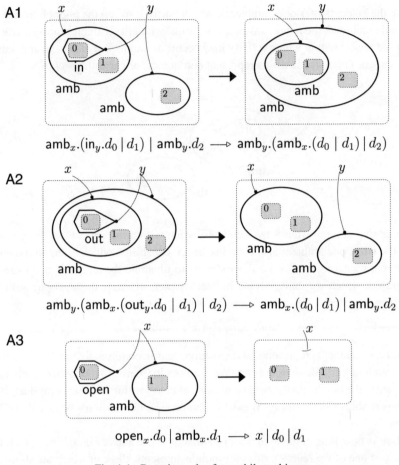

$$\text{amb}_x.(\text{in}_y.d_0 \mid d_1) \mid \text{amb}_y.d_2 \longrightarrow \text{amb}_y.(\text{amb}_x.(d_0 \mid d_1) \mid d_2)$$

$$\text{amb}_y.(\text{amb}_x.(\text{out}_y.d_0 \mid d_1) \mid d_2) \longrightarrow \text{amb}_x.(d_0 \mid d_1) \mid \text{amb}_y.d_2$$

$$\text{open}_x.d_0 \mid \text{amb}_x.d_1 \longrightarrow x \mid d_0 \mid d_1$$

Fig. 1.1. Reaction rules for mobile ambients

should send its contents into the ambient with which it is linked, and then vanish. Also modify the rule so that this occurs even when the send command is not adjacent to the ambient, but may be anywhere outside it. *Hint:* Use two regions, as in the bigraph G at the start of the chapter. To juxtapose two regions but keep them distinct, use '$\parallel$' instead of '$\mid$'. Use '1' to denote the empty bigraph with one region.   □

This concludes our informal introduction to both the structure and the reconfiguration of bigraphs. Our notion of reaction is not complex; nevertheless it can

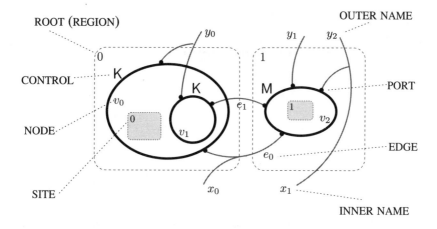

ROOT (REGION)   OUTER NAME   CONTROL   NODE   SITE   PORT   EDGE   INNER NAME

PLACE = ROOT or NODE or SITE

LINK = EDGE or OUTER NAME
POINT = PORT or INNER NAME

Fig. 1.2. Anatomy of bigraphs

represent process calculi such as CCS, mobile ambients and Petri nets. The representation of CCS will be analysed in Chapter 10. Also, with the help of stochastic rates, rules nearly as simple as ours are proving to be useful in modelling biological processes.

Our next task is to define bigraphical structure formally, in the following chapter. It will make precise the anatomy illustrated in Figure 1.2.

2

Defining bigraphs

In Section 2.1 we define bigraphs formally, together with fundamental ways to build with them.

In Section 2.2, using some elementary category theory, we introduce a broader mathematical framework in which bigraphs and their operations can be expressed. The reader can often ignore this generality, but it will yield results which do not depend on the specific details of bigraphs.

In Section 2.3 we explain how the *concrete* place graphs, link graphs and bigraphs over a basic signature each form a category of a certain kind. We then use the tools of the mathematical framework to introduce *abstract* bigraphs; they are obtained from the concrete ones of Section 2.1 by forgetting the identity of nodes and edges.

Throughout this chapter, when dealing with bigraphs we presume an arbitrary basic signature $\mathcal{K}$.

2.1 Bigraphs and their assembly

Notation and terminology We frequently treat a natural number as a finite ordinal, the set of all preceding ordinals: $m = \{0, 1, \ldots, m-1\}$. We write $S \# T$ to mean that two sets S and T are disjoint, i.e. $S \cap T = \emptyset$. We write $S \uplus T$ for the union of sets known or assumed to be disjoint. If f has domain S and $S' \subseteq S$, then $f \upharpoonright S'$ denotes the restriction of f to S'. For two functions f and g with disjoint domains S and T we write $f \uplus g$ for the function with domain $S \uplus T$ such that $(f \uplus g) \upharpoonright S = f$ and $(f \uplus g) \upharpoonright T = g$. We write Id_S for the identity function on the set S.

In defining bigraphs we assume that names, node-identifiers and edge-identifiers are drawn from three infinite sets, respectively $\mathcal{X}$, $\mathcal{V}$ and $\mathcal{E}$, disjoint from each other.

We denote the interfaces, or faces, of bigraphs by I, J, K. Every bigraph will be

14

a pair of a place graph and a link graph, which will be called its *constituents*. We denote bigraphs and their constituents by upper case letters $A, \ldots, H$. □

We begin by defining place graphs and link graphs independently.

Definition 2.1 (concrete place graph) A *concrete place graph*

$$F = (V_F, ctrl_F, prnt_F) : m \to n$$

is a triple having an inner face m and an outer face n, both finite ordinals. These index respectively the *sites* and *roots* of the place graph. F has a finite set $V_F \subset \mathcal{V}$ of *nodes*, a *control map* $ctrl_F : V_F \to \mathcal{K}$ and a *parent map*

$$prnt_F : m \uplus V_F \to V_F \uplus n$$

which is acyclic, i.e. if $prnt_F^i(v) = v$ for some $v \in V_F$ then $i = 0$. □

Definition 2.2 (concrete link graph) A *concrete link graph*

$$F = (V_F, E_F, ctrl_F, link_F) : X \to Y$$

is a quadruple having an inner face X and an outer face Y, both finite subsets of $\mathcal{X}$, called respectively the *inner* and *outer names* of the link graph.[1] F has finite sets $V_F \subset \mathcal{V}$ of *nodes* and $E_F \subset \mathcal{E}$ of *edges*, a *control map* $ctrl_F : V_F \to \mathcal{K}$ and a *link map*

$$link_F : X \uplus P_F \to E_F \uplus Y$$

where $P_F \stackrel{\text{def}}{=} \{(v, i) \mid i \in ar(ctrl_F(v))\}$ is the set of *ports* of F. Thus (v, i) is the ith port of node v. We shall call $X \uplus P_F$ the *points* of F, and $E_F \uplus Y$ its *links*. □

A bigraph is simply the pair of its constituents, a place graph and a link graph:

Definition 2.3 (concrete bigraph) An *interface* for bigraphs is a pair $I = \langle m, X \rangle$ of a place graph interface and a link graph interface. We call m the *width* of I, and we say that I is *nullary, unary* or *multiary* according as m is 0, 1 or >1. A *concrete bigraph*

$$F = (V_F, E_F, ctrl_F, prnt_F, link_F) : \langle k, X \rangle \to \langle m, Y \rangle$$

consists of a concrete place graph $F^{\mathsf{P}} = (V_F, ctrl_F, prnt_F) : k \to m$ and a concrete link graph $F^{\mathsf{L}} = (V_F, E_F, ctrl_F, link_F) : X \to Y$. We write the concrete bigraph as $F = \langle F^{\mathsf{P}}, F^{\mathsf{L}} \rangle$. □

---

[1] An alternative would be to define a link graph interface as an ordinal number k, just like a place graph interface. Thus, instead of alphabetic names, we would represent each name by an ordinal $i \in k$. Our choice to use a special repertoire $\mathcal{X}$ of names is not arbitrary; as explained in Appendix A.2, it yields a distinct technical advantage.

We have now defined all the anatomy of bigraphs, as illustrated in Figure 1.2 at the end of Chapter 1.

We have called our three graphical structures *concrete*; this refers to the fact that their nodes and edges are identified by members of $\mathcal{V}$ and $\mathcal{E}$. We have already used these identifiers in defining a bigraph, to ensure that its place graph and link graph have the same node set and the same control map.

We now define these identifiers to be the *support* of a graphical structure, and we explain how it can be varied in a disciplined way.

Definition 2.4 (support for bigraphs) To each place graph, link graph or bigraph F is assigned a finite set $|F|$, its *support*. For a place graph we define $|F| = V_F$, and for a link graph or bigraph we define $|F| = V_F \uplus E_F$.

For two bigraphs F and G in the same homset, a support translation $\rho : |F| \to |G|$ from F to G consists of a pair of bijections $\rho_V : V_F \to V_G$ and $\rho_E : E_F \to E_G$ that respect structure, in the following sense:

(i) ρ preserves controls, i.e. $ctrl_G \circ \rho_V = ctrl_F$. It follows that ρ induces a bijection $\rho_P : P_F \to P_G$ on ports, defined by $\rho_P((v, i)) \stackrel{\text{def}}{=} (\rho_V(v), i)$.

(ii) ρ commutes with the structural maps as follows:

$$prnt_G \circ (\mathsf{Id}_m \uplus \rho_V) = (\mathsf{Id}_n \uplus \rho_V) \circ prnt_F$$
$$link_G \circ (\mathsf{Id}_X \uplus \rho_P) = (\mathsf{Id}_Y \uplus \rho_E) \circ link_F .$$

Given F and the bijection ρ, these conditions uniquely determine G. We therefore denote G by $\rho \cdot F$, and call it the *support translation of F by ρ*. We call F and G *support equivalent*, and we write $F \simeq G$, if such a support translation exists.

Support translation is defined similarly for place graphs and link graphs.   □

The purpose of interfaces is to enable bigraphs to be *composed*; for this we require the outer face of one to equal the inner face of the other. Examples of composition were shown in Chapter 1; we think of it as placing one bigraph in the context represented by another.

Definition 2.5 (composition and identities) We define composition for place graphs and link graphs separately, and then combine them for the composition of bigraphs.

• If $F : k \to m$ and $G : m \to n$ are two place graphs with $|F| \# |G|$, their composite

$$G \circ F = (V, ctrl, prnt) : k \to n$$

has nodes $V = V_F \uplus V_G$ and control map $ctrl = ctrl_F \uplus ctrl_G$. Its parent map *prnt* is defined as follows: If $w \in k \uplus V_F \uplus V_G$ is a site or node of $G \circ F$ then

$$prnt(w) \overset{\text{def}}{=} \begin{cases} prnt_F(w) & \text{if } w \in k \uplus V_F \text{ and } prnt_F(w) \in V_F \\ prnt_G(j) & \text{if } w \in k \uplus V_F \text{ and } prnt_F(w) = j \in m \\ prnt_G(w) & \text{if } w \in V_G . \end{cases}$$

The identity place graph at m is $\text{id}_m \overset{\text{def}}{=} (\emptyset, \emptyset_{\mathcal{K}}, \text{Id}_m) : m \to m$.[2]

- If $F : X \to Y$ and $G : Y \to Z$ are two link graphs with $|F| \# |G|$, their composite

$$G \circ F = (V, E, ctrl, link) : X \to Z$$

has $V = V_F \uplus V_G$, $E = E_F \uplus E_G$, $ctrl = ctrl_F \uplus ctrl_G$, and its link map *link* is defined as follows: If $q \in X \uplus P_F \uplus P_G$ is a point of $G \circ F$ then

$$link(q) \overset{\text{def}}{=} \begin{cases} link_F(q) & \text{if } q \in X \uplus P_F \text{ and } link_F(q) \in E_F \\ link_G(y) & \text{if } q \in X \uplus P_F \text{ and } link_F(q) = y \in Y \\ link_G(q) & \text{if } q \in P_G . \end{cases}$$

The identity link graph at X is $\text{id}_X \overset{\text{def}}{=} (\emptyset, \emptyset, \emptyset_{\mathcal{K}}, \text{Id}_X) : X \to X$.

- If $F : I \to J$ and $G : J \to K$ are two bigraphs with $|F| \# |G|$, their composite is

$$G \circ F \overset{\text{def}}{=} \langle G^{\mathsf{P}} \circ F^{\mathsf{P}}, G^{\mathsf{L}} \circ F^{\mathsf{L}} \rangle : I \to K$$

and the identity bigraph at $I = \langle m, X \rangle$ is $\langle \text{id}_m, \text{id}_X \rangle$. □

EXERCISE 2.1 Prove for bigraphs that $C \circ (B \circ A) = (C \circ B) \circ A$ when either side is defined. *Hint:* Prove it separately for place graphs and for link graphs, then pair the results. □

We now turn to the second principal way to make larger bigraphs from smaller ones. We can think of composition as putting one bigraph on top of another. We can also put two bigraphs side-by-side. We define this operation, called *juxtaposition*, only when they are disjoint. To be precise:

Definition 2.6 (disjoint graphical structures) Two place graphs F_i ($i = 0, 1$) are *disjoint* if $|F_0| \# |F_1|$. Two link graphs $F_i : X_i \to Y_i$ are *disjoint* if $X_0 \# X_1$, $Y_0 \# Y_1$ and $|F_0| \# |F_1|$. Two bigraphs F_i are *disjoint* if $F_0^{\mathsf{P}} \# F_1^{\mathsf{P}}$ and $F_0^{\mathsf{L}} \# F_1^{\mathsf{L}}$.

In each of the three cases we write $F_0 \# F_1$. □

We now define the juxtaposition of disjoint interfaces and disjoint bigraphs. Juxtaposition is monoidal, i.e. it is associative and has a unit.

---

[2] In contrast to Id, we write id to denote the identity for composition of graphical structures, and more generally for composition of arrows in any kind of category (see Section 2.2).

Definition 2.7 (juxtaposition and units) We define juxtaposition for place graphs and link graphs separately, and then combine them in order to juxtapose bigraphs. In each case we indicate the obvious unit for juxtaposition.

- For place graphs, the juxtaposition of two interfaces m_i $(i = 0, 1)$ is $m_0 + m_1$ and the unit is 0. If $F_i = (V_i, ctrl_i, prnt_i) : m_i \to n_i$ are disjoint place graphs $(i = 0, 1)$, their juxtaposition $F_0 \otimes F_1 : m_0 + m_1 \to n_0 + n_1$ is given by

$$F_0 \otimes F_1 \stackrel{\text{def}}{=} (V_0 \uplus V_1,\ ctrl_0 \uplus ctrl_1,\ prnt_0 \uplus prnt'_1)\,,$$

where $prnt'_1(m_0 + i) = n_0 + j$ whenever $prnt_1(i) = j$.

- For link graphs, the juxtaposition of two disjoint link graph interfaces is $X_0 \uplus X_1$ and the unit is $\emptyset$. If $F_i = (V_i, E_i, ctrl_i, prnt_i) : X_i \to Y_i$ are disjoint link graphs $(i = 0, 1)$, their juxtaposition $F_0 \otimes F_1 : X_0 \uplus X_1 \to Y_0 \uplus Y_1$ is given by

$$F_0 \otimes F_1 \stackrel{\text{def}}{=} (V_0 \uplus V_1,\ E_0 \uplus E_1,\ ctrl_0 \uplus ctrl_1,\ link_0 \uplus link_1)\,.$$

- For bigraphs, the juxtaposition of two disjoint interfaces $I_i = \langle m_i, X_i \rangle$ $(i = 0, 1)$ is $\langle m_o + m_1, X_0 \uplus X_1 \rangle$ and the unit is $\epsilon = \langle 0, \emptyset \rangle$. If $F_i : I_i \to J_i$ are disjoint bigraphs $(i = 0, 1)$, their juxtaposition $F_0 \otimes F_1 : I_0 \otimes I_1 \to J_0 \otimes J_1$ is given by

$$F_0 \otimes F_1 \stackrel{\text{def}}{=} \langle F_0^{\mathsf{P}} \otimes F_1^{\mathsf{P}},\ F_0^{\mathsf{L}} \otimes F_1^{\mathsf{L}} \rangle\,. \qquad \Box$$

This completes our definition of the graphical structures that concern us, together with the fundamental operations upon them.

2.2 Mathematical framework

This section introduces certain kinds of *category*, which serve to classify bigraphs and to develop some of their theory. We assume no previous knowledge of category theory; we shall only use its elementary concepts, explaining them as we introduce them.

Any kind of category deals with two main kinds of entity: *objects* and *arrows*. For example, in the category SET the objects are *sets* $S_1, S_2, S_3, \ldots$ and the arrows are *functions* $f, g, \ldots$ between sets. If a function f takes members of set S_1 to members of set S_2 then one writes $f : S_1 \to S_2$, as in normal mathematical practice. In categories this practice is generalised; each arrow f – which may be quite different from a function – has a *domain* I and a *codomain* J, both objects, and again we write $f : I \to J$. The main categories deployed in this book have objects that are interfaces (of different kinds) and arrows that are graphical structures.

Any kind of category is concerned with the *composition* of two arrows $f : I \to J$ and $h : J \to K$ to produce a third arrow $g = h \circ f : I \to K$. This equation is drawn as a diagram:

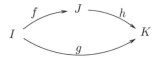

which is said to *commute*, because the two ways of going from I to K mean the same. For example, in Chapter 1 we composed two bigraphs $F : \epsilon \rightarrow \langle 3, \{xy\} \rangle$ and $H : \langle 3, \{xy\} \rangle \rightarrow \langle 2, 0 \rangle$ to yield $G = H \circ F : \epsilon \rightarrow \langle 2, 0 \rangle$.

Different kinds of category may have other operations besides composition, and may have different properties. We shall be concerned with four kinds, which can be arranged in a hierarchy as follows:

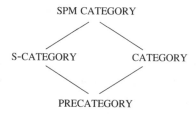

Of these kinds, s-categories are new; the other three are standard. Moving upward to the left ($\nwarrow$) in the hierarchy gains more operations on arrows; moving upward to the right ($\nearrow$) changes composition from a partial to a total operation.

Our work will be mainly with two of these kinds. We shall often be concerned with *concrete* bigraphs, whose explicit support allows us to determine when one bigraph shares nodes and/or edges with another. For this purpose we work mainly in *s-categories*. On the other hand, for *abstract* bigraphs, where support is absent, we work mainly in *symmetric partial monoidal* (or *spm*) *categories*.

Using the hierarchy, we now introduce the features of both spm categories and s-categories, one by one. We begin with categories (Definition 2.8), which lead to spm categories (Definition 2.11); then we introduce precategories (Definition 2.12), which lead to s-categories (Definition 2.13).

Definition 2.8 (category) A *category* **C** has a set of *objects* and a set of *arrows*. We shall often denote objects by I, J, K and arrows by f, g, h. Each arrow f has a *domain* and *codomain*, both objects; if these are I and J then we write $f : I \rightarrow J$, $I = \text{dom}(f)$ and $J = \text{cod}(f)$. We write $\mathbf{C}(I \rightarrow J)$, or just $(I \rightarrow J)$, for the *homset* of I and J, the set of arrows $f : I \rightarrow J$.

For each object I there is an *identity* arrow $\text{id}_I : I \rightarrow I$; we write just id when I

is understood. The *composition* $g \circ f$ of f and g satisfies the following:

(C1) $g \circ f$ is defined iff $\text{cod}(f) = \text{dom}(g)$
(C2) $h \circ (g \circ f) = (h \circ g) \circ f$ when either is defined
(C3) $\text{id} \circ f = f$ and $f = f \circ \text{id}$.   □

Terminology We shall often say that g is a *context for* f, meaning that $g \circ f$ is defined.

We often need to move from one category to another, preserving some structure. Hence the following important notion.

Definition 2.9 (functor) A *functor* $\mathcal{F} : \mathbf{C} \to \mathbf{D}$ between two categories is a function taking objects to objects and arrows to arrows; it takes the arrow $f : I \to J$ in $\mathbf{C}$ to the arrow $\mathcal{F}(f) : \mathcal{F}(I) \to \mathcal{F}(J)$ in $\mathbf{D}$.

More generally, let ϕ be an n-ary partial operation on objects and/or arrows in both $\mathbf{C}$ and $\mathbf{D}$. Then $\mathcal{F}$ *preserves* ϕ if $\mathcal{F}(\phi(x_1, \ldots, x_n)) = \phi(\mathcal{F}(x_1), \ldots, \mathcal{F}(x_n))$, meaning that if the left-hand side is defined then so is the right-hand side.

Similarly, if R is a relation on objects and/or arrows in $\mathbf{C}$, and also in $\mathbf{D}$, then $\mathcal{F}$ *preserves* R if $R(x_1, \ldots, x_n) \Rightarrow R(\mathcal{F}(x_1), \ldots, \mathcal{F}(x_n))$.

Every functor must preserve both composition and identities.   □

The initial requirement simply says that $\mathcal{F}$ preserves the domain and codomain operations, dom and cod. In the case $n = 0$ of 'preserves', ϕ is a single object or arrow in each category, i.e. an identity.

We now proceed in two steps to an *spm category*, an enriched kind of category possessing a form of *product*. A special case of this product is the *juxtaposition* of bigraphs, as defined in Section 2.1.

Definition 2.10 (partial monoidal category) A category is said to be *partial monoidal* when it has a partial *tensor product* $\otimes$ both on objects and on arrows satisfying the following conditions.

On objects, $I \otimes J$ and $J \otimes I$ are either both defined or both undefined.[3] The same holds for $I \otimes (J \otimes K)$ and $(I \otimes J) \otimes K$; moreover, they are equal when defined. There is a *unit* object ϵ, often called the *origin*, for which $\epsilon \otimes I = I \otimes \epsilon = I$ for all I.

On arrows, the tensor product of $f : I_0 \to I_1$ and $g : J_0 \to J_1$ is defined iff $I_0 \otimes J_0$

---

[3] This is a variant of the standard definition, which requires that $I \otimes J$ is always defined. We relax this condition because, in bigraphs, we have chosen to represent open links by names drawn from an infinite alphabet, rather than by ordinal numbers, yielding a much smoother representation of process calculi. Appendix A.2 explains the choice in more detail. We have adopted the strict form of 'monoidal', i.e. the equations are required to hold exactly, not merely up to isomorphism.

and $I_1 \otimes J_1$ are both defined. The following must hold when both sides are defined:

(M1) $f \otimes (g \otimes h) = (f \otimes g) \otimes h$
(M2) $\mathrm{id}_\epsilon \otimes f = f \otimes \mathrm{id}_\epsilon = f$
(M3) $(f_1 \otimes g_1) \circ (f_0 \otimes g_0) = (f_1 \circ f_0) \otimes (g_1 \circ g_0)$.

A functor of partial monoidal categories preserves unit and tensor product. □

In (M1), from the conditions stated, either both sides are defined or both are un-defined. In (M2) both products are defined. Equation (M3) is best explained by a diagram showing composition as vertical connection, and tensor product as hori-zontal juxtaposition:

(M3)

This says that tensor product commutes with composition.

Henceforth we shall use the term 'product' to mean 'tensor product' unless other-wise qualified. We now enrich a partial monoidal category by adding arrows called *symmetries*, which allow the factors in a product to be re-ordered. They obey four laws, explaining how they relate to composition, product and the identities.

Definition 2.11 (spm category) A partial monoidal category is *symmetric (spm)*[4] if, whenever $I \otimes J$ is defined, there is an arrow $\gamma_{I,J} : I \otimes J \to J \otimes I$ called a *symmetry*, satisfying the following equations – illustrated in the diagram below – when the compositions and products are defined:

(S1) $\gamma_{I,\epsilon} = \mathrm{id}_I$
(S2) $\gamma_{J,I} \circ \gamma_{I,J} = \mathrm{id}_{I \otimes J}$
(S3) $\gamma_{I_1,J_1} \circ (f \otimes g) = (g \otimes f) \circ \gamma_{I_0,J_0}$ (for $f : I_0 \to I_1$, $g : J_0 \to J_1$)
(S4) $\gamma_{I \otimes J,K} = (\gamma_{I,K} \otimes \mathrm{id}_J) \circ (\mathrm{id}_I \otimes \gamma_{J,K})$.

A functor between spm categories preserves unit, product and symmetries. □

---

[4] In a previous paper [65] the name 'ssm' was used, connoting symmetric and strict. Here we replace 'ss' by 'sp', for 'symmetric partial', leaving 'strict' to be understood.

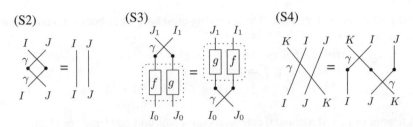

EXERCISE 2.2 In an spm category an arrow is *ground*, or an *agent*, if its domain is the origin ϵ. Define *context expressions* C to build one agent from another, as follows:

$$C ::= [\cdot] \mid (g \otimes C) \mid (C \otimes g) \mid (h \circ C)$$

where g is ground and the products and compositions are well-formed, i.e. their operands are in appropriate homsets. This syntax ensures that every context expression C contains exactly one occurrence of the 'hole' $[\cdot]$. Let $C[a]$ denote the ground bigraph built by C from any ground a: thus $[a] = a$. The homset of a must ensure that $C[a]$ is well-formed.

A particular form of context expression is just $f \circ [\cdot]$. Prove that these particular context expressions are fully general; that is, for every C there exists an arrow f such that $f \circ a = C[a]$ for all a. *Hint:* Use induction on the structure of C.

Which laws of an spm category are needed in the proof?   □

We now introduce the notions of precategory and s-category. We can adapt most details from the notions of category and spm category. The main difference is that composition of two arrows $f : I \to J$ and $g : J \to K$ is not always defined. As we shall see later, this limitation is a price we pay for dealing with the *occurrences* of one bigraph within another. This handling is smooth; at the level of our work, s-categories lose little of the character of an spm category, and the s-category of concrete bigraphs has useful properties not present in the corresponding spm category.

Definition 2.12 (precategory) A *precategory* `C is like a category except that composition of $f$ and $g$ may be undefined even when $\mathrm{cod}(f) = \mathrm{dom}(g)$. We use a tag, as in `C, to distinguish precategories. Composition satisfies the following conditions (the first being weaker than for a category):

(C1′)   if $g \circ f$ is defined then $\mathrm{cod}(f) = \mathrm{dom}(g)$
(C2) $h \circ (g \circ f) = (h \circ g) \circ f$ when either is defined
(C3) $\mathrm{id} \circ f = f$ and $f = f \circ \mathrm{id}$.

We understand C3 to imply that composition of an arrow f with the identities on its domain and codomain is always defined.

A functor between precategories is exactly as a functor between categories. □

Now, an s-category enriches a precategory by adding a partial tensor product and symmetries, just as an spm category enriches a category. It also imposes sharper conditions under which composition and tensor product are defined.

For this purpose we introduce the notion of a set of *support*, generalising the support of bigraphs introduced in Section 2.1. We presuppose an infinite vocabulary S of *support elements*; then we shall associate a finite set of support elements with each arrow. This association will be arbitrary, subject to simple constraints detailed in the following definition.

Definition 2.13 (s-category) An s-category `C is a precategory in which each arrow $f$ is assigned a finite *support* $|f| \subset S$. Further, `C possesses a partial tensor product, unit and symmetries, as in an spm category. The identities id_I and symmetries $\gamma_{I,J}$ are assigned empty support. In addition:

(i) For $f : I \to J$ and $g : J' \to K$, the composition $g \circ f$ is defined iff $J = J'$ and $|f| \,\#\, |g|$; then $|g \circ f| = |f| \uplus |g|$.

(ii) For $f : I_0 \to I_1$ and $g : J_0 \to J_1$, the tensor product $f \otimes g$ is defined iff $I_i \otimes J_i$ is defined ($i = 0, 1$) and $|f| \,\#\, |g|$; then $|f \otimes g| = |f| \uplus |g|$.

The equations (M1)–(M3) and (S1)–(S4) from Definitions 2.10 and 2.11 are required to hold when both sides are defined.

Arrows f and g in the same homset are said to be *support-equivalent*, and we write $f \simeq g$, if there is a bijection $\rho : |f| \to |g|$, called a *support translation*, that respects the structure of f. A functor between s-categories preserves tensor product, unit, symmetries and support equivalence. □

Appendix A.1 shows the 'structure-respecting' conditions that must be satisfied by any support translation in an s-category. We shall not refer to these conditions explicitly; we shall mainly be concerned with them in the specific case of bigraphs, for which the conditions are stated explicitly in Definition 2.4.

We shall soon see that bigraphs over a given basic signature form an s-category. Of course, they have detailed structure (nodes, etc.) not present in an arbitrary s-category, and this admits new features. But there is one important feature that we can capture at the general level of s-categories, and that will be useful for understanding the dynamics of reactive systems in general. It represents one way in which the behaviour of such systems depends upon its spatial configuration. We express it in terms of NAT, the spm category whose objects are natural numbers (considered here as finite ordinals) and whose arrows are functions between them. In NAT we take the tensor product to be addition, with unit 0.

Definition 2.14 (wide s-category) An s-category $`\mathbf{C}$ is *wide* if it is equipped with a functor width : $`\mathbf{C} \to \text{NAT}$.   □

Note that this is really a functor between s-categories, because any spm category is also an s-category with empty supports. The intuition of the width functor is that, for an object I, the ordinal width(I) indexes the 'regions' of I, while for an arrow $f : I \to J$ the function width(f) tells us the unique region of J in which each region of I lies. The width functor tells us no more about the spatial structure of objects and arrows; but as we have seen, bigraphs have a detailed spatial structure defined by their nodes, and this structure certainly yields a width functor.

Some of the work of this book is done at the general level of wide s-categories, and is thus independent of possible variations of the notion of bigraph. In particular they lead in Chapter 7 to a general theory of *wide reactive systems (WRSs)*, including a crucial theorem concerning the congruence of behavioural equivalence. In Section 2.3 we shall see that the width functor for bigraphs allows us to express the *locality* of any potential reaction of a bigraph g, and thereby to determine the contexts in which that reaction can occur.

Let us now relate s-categories with spm categories. As already mentioned, every spm category can be seen immediately as an s-category: one whose supports are all empty. Conversely, from any s-category we obtain an spm category, just by hiding the support. To be precise:

Definition 2.15 (support quotient) For any s-category $`\mathbf{C}$, its *support quotient*

$$\mathbf{C} \overset{\text{def}}{=} {}`\mathbf{C}/\backsimeq$$

is the spm category whose objects are those of $`\mathbf{C}$, and whose arrows $[f] : I \to J$ are support-equivalence classes of the homset $`\mathbf{C}(I \to J)$. The composition of $[f] : I \to J$ with $[g] : J \to K$ is defined as $[g] \circ [f] \overset{\text{def}}{=} [g' \circ f']$, where $f' \in [f]$ and $g' \in [g]$ are chosen with disjoint supports.

The tensor product is defined analogously. The identities and symmetries of $\mathbf{C}$ are singleton equivalence classes since they have empty support.   □

This definition is unambiguous, since the properties of support translation ensure that the construction of a composite or product in $\mathbf{C}$ does not depend upon the choice of representative arrows in $`\mathbf{C}$. We now justify the definition by a theorem.

Theorem 2.16 (support quotient) *The support quotient* $\mathbf{C} = {}`\mathbf{C}/\backsimeq$ *is an spm category. Its construction defines a functor of s-categories*

$$[\cdot] : {}`\mathbf{C} \to \mathbf{C}$$

called the support quotient *functor. If* $`\mathbf{C}$ *is wide, with width functor* width, *then* $\mathbf{C}$

can be enriched to a wide spm category by equipping it with the functor width$: \mathbf{C} \to$ NAT *defined on objects as in* $`\mathbf{C}$ *and on arrows by* width$([f]) \overset{\text{def}}{=}$ width(f).

This completes our mathematical framework. We are now ready to assert that concrete place graphs, link graphs and bigraphs all form s-categories, the latter being a wide s-category.

2.3 Bigraphical categories

In this section we cast concrete bigraphs and their constituent place graphs and link graphs as s-categories. We also cast their corresponding abstract structures as spm categories.

Definition 2.17 (graphical s-categories) A basic signature $\mathcal{K}$ was defined in Definition 1.1. Concrete place graphs, link graphs and bigraphs over an arbitrary signature were defined in Definitions 2.1, 2.2 and 2.3. We now cast each of these kinds of graph as arrows in an s-category, denoted respectively by $`$PG$(\mathcal{K})$, $`$LG$(\mathcal{K})$ and $`$BG$(\mathcal{K})$.

The objects in these three s-categories are called *interfaces*, or *faces*. For place graphs they are natural numbers, for link graphs they are a finite name-sets, and for bigraphs they are pairs of a natural number m and a finite name-set.

Support for the three kinds of graph was defined in Definition 2.4, with support elements $\mathcal{V} \uplus \mathcal{E}$. *Composition* and *identities* were set out in Definition 2.5, and *juxtaposition* and *units* in Definition 2.7, determining *tensor product*.

To complete our definition it remains to define *symmetries* $\gamma_{I,J}$ as follows:

$$\text{in } `\text{PG} : \quad \gamma_{m,n} \overset{\text{def}}{=} (\emptyset, \emptyset, prnt), \quad \text{where} \quad prnt(i) = n+i \ (i \in m)$$
$$\text{and} \quad prnt(m+j) = j \ (j \in n)$$
$$\text{in } `\text{LG} : \quad \gamma_{X,Y} \overset{\text{def}}{=} \text{id}_{X \uplus Y}$$
$$\text{in } `\text{BG} : \quad \gamma_{\langle m,X \rangle, \langle n,Y \rangle} \overset{\text{def}}{=} \langle \gamma_{m,n}, \gamma_{X,Y} \rangle . \qquad \square$$

Thus, if γ is a symmetry of bigraphs, then $\gamma \circ G$ just re-orders the regions of G but leaves its names unchanged.

It is a routine matter to prove that this data defines three s-categories. Moreover, the s-category of bigraphs is easily seen to be wide; this is due to the spatial nature of place graphs, which yields an obvious width functor. We wrap these important results together as a theorem:

Theorem 2.18 (graphical s-categories) $`$PG$(\mathcal{K})$, $`$LG$(\mathcal{K})$ *and* $`$BG$(\mathcal{K})$, *as defined in Definition 2.17, are all s-categories.*

Further, we may equip $`$BG$(\mathcal{K})$ *with a width functor, as follows. For each interface* $I = \langle m, X \rangle$, *define* width$(I) = m$, *and for each bigraph $F$ and any site $i$ of $F$,* *define* width$(F)(i)$ *to be the unique root that is an ancestor of* $i$ *in* $F$. *Then* $`\mathrm{BG}(\mathcal{K})$, *so equipped, is a wide s-category.*

EXERCISE 2.3 What bigraphs exist in a homset of $`\mathrm{BG}(\mathcal{K})$ of the form $(I \to \epsilon)$? Which of these have empty support?   □

Our final task in this chapter is to define the spm category of abstract bigraphs. But we need first to consider a technical point concerning *idle links*: those links to which no points are mapped. Recall that a link is either an outer name or an edge. The reader may think that idle links are useless, but they arise inevitably in our framework.

To see how an idle (outer) *name* may arise, consider the reaction rules illustrated in Chapter 1. Each reaction rule may be written $r \longrightarrow r'$, where r is the redex and r' the reactum. We need r and r' to have the same outer face, because reactions by this rule take the form $C \circ r \longrightarrow C \circ r'$, where C is a context for both r and r'. But the points linked to a name x in r may no longer exist in r', because the reaction discards the nodes of r to which they belong. Examples of this are the rule **B1** for built environments, or the rule **A3** for mobile ambients, both illustrated in Chapter 1. Then idle *edges* also arise; for in the reaction $C \circ r \longrightarrow C \circ r'$ the context C may have an edge e containing only the point x; then e will be an idle edge of $C \circ r'$.

We are now ready to define the wide spm category of abstract bigraphs. In forming these from the concrete ones $`\mathrm{BG}(\mathcal{K})$ we wish to forget support; we also wish to forget idle edges. So it is not quite enough to quotient the concrete bigraphs by support equivalence. For suppose F and G are identical except that F has idle edges, but G has none. Then they are not support-equivalent; the support quotient $[F]$ still has idle edges, although they are unidentified, while $[G]$ has none. We therefore need to quotient by a slightly larger equivalence, as follows:

Definition 2.19 (lean, lean-support quotient) A bigraph is *lean* if it has no idle edges. Two bigraphs F and G are *lean-support equivalent*, written $F \backsimeq G$, if they are support-equivalent ignoring their idle edges. It is easily seen that both composition and tensor product preserve this equivalence.

For the bigraphical s-category $`\mathrm{BG}(\mathcal{K})$, its *lean-support quotient*

$$\mathrm{BG}(\mathcal{K}) \stackrel{\text{def}}{=} `\mathrm{BG}(\mathcal{K})/ \backsimeq$$

is the spm category whose objects are those of $`\mathrm{BG}(\mathcal{K})$ and whose arrows $[\![G]\!] : I \to J$, called *abstract bigraphs*, are lean-support equivalence classes of the homset $(I \to J)$ in $`\mathrm{BG}(\mathcal{K})$. Composition, tensor product, identities and symmetries for the lean-support quotient are defined just as for support quotient in Definition 2.15.

The spm categories $\text{PG}(\mathcal{K})$ of abstract place graphs and $\text{LG}(\mathcal{K})$ of abstract link graphs are constructed similarly. □

We now justify the definition by a theorem.

Theorem 2.20 (abstract bigraphs) *The lean-support quotient* $\text{BG}(\mathcal{K})$ = ˋ$\text{BG}(\mathcal{K})/ \backsimeq$ *is an spm category. Its construction defines a functor of spm categories*

$$\llbracket \cdot \rrbracket : \text{ˋ}\text{BG}(\mathcal{K}) \to \text{BG}(\mathcal{K})$$

called the lean-support quotient *functor. There are similar lean-support quotient functors for place graphs and link graphs, yielding spm categories* $\text{PG}(\mathcal{K})$ *and* $\text{LG}(\mathcal{K})$.

Finally, $\text{BG}(\mathcal{K})$ *equipped with essentially the same width functor as* ˋ$\text{BG}(\mathcal{K})$ *forms a wide spm category.*

This quotient is essential for our theory. In later chapters we shall move back and forth between concrete and abstract bigraphs, according to whether or not we need to identify support elements. For example, Chapter 3 is concerned with the algebra of abstract bigraphs, which does not depend upon support; on the other hand Chapter 5 is concerned with a form of least upper bound for a pair of concrete bigraphs, and this notion is absent for abstract bigraphs because it depends critically upon support.

3

Algebra for bigraphs

In this chapter we show how bigraphs can be built from smaller ones by composition, product and identities. In this we follow process algebra, where the idea is first to determine how distributed systems are assembled *structurally*, and then on this basis to develop their *dynamic* theory, deriving the behaviour of an assembly from the behaviours of its components.

This contrasts with our definition of a bigraph as the pair of a place graph and a link graph. This pairing is important for bigraphical theory, as we shall see later; but it may not reflect how a system designer thinks about a system. The algebra of this chapter, allowing bigraphs to be built from elementary *bigraphs*, is a basis for the synthetic approach of the system-builder.

Our algebraic structure pertains naturally to the abstract bigraphs $\mathrm{BG}(\mathcal{K})$. Much of it pertains equally to concrete bigraphs. Properties enjoyed exclusively by concrete bigraphs are postponed until Chapter 5.

3.1 Elementary bigraphs and normal forms

Notation and convention The *places* of $G : \langle m, X \rangle \to \langle n, Y \rangle$ are its sites m, its nodes and its roots n. The *points* of G are its ports and inner names X. The *links* of G are its edges and outer names Y; the edges are *closed* links, and the outer names are *open* links. A point is said to be *open* if its link is open, otherwise it is *closed*. G is said to be *open* if all its links are open (i.e. it has no edges).

A place with no children, or a link with no points, is called *idle*. Two places with the same parent, or two points with the same link, are called *siblings*.

If an interface $I = \langle m, X \rangle$ has $X = \emptyset$ we may write I as m; if $m = 0$ or $m = 1$ we may write it as X or as $\langle X \rangle$ respectively. When there is no ambiguity, especially in interfaces, we shall often write a name-set $\{x, y, z, \ldots\}$ as $\{xyz \cdots\}$.

The unique bigraph with empty support in $\epsilon \to I$ is often written I.

28

A bigraph $g : \epsilon \to I$, with domain ϵ, is called *ground*; we use lower case letters for ground bigraphs, and write $g : I$. □

We now describe the elementary node-free bigraphs. For each kind we mention in parentheses the Greek letter we shall use most often to denote them, e.g. ϕ for placings.

Definition 3.1 (placing, permutation, merge) A node-free bigraph with no links is a *placing* (ϕ). A placing that is bijective from sites to roots is a *permutation* (π). A placing with one root and n sites is denoted by $merge_n$. □

elementary placings:

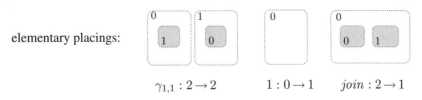

$$\gamma_{1,1} : 2 \to 2 \qquad 1 : 0 \to 1 \qquad join : 2 \to 1$$

All permutations can be built (using composition, product and identities) from the elementary symmetry $\gamma_{1,1}$. All placings can be built from $\gamma_{1,1}, 1$ and $join$. For example, $merge_0 = 1$ and $merge_{n+1} = join \circ (\mathrm{id}_1 \otimes merge_n)$.

Definition 3.2 (linking, substitution, closure) A node-free bigraph with no places is a *linking* (λ). Linkings are generated by composition, product and identities from two basic forms: elementary *substitutions* y / X, and elementary *closures* $/x : x \to \epsilon$, as shown in the diagram.

elementary linkings:

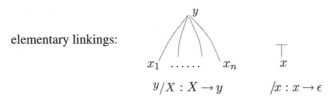

$$y/X : X \to y \qquad /x : x \to \epsilon$$

A *substitution* (σ) is a product of elementary substitutions; a *closure* is a product of elementary closures. A bijective substitution is called a *renaming* (α). We denote the empty substitution from ϵ to x by $x : \epsilon \to x$. □

Note that a closure $/x \circ G$ may create an idle edge, if x is an idle name of G. Intuitively idle edges are 'invisible', and indeed we shall see later how to ignore them.

EXERCISE 3.1 Show that every linking can be built from elementary linkings using identities, composition and product. Is composition necessary for this? □

In any (pre)category an *isomorphism* or *iso* is an arrow $\iota : I \to J$ that has an inverse $\iota^{-1} : J \to I$; that is, $\iota^{-1} \circ \iota = \mathrm{id}_I$ and $\iota \circ \iota^{-1} = \mathrm{id}_J$. Isos are an important class of node-free bigraphs, characterised as follows:

Proposition 3.3 (isomorphism) *Place graph and link graph isos are respectively permutations π and renamings α. Bigraph isos are pairs $\langle \pi, \alpha \rangle$.*

There is only one kind of elementary bigraph that introduces nodes:

Definition 3.4 (ion) For each control $K : n$, the bigraph $K_{\vec{x}} : 1 \to \langle 1, \{\vec{x}\} \rangle$ having a single K-node with ports linked bijectively to n distinct names $\vec{x}$ is called a *discrete ion*.   □

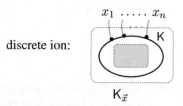

discrete ion:

$K_{\vec{x}}$

Definition 3.5 (atom, molecule) If the site of a discrete K-ion is filled by $1 : 0 \to 1$ (see Definition 3.1), the result is a *discrete atom*, $K_{\vec{x}} \circ 1$; if it is filled by a discrete bigraph (see Definition 3.8 below) $G : I \to \langle 1, Y \rangle$, then it is a *discrete molecule*, $(K_{\vec{x}} \otimes \mathrm{id}_Y) \circ G$.   □

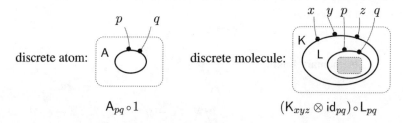

discrete atom:

$A_{pq} \circ 1$

discrete molecule:

$(K_{xyz} \otimes \mathrm{id}_{pq}) \circ L_{pq}$

The diagram shows examples. Note how $K_{xyz} \otimes \mathrm{id}_{pq}$ exports names from the molecule. We shall shortly discuss non-discrete constructions, in which points may be linked.

We can express all bigraphs algebraically in terms of elementary placings, linkings and ions, using composition, product and identities. This applies to both `BG($\mathcal{K}$) and BG($\mathcal{K}$), but in `BG($\mathcal{K}$) we may wish to make support explicit in the algebraic expression of a bigraph. This is easy, because nodes are created only by ions, and edges only by closure. So we need only annotate ions and closures with node- and edge-identifiers respectively, thus: $^{v}K_{\vec{x}}$ and $^{e}/x$.

Given the elements and operations of our algebra, what is its theory? When do two expressions denote the same bigraph? This question has been answered, at least for abstract bigraphs. We omit the proof, but it is worth recording the result here:

Theorem 3.6 (axioms for bigraphs) *Two bigraphical expressions denote the same abstract bigraph if and only if they can be proved equal by the equations of an spm category (Definitions 2.8–2.11), together with the axioms tabulated below.*

In other words, the axioms are both *sound* and *complete*. They say simple things: The place axioms say that *join* is commutative, has a unit and is associative; the link axioms say that the formation of links obeys obvious rules; the node axiom says that we can name ports arbitrarily. Since the ssm axioms are not at all specific to bigraphs, this result means that the *structure* of bigraphs is straightforward, as it should be; we should expect the subtlety of a behavioural model to lie in its *dynamics*.

Symmetry axiom: $\gamma_{\langle m,X\rangle,\langle n,Y\rangle} = \gamma_{m,n} \otimes \mathsf{id}_{X\uplus Y}$

Place axioms: $join \circ \gamma_{1,1} = join$
$join \circ (1 \otimes \mathsf{id}_1) = \mathsf{id}_1$
$join \circ (join \otimes \mathsf{id}_1) = join \circ (\mathsf{id}_1 \otimes join)$

Link axioms: $^{x}/x = \mathsf{id}_x$
$/x \circ x = \mathsf{id}_\epsilon$
$/y \circ {}^{y}/x = /x$
$^{z}/(Y \uplus y) \circ (\mathsf{id}_Y \otimes {}^{y}/X) = {}^{z}/(Y \uplus X)$

Node axiom: $(\mathsf{id}_1 \otimes \alpha) \circ \mathsf{K}_{\vec{x}} = \mathsf{K}_{\alpha(\vec{x})}$

Axioms for bigraphical structure

Let us now return to properties of bigraphs that can be expressed algebraically. We begin with the *occurrence* of one bigraph within another. We adopt the following definition, which applies to both concrete and abstract bigraphs:

Definition 3.7 (occurrence) A bigraph F *occurs* in a bigraph G if the equation $G = C_1 \circ (F \otimes \mathsf{id}_I) \circ C_0$ holds for some interface I and bigraphs C_0 and C_1. $\square$

The identity id_I is important here: it allows nodes of C_1 to have children in C_0 as well as in F, and allows C_1 and C_0 to share links that do not involve F. It appears to be the natural way to define occurrence, as the following exercise suggests.

EXERCISE 3.2 Make sure that the definition implies the right thing, in simple cases: i.e. that F occurs in $F \circ C$, $C \circ F$, $F \otimes C$ and $C \otimes F$. Less trivially, show that a ground bigraph a occurs in a ground bigraph g iff $g = C \circ a$ for some C. Also prove that occurrence is transitive, i.e. if E occurs in F and F occurs in G then E occurs in G. $\square$

We now come to two kinds of bigraph, *prime* and *discrete*, which are important both for the algebraic structure of bigraphs (Proposition 3.9) and for their dynamics (Definition 8.5). In both cases we are concerned with breaking down a bigraph into parts; for example, Proposition 3.9 shows that every bigraph is the composition of a linking with a discrete bigraph.

Definition 3.8 (prime, discrete)   A *prime* bigraph has no inner names and a unary outer face; its homset takes the form $m \to \langle X \rangle$.

A link graph or bigraph is *discrete* if it has no closed links, and its link map is bijective. Thus it is open, no two points are siblings, and no name is idle. $\square$

An important prime is $merge_n: n \to 1$, where $n \geq 0$; see Definition 3.1. It has no nodes, and maps n sites to a single root. A bigraph $G: m \to \langle n, X \rangle$ with no inner names can be merged into a prime $(merge \otimes \mathrm{id}_X) \circ G$. As here, we shall usually omit the subscript n from $merge$.

Note the absence of inner names in a prime bigraph. This ensures the unique decomposition of a bigraph into a linking and discrete primes, as follows:

Proposition 3.9 (discrete normal form)   *Every bigraph* $G: \langle m, X \rangle \to \langle n, Z \rangle$ *can be expressed uniquely, up to a renaming on* Y, *as*

$$G = (\mathrm{id}_n \otimes \lambda) \circ D$$

where $\lambda: Y \to Z$ *is a linking and* $D: \langle m, X \rangle \to \langle n, Y \rangle$ *is discrete. Further, every discrete* D *may be factored uniquely, up to permutation of the sites of each factor, as*

$$D = \alpha \otimes ((P_0 \otimes \cdots \otimes P_{n-1}) \circ \pi)$$

with α *a renaming, each* P_i *prime and discrete, and* π *a permutation of all the sites.*

Note that a renaming α is discrete but not prime, since it has zero width and also has inner names; this explains why a renaming is needed in the prime factorisation. In the special case that D is ground, the result simplifies as follows:

Corollary 3.10 (ground discrete normal form) *A ground bigraph $g : \langle n, Z \rangle$ can be expressed uniquely, up to renaming on Y, as $g = (\mathrm{id}_n \otimes \lambda) \circ (d_0 \otimes \cdots \otimes d_{n-1})$, where $\lambda : Y \to Z$ is a linking and the d_i are discrete primes.*

This analysis of a bigraph into smaller discrete ones is crucial for the proof that our algebraic theory is complete (Theorem 3.6). It can be seen as extracting all non-trivial linking from a bigraph G at the very first step. But it may not be how a designer would wish to build a bigraph from smaller ones. Instead, she may prefer to push all linking – both substitutions and closures – inwards as far as possible. We shall shortly see how to break down a bigraph in this alternative way.

3.2 Derived operations

Notation We often omit '$\ldots \otimes \mathrm{id}_I$' in a composition $(F \otimes \mathrm{id}_I) \circ G$ when there is no ambiguity; for example we write $merge \circ G$ for $(merge \otimes \mathrm{id}_X) \circ G$.

Given a linking $\lambda : Y \to Z$, we may wish to apply it to a bigraph $G : I \to \langle m, X \rangle$ with fewer names, i.e. $Y = X \uplus X'$. Then we may write $\lambda \circ G$ for $(\mathrm{id}_m \otimes \lambda) \circ (G \otimes X')$ when m and X' can be understood from the context. $\square$

If $X = \{x_1, \ldots, x_n\}$ we shall write $/X$ to mean $/x_1 \otimes \cdots \otimes /x_n$.

We now generalise the tensor product. We define an operation that comes closer to the 'parallel composition' of process calculi by allowing names to be shared.

Definition 3.11 (parallel product) The *parallel product* $\parallel$ is given on interfaces by
$$\langle m, X \rangle \parallel \langle n, Y \rangle \overset{\text{def}}{=} \langle m + n, X \cup Y \rangle .$$

Now let $G_i : I_i \to J_i$ $(i = 0, 1)$ be two bigraphs with disjoint supports. Denote the link map of G_i by $link_i$ $(i = 0, 1)$, and assume further that $link_0 \cup link_1$ is a function. Then the parallel product
$$G_0 \parallel G_1 : I_0 \parallel I_1 \to J_0 \parallel J_1$$

is defined just as tensor product, except that its link map allows name-sharing. $\square$

Let X_i, Y_i be the names of I_i, J_i respectively $(i = 0, 1)$. Because the supports of G_i are disjoint, the condition that $link_0 \cup link_1$ is a function amounts to requiring that, for every inner name $x \in X_0 \cap X_1$, there exists an outer name $y \in Y_0 \cap Y_1$ such that $link_0(x) = link_1(x) = y$. Thus tensor product is the special case in which $X_0 \cap X_1 = Y_0 \cap Y_1 = \emptyset$.

Proposition 3.12 (parallel product) *The parallel product of bigraphs is associative; that is, $F \parallel (G \parallel H) = (F \parallel G) \parallel H$ when either side is defined. It also has*

id_ϵ *as unit. Furthermore it satisfies the 'bifunctorial' property when both sides are defined:*

$$(F_1 \parallel G_1) \circ (F_0 \parallel G_0) = (F_1 \circ F_0) \parallel (G_1 \circ G_0) .$$

Proof   Straightforward from the definition, noting that the condition on link maps is satisfied on one side iff it is satisfied on the other side.   □

The reader may be concerned that $F \parallel G$ is only defined when $link_F \cup link_G$ is a function. Indeed, in previous work $F \parallel G$ was permitted only when the inner faces of F and G are disjoint, ensuring $link_F \# link_G$ and thus implying our constraint. However, the useful bifunctorial property is then lost.

From another point of view, the present definition is natural; for it can be shown that the constraint on link maps holds if and only if there are bigraphs F' and G' and a substitution σ, with all three inner faces disjoint, such that $F = F' \parallel \sigma$, $G = \sigma \parallel G'$, and $F \parallel G = F' \parallel \sigma \parallel G'$. Thus, given the disjointness of supports, $F \parallel G$ is defined iff the two bigraphs treat their open inner names the same.

Notation   Parallel product allows further convenient abbreviations. For example, if $X = \{x_1, \ldots, x_n\}$ we define $y/X \stackrel{\text{def}}{=} y/x_1 \parallel \cdots \parallel y/x_n$. Also, if G has outer face $\langle n, X \uplus Z \rangle$, we shall write $y/X \circ G$ to mean $(y/X \parallel id_I) \circ G$, where $I = \langle n, Z \rangle$. This makes sense even if $y \in X \uplus Z$.   □

It is common to nest, inside an ion, a bigraph of width 1 that shares names with the ion. We therefore define a *nesting* operation as follows:

Definition 3.13 (nesting)   Let $F : I \to \langle m, X \rangle$ and $G : m \to \langle n, Y \rangle$ be bigraphs. Define the *nesting* $G.F : I \to \langle n, X \cup Y \rangle$ by:

$$G.F \stackrel{\text{def}}{=} (id_X \parallel G) \circ F .$$ □

Example 3.14 (nesting)   The figure below uses nesting to describe a non-discrete version of the discrete molecule shown earlier. It can be written $(K_{xyz} \parallel id_{yz}) \circ L_{yz}$, using parallel product to create the sharing of names. With the nesting operation we can also write it as $K_{xyz}.L_{yz}$.   □

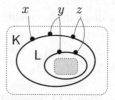

molecule: $(K_{xyz} \parallel id_{yz}) \circ L_{yz} = K_{xyz}.L_{yz}$

Nesting will be found to express the prefixing operation of CCS.

Notation If A is an atomic control then we may abbreviate the atom A.1 to just A; this is justified because an atomic node can only contain 1. □

EXERCISE 3.3 Prove that nesting is associative; that is, $H.(G.F) = (H.G).F$ for $F: I \to \langle k, X \rangle$, $G: k \to \langle m, Y \rangle$ and $H: m \to \langle n, Z \rangle$. *Hint:* Expand the definition of nesting, then use associativity of parallel product and the bifunctorial property. □

We now derive a form of parallel product that produces bigraphs of unit width:

Definition 3.15 (merge product) The *merge product* $|$ is defined on interfaces by $\langle m, X \rangle \mid \langle n, Y \rangle \stackrel{\text{def}}{=} \langle X \cup Y \rangle$. On bigraphs, under the same condition as for parallel product, it is defined by

$$G_0 \mid G_1 \stackrel{\text{def}}{=} merge \circ (G_0 \parallel G_1) \colon I_0 \parallel I_1 \to J_0 \mid J_1 \,. \qquad \square$$

Proposition 3.16 (merge product) *Merge product is associative, and (on bigraphs of unit width) it has 1 as unit.*

By introducing derived products and nesting, we have clothed the categorical operations – composition and tensor product – in a way that yields convenient algebraic expression. As we shall soon see, this brings us closer to the form of expression found in process calculi. Thus we have exposed spm categories as a foundation for these calculi. One advantage, already mentioned, has been the existence of a normal form (Proposition 3.9) that enables the proof of algebraic completeness (Theorem 3.6).

However, we can now show that our derived operations – though they may not support a completeness theorem – allow us to break down a bigraph in the alternative way we mentioned, pushing linking inwards. It works for arbitrary bigraphs, but here we shall give it just for ground bigraphs, as another corollary of Proposition 3.9:

Corollary 3.17 (ground connected normal form) *A ground bigraph $g: \langle n, Z \rangle$ can be expressed uniquely, up to renaming on Y, as $g = (\text{id}_{\langle n, Z \rangle} \otimes /Y) \circ (p_0 \parallel \cdots \parallel p_{n-1})$, where the p_i are prime and each closed link $y \in Y$ has ports in more than one p_i.*

This form of factorisation – sharing names as deeply as possible – can be continued into the primes p_i by means of merge product and nesting. Here is an example, for a ground bigraph used in Chapter 1; we assume that K is atomic.

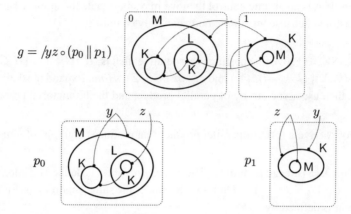

$$g = /yz \circ (p_0 \parallel p_1)$$

You may check that $p_0 = M_y.(/x \circ (K_{yx}.1 \mid L.(K_{xz}.1)))$ and $p_1 = K_{zy}.(M_z.1).$[1]

Example 3.18 (CCS redexes) We shall use the process calculus CCS as a running example throughout this work. We begin with the redex of the usual CCS reaction rule, which we shall study in detail in Chapter 8, as a good example of an algebraic expression. In the notation of CCS, the reaction rule takes the form

$$(x.P + A) \mid (\overline{x}.Q + B) \longrightarrow P \mid Q$$

where P, Q, A, B are *parameters*, i.e. arbitrary CCS expressions. This parametric-ity will be represented as four sites in a non-ground bigraph R; see the diagram below. The meaning of the rule is that an interaction between x and $\overline{x}$ can occur, and if so then the alternatives A and B will be discarded.

$$\text{alt.} (\text{send}_x \mid \text{id}_1) \mid \text{alt.} (\text{get}_x \mid \text{id}_1)$$

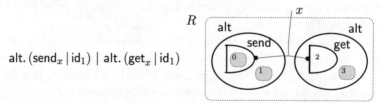

Note that 'send' (sending) and 'get' (receiving) are controls of arity 1, and 'alt' representing summation has arity 0. The algebraic expression of R, as shown, makes good use of the nesting operation. Note that the redex R is prime. It may be surprising that merge product not only represents what is called 'parallel com-position' in CCS, but also (together with alt) represents summation. In Chapter 10 we shall see how this works; essentially, the reaction rule provides the difference in meaning between these two operations.

---

[1] These expressions contain '.1' many times. This is necessary when an empty node has non-atomic control, such as K or M here.

The parametric rule generates an infinite family of *ground* redexes, once the parameters are supplied as ground bigraphs. It turns out that it is enough to assume these parameters to be discrete; so, since the inner width (i.e. width of inner face) of R is 4, these parameters form a single parameter $d : \langle 4, Y \rangle = d_0 \otimes d_1 \otimes d_2 \otimes d_3$, with $d_i : \langle Y_i \rangle$, where $Y = \biguplus_i Y_i$. Thus each ground redex can be expressed as

$$R.d = \mathsf{alt}.(\mathsf{send}_x.d_0 \mid d_1) \mid \mathsf{alt}.(\mathsf{get}_x.d_2 \mid d_3) \,. \qquad \square$$

To end this chapter, let us use the CCS redex $R = \mathsf{alt}.(\mathsf{send}_x \mid \mathsf{id}) \mid \mathsf{alt}.(\mathsf{get}_x \mid \mathsf{id})$ to illustrate another phenomenon. We shall meet it in Definition 8.6 and Proposition 8.14 to characterise certain well-behaved transition systems, including the one we derive for CCS. The reader may safely ignore it until then, but we analyse it here because it is a structural property with some intrinsic interest.

We shall need to deal with cases in which a bigraph R – especially a redex – occurs in the composition $G = B \circ A$ of two bigraphs, but not in either A or B alone. Indeed, this is exactly what gives rise to communication in CCS; for if p and q are (bigraphs representing) CCS processes, then p may contain $\mathsf{alt}.(\mathsf{send}_x \mid \mathsf{id})$ while q contains $\mathsf{alt}.(\mathsf{get}_x \mid \mathsf{id})$. In this case we have $G = p \mid q$, $A = p$ and $B = \mathsf{id}_1 \mid q$, so the interface between A and B is unary.

But there are other ways to decompose the CCS redex R. For example, we have $R = Q \circ P$ where $P = \mathsf{send}_x \parallel \mathsf{get}_x$ and $Q = \mathsf{alt} \mid \mathsf{alt} \mid \mathsf{id}_x$, so the interface between P and Q may be multiary. In this case, it turns out that if R occurs in $G = B \circ A$, where A has a unary outer face, then this occurrence cannot arise from an occurrence of P in A and Q in B.

This phenomenon will affect how we derive transition systems, e.g. for CCS, so we need to treat it more formally.

Definition 3.19 (split, tight) A *split for* F is a pair A, B such that F occurs in $B \circ A$ and both $|A| \cap |F|$ and $|B| \cap |F|$ are non-empty. The split is *m-ary* if A has an m-ary outer face. The split is *tight* if some port in $|A| \cap |F|$ is linked to a port in $|B| \cap |F|$.

Finally, F is *tight* if every unary split for F is tight. $\qquad \square$

The notion of a split helps to address the question: If a bigraph F can be split into two parts across the boundary of a composition, then how are the two parts of F related? It depends upon the interface of the composition. Our definition of tightness is a little arbitrary, but will help to measure how 'tightly knit' is each redex in a bigraphical reactive system.

For example, consider any split A, B for R, the CCS redex. In general there need be no link between the two parts; we may have $R = B \circ A$ where $A = \mathsf{send}_x \parallel \mathsf{get}_x$ and $B = \mathsf{alt} \mid \mathsf{alt} \mid \mathsf{id}_x$, and no port of A is linked to a port of B (indeed B has no ports). But note that the interface of the split is not unary. If we consider only unary splits, we find that there is always a linked pair of ports of R in opposite parts of the composition. So R is tight.

EXERCISE 3.4 Prove that the CCS redex is tight.

Rules A1–A3 for mobile ambients and B1–B3 for the built environment are given in Chapter 1; which of their redexes are tight?   □

4

Relative and minimal bounds

This chapter introduces an important structural notion at the general[1] level of a precategory. We begin with some motivation from bigraphs.

Structural analysis for bigraphs is more challenging than it is for algebraic terms. Terms are tree-like, and trees enjoy the property that, for two subtrees of a larger tree, either they are disjoint or one is contained in the other. This is not the case with bigraphs. For example, consider the built environment of Example 1.2; one may consider one subsystem consisting of the agents and the computers, and another consisting of the rooms and the agents. They have a non-trivial intersection: the agents.

This situation can be represented generally in a category or precategory, but let us restrict attention to bigraphs. A bigraph, even a ground bigraph, can often be decomposed in two ways; for example $g = C_0 \circ f_0 = C_1 \circ f_1$. We say that f_0 and f_1 both *occur* in g. Do these *occurrences* overlap? What, if any, is the smallest part h of g that contains them both, i.e. $g = D \circ h$, with $h = D_i \circ f_i$ and $C_i = D \circ D_i$ $(i = 0, 1)$?

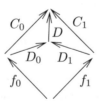

In abstract graphs this question has no definite answer. But in the dynamic theory of bigraphs we shall need answers to such questions. They arise in two distinct ways.

---

[1] The words 'abstract' and 'general' can be confused. They are often used as synonyms, but in this work 'abstract/concrete' distinguishes only between graphs in which the nodes and edges are unidentified and those in which they are identified. On the other hand 'general/specific' represents a spectrum from lesser to greater definition; for example, it proceeds from 'precategory' through 's-category', then through the class of all bigraphical s-categories, then to any specific bigraphical s-category such as $\mathrm{BG}_{\mathrm{ccs}}$ or $^{\backprime}\mathrm{BG}_{\mathrm{ccs}}$.

First, two reconfigurations – or *reactions* as we shall call them – of a bigraph g may be possible; this means that two different *redexes* – the parts to be reconfigured – may occur in g. If they overlap, then one reaction may preclude the other, forming what is known as a critical pair; we have to analyse such possible *conflicts*. Second, a system may be able to contribute to a reaction – it may contain part of a redex – and we wish to know whether the environment contains the missing part, so that they can jointly react; we have to analyse such *potential* reactions. We would like to know, for a given potential reaction, what is the minimal environment that permits it to occur.

This motivates the notion of *relative pushout* (RPO), which we develop here in the general framework of an arbitrary precategory.

Notation While we are working at this general level, we revert to using lower case letters for arrows in this chapter. We shall frequently use $\vec{f}$ to denote a pair f_0, f_1 of arrows. If their domains coincide the pair is a *span*, if their codomains coincide it is a *cospan*. If the shared domain of a span $\vec{f}$ is H and the codomains are I_0 and I_1, then we may write $\vec{f} : H \to \vec{I}$, with a dual notation for cospans. We shall also use $\vec{f} \circ g$ to mean the span $f_0 \circ g, f_1 \circ g$, with a dual notation for cospans.   □

Definition 4.1 (bound, consistent) If $\vec{f}$ is a span and $\vec{g}$ a cospan such that $g_0 \circ f_0 = g_1 \circ f_1$, then we call $\vec{g}$ a *bound* for $\vec{f}$. If $\vec{f}$ has a bound it is said to be *consistent*.   □

Before defining relative pushouts, we recall the standard notion of pushout:

Definition 4.2 (pushout) A *pushout* for a span $\vec{f}$ is a bound $\vec{h}$ for $\vec{f}$ such that, for any bound $\vec{g}$, there is a unique arrow h such that $h \circ \vec{h} = \vec{g}$.   □

We are now ready for the main definition of this chapter:

Definition 4.3 (relative pushout) Let $\vec{g}$ be a bound for $\vec{f}$. A *bound for $\vec{f}$ relative to $\vec{g}$* is a triple $(\vec{h}, h)$ of arrows such that $\vec{h}$ is a bound for $\vec{f}$ and $h \circ \vec{h} = \vec{g}$. We may call the triple a *relative bound* when $\vec{g}$ is understood.

A *relative pushout (RPO) for $\vec{f}$ relative to $\vec{g}$* is a relative bound $(\vec{h}, h)$ such that for any relative bound $(\vec{k}, k)$ there is a unique arrow j for which $j \circ \vec{h} = \vec{k}$ and $k \circ j = h$. (See the right-hand diagram.)

We say that a precategory *has RPOs* if, whenever a span has a bound, it also has an RPO relative to that bound.   □

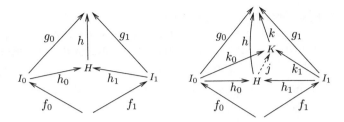

We shall often omit the word 'relative'; for example we may call $(\vec{h}, h)$ a bound (or RPO) for $\vec{f}$ to $\vec{g}$.

The more familiar notion, a pushout, is a bound $\vec{h}$ for $\vec{f}$ such that *for any* bound $\vec{g}$ there exists an h which makes the left-hand diagram commute. Thus a pushout is a *least* bound, while an RPO provides a *minimal* bound relative to a given bound $\vec{g}$.

Suppose that we can construct an RPO $(\vec{h}, h)$ for $\vec{f}$ to $\vec{g}$; what happens if we try to iterate the construction? More precisely, is there an RPO for $\vec{f}$ to $\vec{h}$? The answer lies in the following important concept:

Definition 4.4 (idem pushout) If $\vec{f}: H \to \vec{I}$ is a span, then a cospan $\vec{g}: \vec{I} \to J$ is an *idem pushout (IPO)* for $\vec{f}$ if $(\vec{g}, \mathrm{id}_J)$ is an RPO for $\vec{f}$ to $\vec{g}$. □

The attempt to iterate the RPO construction will yield the *same* bound (up to isomorphism); the minimal bound for $\vec{f}$ to any bound $\vec{g}$ is reached in just one step. This is assured by the first two parts of the following proposition, which summarises the essential properties of RPOs and IPOs on which our work relies.

Proposition 4.5 (properties of RPOs) *In any precategory* `C:

(1) If an RPO for $\vec{f}$ to $\vec{g}$ exists, then it is unique up to isomorphism.

(2) If $(\vec{h}, h)$ is an RPO for $\vec{f}$ to $\vec{g}$, then $\vec{h}$ is an IPO for $\vec{f}$.

(3) If $\vec{h}$ is an IPO for $\vec{f}$, and an RPO exists for $\vec{f}$ to $h \circ \vec{h}$, then the triple $(\vec{h}, h)$ is such an RPO.

(4) Suppose that the diagram below commutes, and that f_0, g_0 has an RPO to the pair $h_1 \circ h_0, f_2 \circ g_1$. Then

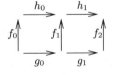

    (a) if the two squares are IPOs, so is the rectangle;
    (b) if the rectangle and left square are IPOs, so is
        the right square.

(5) If `C is an s-category, then any support translation of an RPO is an RPO.

(6) Every pushout is an IPO.

Proof (partial) We prove (1) here. We pose (2) and (3) as Exercises 4.1 and 4.2.

For (1), assume that $(\vec{h}, h)$ is an RPO for $\vec{f}$ to $\vec{g}$, with mediating object H. We must show that $(\vec{k}, k)$, with mediating object K, is also an RPO iff there is an iso $\iota : H \to K$ such that $k \circ \iota = h$ and $\vec{k} = \iota \circ \vec{h}$.

($\Rightarrow$)   Assume that $(\vec{k}, k)$ is also an RPO. Each of the two RPOs is a relative bound; by comparing each with the other, or with itself, we first deduce three properties:

$$\text{there exists unique } x : H \to K \text{ such that } \vec{k} = x \circ \vec{h} \text{ and } k \circ x = h \; ; \tag{a}$$
$$\text{there exists unique } y : K \to H \text{ such that } \vec{h} = y \circ \vec{k} \text{ and } h \circ y = k \; ; \tag{b}$$
$$\text{there exists unique } z : H \to H \text{ such that } \vec{h} = z \circ \vec{h} \text{ and } h \circ z = h \; . \tag{c}$$

It then follows that $y \circ x = \text{id}$, since both satisfy the equations of (c). Similarly we find $x \circ y = \text{id}$. Hence x is an iso, readily seen to have the required property.

($\Leftarrow$)   Assume an iso $\iota : H \to K$ with inverse ι', such that $\iota \circ \vec{h} = \vec{k}$ and $k \circ \iota = h$. Let $(\vec{\ell}, \ell)$ be any relative bound. Then, since $(\vec{h}, h)$ is an RPO, there exists unique $z : H \to L$ such that $z \circ \vec{h} = \vec{\ell}$ and $\ell \circ z = h$.

To prove $(\vec{k}, k)$ an RPO we require a unique $w : K \to L$ satisfying the equations $\vec{\ell} = w \circ \vec{k}$ and $l \circ w = k$. Now $\vec{\ell} = (z \circ \iota') \circ \vec{k}$ and $\ell \circ (z \circ \iota') = k$; thus $w = z \circ \iota'$ satisfies the equations. Moreover, for any w' satisfying the equations we find $\vec{\ell} = (w' \circ \iota) \circ \vec{h}$ and $\ell \circ (w' \circ \iota) = h$, hence by the unicity of z we have $(w' \circ \iota) = z$. Therefore $w = w'$, ensuring unicity of w.   □

EXERCISE 4.1 Prove (2) in Proposition 4.5. That is, assume that $(\vec{h}, h)$ is an RPO for $\vec{f}$ relative to $\vec{g}$, and prove that $\vec{h}$ is an IPO for $\vec{f}$.   □

EXERCISE 4.2 Prove (3) in Proposition 4.5. That is, assume that $\vec{h}$ is an IPO for $\vec{f}$, and that an RPO exists for $\vec{f}$ relative to $h \circ h_0, h \circ h_1$; then prove that $(\vec{h}, h)$ is such an RPO.   □

These properties are powerful; for example, they will enable us to define behavioural equivalences which are *congruences*, i.e. they are preserved by composition and tensor product, and hence by all derived operations such as parallel and merge products, nesting, substitution and merging. Thus, if a subsystem is replaced by a congruent subsystem, then the behaviour of the whole system is unchanged. This will be illustrated for both Petri nets in Chapter 9 and CCS in Chapter 10, thus confirming existing theory for these process models.

These benefits only fully accrue in a precategory that *has RPOs*, i.e. it has an RPO for every bounded span. In Chapter 5 we shall show that the s-category of concrete bigraphs over any basic signature has RPOs.

However, we need more than this. In Chapter 6 we shall define s-categories of bigraphs that obey a wide range of so-called *sorting disciplines*; these often impose structural constraints, which may preclude the existence of (some or all) RPOs. Such a discipline `A typically consists of an s-category of bigraphs whose places – or whose points and links – have been assigned certain sorts, and the only bigraphs permitted are those that satisfy a structural constraint expressed in terms of the sorts. A simple example is when each place is assigned one of the sorts 'red' or 'blue', and the admissible bigraphs are those in which the parent of each node v has a different colour from v, while the parent of each site s has the same colour as s.

As we shall see in Chapter 6, every sorted bigraphical s-category `A is built on a basic signature $\mathcal{K}$, and has a functor

$$`\mathcal{U} : `A \to `BG(\mathcal{K})$$

called a *forgetful* functor, because it forgets the sorts of `A.[2] We want `A to be well-behaved; in particular, to have RPOs. A sufficient condition for this is that the functor `$\mathcal{U}$ is safe, according to the following general definition:

Definition 4.6 (safe functors and sorting) A functor $\mathcal{F} : `A \to `B$ of s-categories is *safe* if it creates RPOs and isomorphisms, and also reflects identities, products and pushouts. These properties are defined as follows, where we write $\mathcal{F}(\vec{f})$ to mean $\mathcal{F}(f_0), \mathcal{F}(f_1)$:

- $\mathcal{F}$ *creates RPOs* if, given a span $\vec{f}$ bounded by $\vec{h}$ in `A, any RPO in `B for $\mathcal{F}(\vec{f})$ relative to $\mathcal{F}(\vec{h})$ has an $\mathcal{F}$-preimage that is an RPO for $\vec{f}$ relative to $\vec{h}$.[3]
- $\mathcal{F}$ *creates isomorphisms* if, for any object I_0 in `A and isomorphism $\kappa : \mathcal{F}(I_0) \to K_1$ in `B, there is a unique object I_1 and isomorphism $\iota : I_0 \to I_1$ in `A such that $\mathcal{F}(\iota, I_1) = (\kappa, K_1)$.
- $\mathcal{F}$ *reflects identities* if, whenever f is an arrow in `A such that $\mathcal{F}(f)$ is an identity, then f is itself an identity.
- $\mathcal{F}$ *reflects products* if, whenever $\mathcal{F}(g) = \mathcal{F}(f_0) \otimes \mathcal{F}(f_1)$, then also $g = f_0 \otimes f_1$.
- $\mathcal{F}$ *reflects pushouts* if, for $\vec{f}$ bounded by $\vec{g}$ in `A, whenever $\mathcal{F}(\vec{g})$ is a pushout for $\mathcal{F}(\vec{f})$ then $\vec{g}$ is a pushout for $\vec{f}$.

A sorting discipline is *safe* if its forgetful functor is safe. □

These conditions are not necessarily independent. They are chosen with a view to deriving transition systems. At least one of the conditions is implied by one or more of the others; the reader may enjoy the puzzle of verifying this.

---

[2] A similar functor $\mathcal{U} : A \to BG(\mathcal{K})$ of spm categories exists for abstract bigraphs, where **A** is the lean-support quotient of `A.

[3] This RPO-preimage may not be unique; it may vary by an iso at the mediating object.

The following is important for deriving transition systems for sorted bigraphs:

Proposition 4.7 (transferring RPOs) *Let* $\mathcal{F} : {}^{\backprime}\mathbf{A} \to {}^{\backprime}\mathbf{B}$ *create RPOs, and assume that* ${}^{\backprime}\mathbf{B}$ *has RPOs. Then*

(1) ${}^{\backprime}\mathbf{A}$ *has RPOs.*

(2) $\mathcal{F}$ *preserves RPOs; that is, if* $(\vec{g}, g)$ *is an RPO in* ${}^{\backprime}\mathbf{A}$ *for* $\vec{f}$ *relative to* $\vec{h}$, *then* $\mathcal{F}(\vec{g}, g)$ *is an RPO in* ${}^{\backprime}\mathbf{B}$ *for* $\mathcal{F}(\vec{f})$ *relative to* $\mathcal{F}(\vec{h})$.

Proof (outline) The first part is immediate from the definition. For the second part, first construct an RPO $(\vec{k}', k')$ in ${}^{\backprime}\mathbf{B}$ for $\mathcal{F}(\vec{f})$ relative to $\mathcal{F}(\vec{h})$. Then $\mathcal{F}$ creates from this an RPO $(\vec{k}, k)$ in ${}^{\backprime}\mathbf{A}$ for $\vec{f}$ relative to $\vec{h}$. By Proposition 4.5(1), this RPO coincides with the given RPO $(\vec{g}, g)$ up to an isomorphism between their mediating interfaces. Hence, since functors preserve isomorphism, $(\vec{k}', k')$ coincides similarly with $\mathcal{F}(\vec{g}, g)$, and the latter is therefore itself an RPO in ${}^{\backprime}\mathbf{B}$.   □

The last four conditions for safety, when satisfied by a sorting discipline (Chapter 6) will allow us to make its derived transition system more tractable. It will turn out that a quite wide class of sorting disciplines satisfy the five conditions, including our formulation of both Petri nets and CCS in bigraphs.

Here is another property that will be useful later:

Proposition 4.8 (creating IPOs) *If a functor* $\mathcal{F}$ *is safe then it creates IPOs; that is, if* $\vec{g}$ *bounds* $\vec{f}$, *and* $\mathcal{F}(\vec{g})$ *is an IPO for* $\mathcal{F}(\vec{f})$, *then* $\vec{g}$ *is an IPO for* $\vec{f}$.

Proof We have that $(\mathcal{F}(\vec{g}), \mathsf{id})$ is an RPO for $\mathcal{F}(\vec{f})$ to $\mathcal{F}(\vec{g})$. Since $\mathcal{F}$ creates RPOs, there is an RPO $(\vec{h}, h)$ for $\vec{f}$ to $\vec{g}$, and this RPO is a preimage of the RPO $(\mathcal{F}(\vec{g}), \mathsf{id})$.

But $\mathcal{F}$ reflects identities, and $\mathcal{F}(h) = \mathsf{id}$, so h is an identity. It follows that $\vec{h} = \vec{g}$, and hence $\vec{g}$ is an IPO as required.   □

It will be useful to have a sufficient condition for a functor to reflect pushouts. For this we need a standard categorical notion:

Definition 4.9 (op-cartesian)

Let $\mathcal{F} : {}^{\backprime}\mathbf{A} \to {}^{\backprime}\mathbf{B}$ be a functor. An arrow $f : I \to J$ in ${}^{\backprime}\mathbf{A}$ is said to be *op-cartesian for* $\mathcal{F}$ if, for all $h : I \to K$ and g' such that $\mathcal{F}(h) = g' \circ \mathcal{F}(f)$, there exists unique g such that $\mathcal{F}(g) = g'$ and $h = g \circ f$.   □

$$\left(\begin{array}{ccc} h\nearrow & {}^{\wedge}_{\vdots}g & g'\Big\uparrow \quad \Big\uparrow \mathcal{F}(h) \\ & \Big\uparrow f & \mathcal{F}(f)\Big\uparrow \end{array} \right)$$

Proposition 4.10 (reflecting pushouts) *If every arrow in the domain of a functor* $\mathcal{F}$ *is op-cartesian then* $\mathcal{F}$ *reflects pushouts.*

EXERCISE 4.3 Prove Proposition 4.10. *Hint:* You need to use the op-cartesian property more than once. □

We are now ready to apply these general notions, first to unsorted bigraphs in Chapter 5 and then to sorted bigraphs in Chapter 6.

5

Bigraphical structure

This chapter refines the structural analysis of concrete bigraphs. In Section 5.1 we establish some properties for concrete bigraphs, including RPOs. In Section 5.2 we enumerate all IPOs for a given span. Finally, in Section 5.3 we show that RPOs do not exist in general for abstract bigraphs.

5.1 RPOs for bigraphs

We begin with a characterisation of epimorphisms (epis) and monomorphisms (monos) in bigraphs. These notions are defined in a precategory just as in a category, as follows:

Definition 5.1 (epi, mono) An arrow f in a precategory is *epi* if $g \circ f = h \circ f$ implies $g = h$. It is *mono* if $f \circ g = f \circ h$ implies $g = h$. □

Proposition 5.2 (epis and monos in concrete bigraphs) *A concrete place graph is epi iff no root is idle; it is mono iff no two sites are siblings. A concrete link graph is epi iff no outer name is idle; it is mono iff no two inner names are siblings.*

A concrete bigraph G is an epi (resp. mono) iff its place graph G^P and its link graph G^L are so.

EXERCISE 5.1 Prove the above proposition, at least for the case of epi link graphs. *Hint:* Make the following intuition precise: if G and H differ then, when composed with F, the difference can be hidden if and only if F has an idle name. □

The proposition fails for *abstract* bigraphs, suggesting that concrete bigraphs have more tractable structure. We shall now provide further evidence for this by constructing RPOs for them.

The construction of RPOs in `Bg is made easier by the fact that we can construct them separately for `Pg and `Lg and then pair them. Moreover the constructions for place graphs and link graphs have much in common. We shall first discuss informally, with examples, how it works for link graphs. Then we shall present the formal construction for both link graphs and place graphs without further discussion. We prove the validity of the link graph construction; the proof for place graphs is similar.

Pushouts were defined in Definition 4.2. Our construction of RPOs in bigraphs adapts the standard construction of pushouts in the category of sets and functions, which we now recall.

Example 5.3 (pushouts for functions) Let $\vec{f}: R \to \vec{S}$ be a span of functions between sets. What cospan $\vec{g}: \vec{S} \to T$ is a pushout? (For simplicity, assume $S_0 \# S_1$.) To ensure $g_0 \circ f_0 = g_1 \circ f_1$ we must equate $g_0(y_0)$ and $g_1(y_1)$ whenever, for some $x \in R$, $f_0(x) = y_0$ and $f_1(x) = y_1$. To ensure a pushout, we must equate no more than these.

To make this precise, define the least equivalence relation $\equiv$ on $S_0 \uplus S_1$ such that $y_0 \equiv y_1$ whenever, for some x, we have $f_i(x) = y_i$ $(i = 0, 1)$. Then for each $y \in S_0$ define $g_0(y) \stackrel{\text{def}}{=} [y]_\equiv$, the equivalence class of y; similarly for $g_1(y)$ when $y \in S_1$. This completes the pushout construction. $\square$

A similar equivalence relation arises in the more complex setting of RPOs for concrete bigraphs, which is the main topic of this chapter. We therefore switch back to our convention of using upper case letters, usually A–H, for bigraphs and their constituents.

Example 5.4 (RPOs for link graphs) We shall now illustrate the RPO construction for link graphs with the example in Figure 5.1, showing a span $\vec{A}$ bounded by a cospan $\vec{D}: \vec{X} \to Z$. We assume the interfaces $X_0 = \{x_0, y_0, z_0\}$ and $X_1 = \{x_1, y_1, z_1, w_1\}$ to be disjoint as in the previous example, to ease the discussion. We wish to form an RPO $(\vec{B}, B)$, where $\vec{B}: \vec{X} \to \hat{X}$ and $B: \hat{X} \to Z$.

nodes and edges: We assign to B_0 and B_1 as few nodes and edges as possible to achieve a bound. Assign to B_0 all those in A_1 but not in A_0, and similarly for B_1. B gets all those in $\vec{D}$ but not in $\vec{A}$. Thus B_0 gets v_4, B_1 gets v_3 and e_0, and B gets v_5 and e_1. The shapes of nodes reflect this assignment; for example round nodes are shared by A_0 and A_1.

interface: We have to decide, for $i \in \{0, 1\}$, which members of X_i will be linked in B_i to an outer name in $\hat{X}$. We cannot export $z_1, w_1 \in X_1$ in this way, since their links each contain a port that is closed in A_0, so we would lose

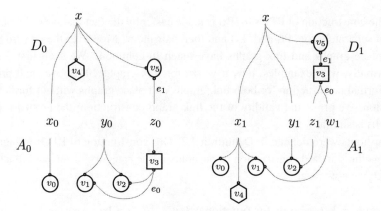

Fig. 5.1. A bounded span $\vec{D}$ for $\vec{A}$

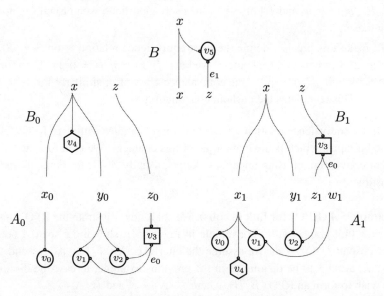

Fig. 5.2. An RPO $(\vec{B}, B)$ for $\vec{A}$ to $\vec{D}$

the commutation $B_0 \circ A_0 = B_1 \circ A_1$. But $\{x_0, y_0, z_0, x_1, y_1\}$ can all be exported to $\hat{X}$.

We then have to decide which of these five should share links in $\hat{X}$. In the jargon of Example 5.3, we look for the smallest equivalence that equates any pair of these names sharing a point in $\vec{A}$; commutation requires us to give such a pair the same link in $\hat{X}$. Readers can check that $\{x_0, y_0, x_1, y_1\}$ must share a link, but z_0 should have a separate link. We choose x, z as names for these links.

links: It remains only to assign links to the ports in $\vec{B}$ and all the points in B. This assignment is dictated uniquely by the commutation equations.

The completed RPO is shown in Figure 5.2. □

EXERCISE 5.2 Suppose that, in Figure 5.1, the link from v_2 to y_0 is replaced by a link from v_2 to some new outer name y, and that we declare $link_{D_0}(y) = x$. From the informal construction in Example 5.4, determine how the RPO $(\vec{B}, B)$ should change, if at all. □

Notation When considering a span $\vec{A} \colon W \to \vec{X}$ of link graphs we shall adopt a naming convention for nodes, ports and edges. We denote the node set of A_i ($i = 0, 1$) by V_i, and denote $V_0 \cap V_1$ by V_2. We shall use $v_i, v'_i, \ldots$ to range over V_i ($i = 0, 1, 2$). Similarly we use $p_i \in P_i$ and $e_i \in E_i$ for ports and edges ($i = 0, 1, 2$). We use q_i for points, i.e. $q_i \in W \uplus P_i$. When there is no ambiguity we write $A(q)$ instead of $link_A(q)$. We use $\bar{\imath}$ to mean $1 - i$ for $i \in \{0, 1\}$.

We define $X_0 + X_1 \overset{\text{def}}{=} \{(i, x) \mid x \in X_i, i \in \{0, 1\}\}$, the disjoint sum of two sets. This differs from $X_0 \uplus X_1$, which asserts that X_0 and X_1 are already disjoint. By $X \setminus Y$ we denote the elements of X not in Y. □

Before giving the formal RPO construction, let us summarise the intuition gained from Example 5.4. To construct an RPO $(\vec{B}, B)$ for $\vec{A}$ relative to a bound $\vec{D}$, we first truncate $\vec{D}$ by removing its outer names, and all nodes and edges not present in $\vec{A}$. (Support is essential for this purpose, in order to identify nodes and edges.) Then for the outer names of $\vec{B}$, we create a name for each link severed by the truncation, equating these new names only when required to ensure that $B_0 \circ A_0 = B_1 \circ A_1$.

Construction 5.5 (RPOs in link graphs) Let the span $\vec{A} \colon W \to \vec{X}$ be bounded by $\vec{D} \colon \vec{X} \to Z$. We construct an RPO $(\vec{B} \colon \vec{X} \to \hat{X}, B \colon \hat{X} \to Z)$ for $\vec{A}$ relative to $\vec{D}$ in three stages, using the notational conventions introduced above.

nodes and edges: If V_i are the nodes of A_i ($i = 0, 1$) then the nodes of D_i are $(V_{\bar{\imath}} \setminus V_2) \uplus V_3$ for unique V_3. Define the nodes of B_i and B to be $V_{\bar{\imath}} \setminus V_2$ ($i = 0, 1$) and V_3 respectively. Edges are treated exactly analogously, and ports inherit the analogous treatment from nodes.

interface: Construct the outer names $\hat{X}$ of $\vec{B}$ as follows. First, define the names in each X_i that must be mapped into $\hat{X}$:

$$X_i' \stackrel{\text{def}}{=} \{x \in X_i \mid D_i(x) \in E_3 \uplus Z\}\,.$$

Next, on the disjoint sum $X_0' + X_1'$, define $\cong$ to be the smallest equivalence for which $(0, x_0) \cong (1, x_1)$ whenever $A_0(q) = x_0$ and $A_1(q) = x_1$ for some point $q \in W \uplus P_2$. Then define $\hat{X}$ up to isomorphism as follows:

$$\hat{X} \stackrel{\text{def}}{=} (X_0' + X_1')/\!\cong\,.$$

For each $x \in X_i'$ we denote by $\widehat{i, x}$ the name in $\hat{X}$ corresponding to the $\cong$-equivalence class of (i, x).

links: Define B_0 to simulate D_0 as far as possible (B_1 is similar):

$$\text{For } x \in X_0: \qquad B_0(x) \stackrel{\text{def}}{=} \begin{cases} \widehat{0, x} & \text{if } x \in X_0' \\ D_0(x) & \text{if } x \notin X_0' \end{cases}$$

$$\text{For } p \in P_1 \setminus P_2: \quad B_0(p) \stackrel{\text{def}}{=} \begin{cases} \widehat{1, x} & \text{if } A_1(p) = x \in X_1 \\ D_0(p) & \text{if } A_1(p) \notin X_1\,. \end{cases}$$

Finally define B, to simulate the common part of D_0 and D_1:

$$\text{For } \hat{x} \in \hat{X}: \quad B(\hat{x}) \stackrel{\text{def}}{=} D_i(x) \text{ where } x \in X_i \text{ and } \widehat{i, x} = \hat{x}$$
$$\text{For } p \in P_3: \quad B(p) \stackrel{\text{def}}{=} D_i(p)\,. \qquad\qquad\qquad \square$$

To prove this definition sound we have to show that the right-hand sides in the clauses defining link maps B_i and B are well-defined links in B_i and B respectively:

Lemma 5.6 *The definition in Construction 5.5 is sound.*

Proof   The second clause defining $B_0(x)$ is sound, since if $x \notin X_0'$ then by definition $D_0(x) \in E_1 \setminus E_2$, which is indeed the port set of B_0. Similar reasoning applies to the second clause defining $B_0(p)$.

The first clause defining $B_0(p)$ is sound, since if $A_1(p) = x$ with $p \in P_1 \setminus P_2$ then we have $x \in X_1'$; for if not, then $D_1(x) \in E_0 \setminus E_2$, which is impossible since $D_1 \circ A_1 = D_0 \circ A_0$.

Finally, the clauses defining B are sound because the right-hand sides are independent of the choice of i and of x; this is seen by appeal to the definition of $\cong$ and the equation $D_1 \circ A_1 = D_0 \circ A_0$. $\qquad\qquad\qquad \square$

The full justification of our construction lies in the following lemma and theorem, both of which are proved in Appendix A.3:

Lemma 5.7 *As defined in Construction 5.5, $(\vec{B}, B)$ is a bound for $\vec{A}$ relative to $\vec{D}$.*

Theorem 5.8 (RPOs in link graphs) `LG(K) has RPOs; that is, whenever a span $\vec{A}$ of link graphs has a bound $\vec{D}$, there exists an RPO for $\vec{A}$ to $\vec{D}$. Moreover Construction 5.5 yields such an RPO.*

We now proceed to the analogous construction of an RPO for a span $\vec{A}\colon h \to \vec{m}$ of place graphs. It closely resembles the one for link graphs, though is a little simpler, so we present it without introductory discussion.

Notation We name nodes just as we did for link graphs. We use r_i, r_i' to range over the roots m_i of A_i ($i = 0, 1$). We shall also use $w, w', \ldots$ to range over $h \uplus V_2$, where h is the domain of each A_i, because shared sites behave just like shared nodes. When there is no ambiguity we write $A(w)$ instead of $prnt_A(w)$. $\square$

Construction 5.9 (RPOs in place graphs) An RPO $(\vec{B}\colon \vec{m} \to \hat{m},\ B\colon \hat{m} \to p)$, for a span $\vec{A}\colon h \to \vec{m}$ in `PG relative to a bound $\vec{D}\colon \vec{m} \to p$, will be built in three stages.

nodes: If V_i are the nodes of A_i ($i = 0, 1$) then the nodes of D_i are $V_{\bar{i}} \setminus V_2 \uplus V_3$ for unique V_3. Define the nodes of B_i and B to be $V_{\bar{i}} \setminus V_2$ ($i = 0, 1$) and V_3 respectively.

interface: Construct the shared codomain $\hat{m}$ of $\vec{B}$ as follows. First, define the roots in each m_i that must be mapped into $\hat{m}$:

$$m_i' \overset{\text{def}}{=} \{r \in m_i \mid D_i(r) \in V_3 \uplus p\} \ .$$

Now on the disjoint sum $m_0' + m_1'$, define $\cong$ as the smallest equivalence for which $(0, r_0) \cong (1, r_1)$ whenever $A_0(w) = r_0$ and $A_1(w) = r_1$ for some shared place $w \in h \uplus V_2$. Then define $\hat{m}$ up to isomorphism by $\hat{m} \overset{\text{def}}{=} (m_0' + m_1')/\!\cong$. For each $r \in m_i'$ we denote the $\cong$-equivalence class of (i, r) by $\widehat{i, r}$.

parents: Define B_0 to simulate D_0 as far as possible (B_1 is similar):

$$\text{For } r \in m_0: \qquad B_0(r) \overset{\text{def}}{=} \begin{cases} \widehat{0, r} & \text{if } r \in m_0' \\ D_0(r) & \text{if } r \notin m_0' \end{cases}$$

$$\text{For } v \in V_1 \setminus V_2: \qquad B_0(v) \overset{\text{def}}{=} \begin{cases} \widehat{1, r} & \text{if } A_1(v) = r \in m_1 \\ D_0(v) & \text{if } A_1(v) \notin m_1 \ . \end{cases}$$

Finally define B, to simulate the common part of D_0 and D_1:

$$\text{For } \hat{r} \in \hat{m}: \quad B(\hat{r}) \overset{\text{def}}{=} D_i(r) \ \text{ where } \widehat{i, r} = \hat{r}$$
$$\text{For } v \in V_3: \quad B(v) \overset{\text{def}}{=} D_i(v) \ .$$

$\square$

Much as for link graphs, one must check that this definition is sound, i.e. that the right-hand sides in the clauses defining the parent maps B_0 and B are well-defined places in B_0 and B respectively. The following is proved just like Theorem 5.8:

Theorem 5.10 (RPOs in place graphs) `PG($\mathcal{K}$) has RPOs; that is, whenever a span $\vec{A}$ of place graphs has a bound $\vec{D}$, there exists an RPO $(\vec{B}, B)$ for $\vec{A}$ to $\vec{D}$. Moreover Construction 5.9 yields such an RPO.*

Finally, we combine our two constructions by pairing:

Corollary 5.11 (RPOs in bigraphs) `BG($\mathcal{K}$) has RPOs. In fact, if a span $\vec{A}$ of bigraphs has a bound $\vec{D}$, then the following is an RPO for $\vec{A}$ to $\vec{D}$:*

$$(\vec{B}, B) \stackrel{\text{def}}{=} (\langle B_0^{\mathsf{P}}, B_0^{\mathsf{L}} \rangle, \langle B_1^{\mathsf{P}}, B_1^{\mathsf{L}} \rangle, \langle B^{\mathsf{P}}, B^{\mathsf{L}} \rangle)$$

where $(\vec{B^{\mathsf{P}}}, B^{\mathsf{P}})$ is an RPO for $\vec{A^{\mathsf{P}}}$ to $\vec{D^{\mathsf{P}}}$ and $(\vec{B^{\mathsf{L}}}, B^{\mathsf{L}})$ is an RPO for $\vec{A^{\mathsf{L}}}$ to $\vec{D^{\mathsf{L}}}$.

Proof It is only necessary to manipulate pairings of place graphs and link graphs. It is crucial that the node sets in the components of $(\vec{B^{\mathsf{P}}}, B^{\mathsf{P}})$ are identical with those in $(\vec{B^{\mathsf{L}}}, B^{\mathsf{L}})$, and hence the pairing of RPOs is defined. □

5.2 IPOs in bigraphs

To prepare for the derivation of labelled transition systems, we have to characterise all the IPOs for a given span $\vec{A}$ of bigraphs.

Although IPOs are defined as a special case of RPOs, their construction is more complex than that for RPOs. For RPOs, we had only to construct a single RPO for $\vec{A}$ relative to a given bound $\vec{D}$; in contrast, for IPOs we want to enumerate a *family*, consisting of the lower squares of all the RPOs for $\vec{A}$ as its bound $\vec{D}$ varies.

The reader may safely omit this section at first reading. When we need specific IPOs later we shall present them explicitly. Readers may then check that they are instances of the present general construction. We shall only give the construction for link graphs; it can be easily adapted to place graphs.

How does a link graph RPO $(\vec{B}, B)$ vary, for a fixed span $\vec{A}$ relative to a varying bound $\vec{D}$? It turns out that there are conditions under which $\vec{B}$ remains fixed and only B varies, so that in this case $\vec{B}$ is a pushout.[1] Since our applications in later chapters will satisfy these conditions, we shall be content here to derive a single distinguished IPO for a given span; but we shall indicate when others exist, and how to construct them from the distinguished one.

The first step is to establish when a span is consistent, i.e. has any bound at all.

---

[1] It is not true in every precategory, or even every category, that a unique IPO is a pushout. But the implication does hold in link graphs, and indeed in bigraphs.

Definition 5.12 (consistency conditions) We define three *consistency* conditions on a span $\vec{A} : W \to \vec{X}$. We use q to range over arbitrary points and q_2 to range over $W \uplus P_2$, the shared points.

CL0 If $v \in V_2$ then $ctrl_0(v) = ctrl_1(v)$.

CL1 If $A_i(q) \in E_2$ then $q \in W \uplus P_2$ and $A_{\bar{\imath}}(q) = A_i(q)$.

CL2 If $A_i(q_2) \in E_i \setminus E_2$ then $A_{\bar{\imath}}(q_2) \in X_{\bar{\imath}}$, and if also $A_{\bar{\imath}}(q) = A_{\bar{\imath}}(q_2)$ then $q \in W \uplus P_2$ and $A_i(q) = A_i(q_2)$. $\qquad\square$

Let us express CL1 and CL2 in words. If $i = 0$, CL1 says that if the link of any point q in A_0 is closed and shared with A_1, then q is also shared and has the same link in A_1. CL2 says, on the other hand, that if the link of a shared point q_2 in A_0 is closed and *unshared*, then its link in A_1 must be open, and further that any peer of q_2 in A_1 must also be its peer in A_0.

We shall find that the consistency conditions are necessary and sufficient for at least one IPO to exist. Necessity is straightforward:

Proposition 5.13 (consistency in link graphs) *If the span $\vec{A}$ has a bound, then the consistency conditions hold.*

Before going further, it will be helpful to look at simple examples.

Example 5.14 (consistent link graphs) Figure 5.1 shows a span $\vec{A}$ bounded by a cospan $\vec{D}$. Nodes v_0, v_1 and v_2 are shared.

Another example is the span $\vec{A} : \emptyset \to \vec{X}$ with bound $\vec{B}$ as shown in Figure 5.3, where $X_0 = \{x_0, y_0, z_0\}$ and $X_1 = \{x_1, y_1\}$. Nodes and edges with subscript 2 are shared; round nodes are unshared.

Controls are not shown in either example. $\qquad\square$

EXERCISE 5.3 Prove Proposition 5.13, and check the consistency conditions for $\vec{A}$ in Figure 5.3. $\qquad\square$

We shall now construct a distinguished IPO for any span $\vec{A}$ satisfying the consistency conditions of Definition 5.12.

Construction 5.15 (an IPO in link graphs) Assume the consistency conditions for the span $\vec{A} : W \to \vec{X}$. We define an IPO $\vec{C} : \vec{X} \to Y$ for $\vec{A}$ as follows.

nodes and edges: Take the nodes and edges of C_i to be $V_{\bar{\imath}} \setminus V_2$ and $E_{\bar{\imath}} \setminus E_2$.

interface: For $i = 0, 1$, define $X_i' \subseteq X_i$, the names to be mapped to the codomain Y, by

$$X_i' \overset{\text{def}}{=} \{x_i \in X_i \mid \forall q \in W \uplus P_2.\ A_i(q) = x_i \Rightarrow A_{\bar{\imath}}(q) \in X_{\bar{\imath}}\} .$$

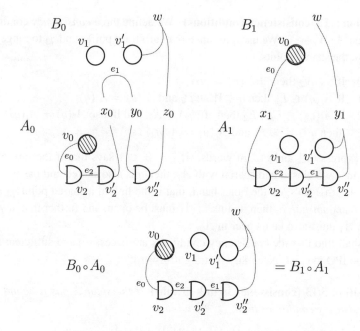

Fig. 5.3. A consistent span $\vec{A}$ of link graphs, with bound $\vec{B}$

Now on the disjoint sum $X_0' + X_1'$, define $\simeq$ as the smallest equivalence such that $(0, x_0) \simeq (1, x_1)$ whenever $A_0(q) = x_0$ and $A_1(q) = x_1$ for some $q \in W \uplus P_2$. Then define Y up to isomorphism by $Y \stackrel{\text{def}}{=} (X_0' + X_1')/\simeq$. For each $x \in X_i'$ we denote the $\simeq$-equivalence class of (i, x) by $\widehat{i, x}$.

links: Define the link maps $C_0 : X_0 \to Y$ as follows (C_1 is similar):

For $x \in X_0$:
$$C_0(x) \stackrel{\text{def}}{=} \begin{cases} \widehat{0, x} & \text{if } x \in X_0' \\ A_1(q) & \text{if } x \in X_0 \setminus X_0', \text{ for } q \in W \uplus P_2 \text{ with } A_0(q) = x \end{cases}$$
For $p \in P_1 \setminus P_2$:
$$C_0(p) \stackrel{\text{def}}{=} \begin{cases} \widehat{1, x} & \text{if } A_1(p) = x \in X_1 \\ A_1(p) & \text{if } A_1(p) \notin X_1 . \end{cases}$$

$\square$

This is a distinguished IPO, but in general there are others for a given span. We shall not need them, but it is interesting (and not obvious!) that they can all be obtained from the distinguished one, as follows. Suppose $\vec{C}$ is constructed as above for the span $\vec{A}$, and suppose A_0 has an idle name x. You can easily check that x

is open in C_0, i.e. $C_0(x) = y \in Y$. Suppose also that C_0 has an edge e. Then if instead we set $C_0(x) = e$, and remove y from Y, it can be shown that we still have an IPO. This variation is called the *elision* of x into C_0. Elision can be performed independently for each idle name x in A_0, choosing an arbitrary edge in C_0; similarly in A_1 and C_1. This can yield a lot of IPOs! But the number is finite, and usually very small.

Indeed, there are two cases when the span $\vec{A}$ has a unique IPO. The first is when both members are epi (no idle names). The second is when one member – say A_0 – is both epi and open. For then, as in the first case, there can be no variation for a name of A_0. Also, since A_0 is open it follows that C_1 is also open (see below), so it has no edges to permit elision of any idle name of A_1.

EXERCISE 5.4 If $\vec{C}$ is an IPO for $\vec{A}$ and A_0 is open, then prove that C_1 is also open. *Hint:* Consider how any edge e in C_1 arises from the IPO construction. □

After this brief tour of undistinguished IPOs, let us prove that our construction of the distinguished one is valid.

Theorem 5.16 (characterising IPOs for link graphs) *Assume that $\vec{A}$ obeys the consistency conditions. Then Construction 5.15 is sound and yields an IPO for $\vec{A}$.*

Proof (outline) For soundness, in the second clause for $C_0(x)$ we must ensure that $q \in W \uplus P_2$ exists such that $A_0(q) = x$, and that each such q yields the same value $A_1(q)$ in $P_1 \setminus P_2$; also in the first clause for $C_0(q)$ we must ensure that $x \in X_1'$. The consistency conditions do ensure this, and also that $C_0 \circ A_0 = C_1 \circ A_1$.

Now recall that a bound $\vec{B}$ for $\vec{A}$ is an IPO iff it forms the legs of an RPO relative to some bound $\vec{D}$. Since $\vec{C}$ is such a bound, take $\vec{D} = \vec{C}$ and apply Construction 5.5, to construct the RPO $(\vec{B}, B)$ relative to $\vec{C}$. To complete the proof, show that $\vec{B} = \vec{C}$ up to isomorphism. □

The reader may like to check the IPO construction by confirming that the bound illustrated in Figure 5.3 is in fact an IPO.

Corollary 5.17 (consistency) *The consistency conditions are necessary and sufficient for consistency.*

Proof Proposition 5.13 already ensured necessity; sufficiency follows from the theorem, since an IPO is a bound. □

We shall not give details of IPOs for place graphs. The construction of distinguished IPOs is entirely analogous. Also, elisions are analogous; just as in link graphs we get other IPOs by eliding idle names into edges, so in place graphs we get other IPOs by eliding idle roots into nodes.

We can now assert the result for bigraphs that we would expect:

Proposition 5.18 (IPOs for bigraphs) *A bound $\vec{C}$ for a span $\vec{A}$ is an IPO in* `BG($\mathcal{K}$) *if and only if $\vec{C}^{\mathrm{P}}$ is an IPO for $\vec{A}^{\mathrm{P}}$ in* `PG($\mathcal{K}$) *and $\vec{C}^{\mathrm{L}}$ is an IPO for $\vec{A}^{\mathrm{L}}$ in* `LG($\mathcal{K}$).

We end this section with five important properties of IPOs that we shall need later. The first is that several qualities of a span are inherited by a cospan which is an IPO. We omit the proof, which is by routine inspection of the IPO constructions. We say A is 'place-epi' if its place graph is epi, etc.

Proposition 5.19 (IPOs inherit qualities) *Let $\vec{A}$ have an IPO $\vec{B}$. If A_0 is node-free, or place-epi, or link-epi, or discrete, or open, then B_1 has the same quality.*

The second property is that tensor product preserves IPOs.

Proposition 5.20 (tensor IPO) *In* `BG($\mathcal{K}$), *let $\vec{C}$ be an IPO for $\vec{A}$ and $\vec{D}$ be an IPO for $\vec{B}$, with $\vec{A} \# \vec{B}$. Then, provided the products exist, the cospan $(C_0 \otimes D_0, C_1 \otimes D_1)$ is an IPO for the span $(A_0 \otimes B_0, A_1 \otimes B_1)$.*

An important corollary is:

Corollary 5.21 (tensor IPOs with identities) *Let $A : I' \to I$ and $B : J' \to J$, where $A \# B$ and also $\{I, I'\} \# \{J, J'\}$. Then the cospan $(\mathrm{id}_I \otimes B, A \otimes \mathrm{id}_J)$ is an IPO for the span $(A \otimes \mathrm{id}_{J'}, \mathrm{id}_{I'} \otimes B)$. See diagram (1).*

$$
\begin{array}{ccc}
(1) & & \\
I \otimes J' \xrightarrow{\ \mathrm{id} \otimes B\ } I \otimes J & \qquad (2) & I \xrightarrow{\ \mathrm{id} \otimes b\ } I \otimes J \\
A \otimes \mathrm{id} \uparrow \qquad \uparrow A \otimes \mathrm{id} & & a \uparrow \quad \uparrow a \otimes \mathrm{id} \\
I' \otimes J' \xrightarrow{\ \mathrm{id} \otimes B\ } I' \otimes J & & \epsilon \xrightarrow{\quad b \quad} J
\end{array}
$$

In particular if $I' = J' = \epsilon$ then $A = a$ and $B = b$ are ground, and the IPO is as in diagram (2).

Our third property is that support equivalence preserves IPOs. The proof is straightforward, capturing the idea that the definition of IPO exploits no property of supports except their disjointness.

Proposition 5.22 (support translation of IPOs) *Let $\vec{A}$ and $\vec{B}$ be a span and co-span whose support is in the domain of a support translation ρ. Then $\rho \cdot \vec{B}$ is an IPO for $\rho \cdot \vec{A}$ iff $\vec{B}$ is an IPO for $\vec{A}$.*

The fourth property is:

Proposition 5.23 (unique IPOs are pushouts) *If a span $\vec{A}$ has exactly one IPO up to isomorphism, then this IPO is a pushout.*

One might expect this property to hold in any precategory, but in fact it does not. The interested reader may enjoy trying to find a counter-example. This is not so easy, and fortunately we do not need that negative result.

EXERCISE 5.5 Show that (A, A) has a unique IPO up to isomorphism, and that it takes the form $(\mathsf{id}, \mathsf{id})$ if and only if A is epi. □

For our fifth property, first recall from Definition 2.19 the notion of leanness, and the lean-support quotient functor $[\![\cdot]\!]$ established in Theorem 2.20. To prepare for transferring transitions from concrete to abstract bigraphs via this functor we assert a simple relation between IPOs and leanness. Let us write A^E for the result of adding a set E of fresh idle edges to a bigraph A. Then

Proposition 5.24 (IPOs, idle edges and leanness) *For any span $\vec{A}$ and cospan $\vec{B}$ of concrete bigraphs:*

(1) If $\vec{B}$ is an IPO for $\vec{A}$, and A_1 is lean, then B_0 is lean.
(2) For any fresh set E of edges, $\vec{B}$ is an IPO for $\vec{A}$ iff (B_0, B_1^E) is an IPO for (A_0^E, A_1).

5.3 Abstract bigraphs lack RPOs

We end this chapter by showing that we cannot rely on the existence of RPOs in abstract bigraphs, where support is forgotten. We give here a counter-example for abstract link graphs; it easily extends to bigraphs.

Example 5.25 (abstract link graphs lack RPOs) Figure 5.4 shows a span (a, a) of ground link graphs, bounded by a cospan (G, G). Note that $G \circ a$ consists of two L-nodes each joined by a closed link to a K node. The diagram also shows two relative bounds for the span relative to the cospan; these are $(\vec{C}, C)$ and $(\vec{D}, D)$.

Ignoring the dashed arrows, the diagram is easily seen to commute. It shows the legs $\vec{B}$ of an assumed RPO $(\vec{B}, B)$ for the span relative to the cospan (B is not shown). For this RPO to exist there must be mediating arrows $\widehat{C}$ and $\widehat{D}$ to the two relative bounds. But these cannot both exist. For if $\widehat{D} \circ \vec{B} = \vec{D}$ then the B_i contain no nodes, and in that case no value of $\widehat{C}$ can achieve $\widehat{C} \circ \vec{B} = \vec{C}$, since the K-nodes in the C_i have different names. □

Thus, by taking $\vec{A} = (a, a)$ and $\vec{G} = (G, G)$ as in the example, we have proved:

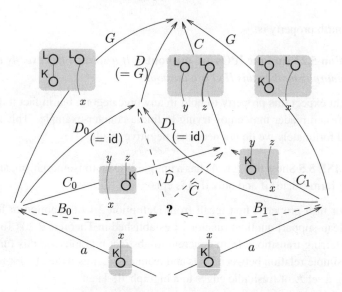

Fig. 5.4. A bounded span of abstract link graphs with no RPO

Proposition 5.26 (abstract link graphs lack RPOs) *In* `LG($\mathcal{K}$) *there is a span $\vec{A}$ of abstract link graphs, and a bound $\vec{G}$ for it, such that no RPO exists from $\vec{A}$ to $\vec{G}$.*

EXERCISE 5.6 (1) Amplify the final sentence in Example 5.25: Why can no value of $\widehat{C}$ achieve the equations $\widehat{C} \circ \vec{B} = \vec{C}$?

(2) What goes wrong if we try to use this counter-example to refute the existence of RPOs in *concrete* link graphs?   □

6

Sorting

Just as in universal algebra, different signatures will be used for different applications of bigraphs. So far our signatures are basic; they assign only an arity to each control. By analogy with the constructors of *many-sorted* algebra, we can also classify our controls by means of *sorts*. But the analogy is not exact, because bigraphs have two degrees of freedom: we can classify places or we can classify links.

6.1 Place sorting and CCS

Let us begin with the classification of places.

Definition 6.1 (place sorting) A *place sorting*

$$\Sigma = (\Theta, \mathcal{K}, \Phi)$$

has a non-empty set Θ of *sorts*, and a signature $\mathcal{K}$ *place-sorted* over Θ, i.e. assigning a sort to each control. An interface is Σ-*sorted* if each of its places is assigned a sort in Θ.

Using $\mathcal{K}$, a bigraph over Σ may be augmented by sorts assigned to its nodes. The third component Φ of Σ, a *formation rule*, is a property of such augmented bigraphs that is satisfied by the identities and symmetries and preserved by composition and product. The augmented bigraphs satisfying Φ are called Σ-*sorted*; they constitute the s-category `BG(Σ) and the spm category BG(Σ) of, respectively, concrete and abstract Σ-sorted bigraphs. □

We write a Σ-sorted interface of width n as $\langle \vec{\theta}, X \rangle$, where $\vec{\theta} = \theta_0 \cdots \theta_{n-1}$ lists the sorts θ_i assigned to each $i \in n$. When Σ is understood, the Σ-sorted bigraphs are often called *place-sorted*. Note that the case $\Theta = \{\theta\}$, a singleton, with Φ vacuous, exactly represents the unsorted bigraphical s-category over $\mathcal{K}$. This corresponds exactly to the situation in many-sorted algebra, in which a single-sorted algebra is effectively unsorted.

Let us now look at functors that relate sorted to unsorted bigraphs, and concrete to abstract bigraphs. These remarks apply equally to link sorting, which is the subject of Section 6.2. Let $\mathcal{K}$ be the basic signature underlying a place sorting Σ. There is clearly a forgetful functor

$$`\mathcal{U} : `\text{Bg}(\Sigma) \rightarrow `\text{Bg}(\mathcal{K})$$

which deletes place sorts from the places in both interfaces and bigraphs. In this book we are only concerned with the case in which `$\text{Bg}(\Sigma)$ has RPOs. This will be ensured by Proposition 4.7, provided that we can prove that Σ is safe (Definition 4.6).

Now recall from Definition 2.19 and Theorem 2.20 the lean-support quotient functor

$$[\cdot] : `\text{Bg}(\Sigma) \rightarrow \text{Bg}(\Sigma)$$

that forgets the identity of nodes and discards idle edges in unsorted bigraphs. There is clearly a similar quotient functor for sorted ones. There is also an obvious functor $\mathcal{U} : \text{Bg}(\Sigma) \rightarrow \text{Bg}(\mathcal{K})$ that forgets sorting for abstract bigraphs. Indeed, with the help of Definition 2.4 it can be shown that the following diagram of functors commutes:

$$
\begin{array}{ccc}
`\text{Bg}(\Sigma) & \xrightarrow{\ `\mathcal{U}\ } & `\text{Bg}(\mathcal{K}) \\
{\scriptstyle [\cdot]}\Big\downarrow & & {\scriptstyle [\cdot]}\Big\downarrow \\
\text{Bg}(\Sigma) & \xrightarrow{\ \mathcal{U}\ } & \text{Bg}(\mathcal{K})
\end{array}
$$

Returning now to place sorting, there is a wide range of possibilities for the formation rule Φ. There are non-trivial sortings even when Θ is a singleton (i.e. places are effectively unsorted), because Φ may restrict bigraphs to an arbitrary sub-(s-)category. For this chapter we shall be concerned with abstract bigraphs, except when we discuss the safety of sortings.

There is one useful constraint that Φ can impose, even when Θ is a singleton:

Definition 6.2 (hardness)   A sort θ in a sorting Σ is *hard* if Σ requires that no root with sort θ is idle. An agent $a : I$ is *hard* if all sorts in I are hard – and hence a has no idle roots.   □

Hardness makes transition systems simpler, as we shall see later. It has been useful for the modelling of process calculi in bigraphs.

The translation of CCS into bigraphs provides a non-trivial example of place sorting. Let us first recall CCS processes:

Definition 6.3 (syntax for finite CCS) We shall let P, Q range over *processes* and A, B over *alternations* (sums); each *alternate* (or summand) of an alternation is a process guarded by an action μ of the form x or $\bar{x}$, where x names a channel. The syntax is:

$$
\begin{aligned}
P &::= & A \mid \nu x P \mid P \mid P \\
A &::= & \mathbf{0} \mid \mu.P \mid A + A \\
\mu &::= & \bar{x} \mid x \quad .
\end{aligned}
$$

The *restriction* $\nu x P$ defines P as the scope of the name x; a name-occurrence in a process is *free* iff it is not scoped by ν. We say P and Q are *alpha-equivalent*, written $P \equiv_\alpha Q$, if they differ only in a change of their restricted names. □

Our treatment of CCS here will be confined to finite processes. Infinite processes are typically introduced by a set $\{D_i \overset{\text{def}}{=} P_i \mid i \in I\}$ of *process definitions*, where the process identifiers D_i may appear in any of the defining expressions P_i. There is more than one way to handle these in bigraphs; one proposal is described in Section 11.2.

As usual, we define a structural congruence over CCS terms:

Definition 6.4 (structural congruence) *Structural congruence* over CCS terms is the smallest equivalence $\equiv$ preserved by all term constructions, and such that

(1) $P \equiv_\alpha Q$ implies $P \equiv Q$, and $A \equiv_\alpha B$ implies $A \equiv B$;
(2) '$\mid$' and '$+$' are associative and commutative under $\equiv$, and $A + \mathbf{0} \equiv A$;
(3) $\nu x \nu y P \equiv \nu y \nu x P$;
(4) $\nu x P \equiv P$ and $\nu x (P \mid Q) \equiv P \mid \nu x Q$ for any x not free in P;
(5) $\nu x (A + \mu.P) \equiv A + \mu.\nu x P$ for any x not free in A or μ.

□

This is standard, except for two things. First, we do not have $P \mid \mathbf{0} \equiv P$; but we shall find that these two terms translate into bisimilar bigraphs. Second, equation (5) is not standard for CCS structural congruence; but the processes have identical transitions, and indeed we shall translate them into the same bigraph.

To prepare for translating CCS into bigraphs, we first define a class of place sortings suggested by the two-sorted syntax of CCS itself.

Definition 6.5 (stratified place sorting) A place sorting $\Sigma = (\Theta, \mathcal{K}, \Phi)$ is *stratified* if, for some function $\phi : \Theta \to \Theta$, the formation rule Φ requires that

all children of a root $r : \theta$ have sort θ ;
all children of a node $v : \theta$ have sort $\phi(\theta)$.

The CCS stratified sorting Σ_{ccs} has $\Theta = \{\text{p}, \text{a}\}$ (for processes and alternations), with $\phi(\text{p}) = \text{a}$ and $\phi(\text{a}) = \text{p}$; it is also hard for sort p.   □

EXERCISE 6.1 Check that the formation rule for stratified sorting is preserved by composition and tensor product, and satisfied by identities.   □

We are now ready for the translation of CCS into the two-sorted category $\text{BG}(\Sigma_{\text{ccs}})$. The idle prime $1 : \text{a}$ has a special role; it will represent the empty alternation. Then the atom nil $\overset{\text{def}}{=}$ alt.1 will represent the null process. We shall map CCS processes and alternations respectively into ground homsets $\epsilon \to \langle \text{p}, X \rangle$ and $\epsilon \to \langle \text{a}, X \rangle$. For this purpose we define two families of translation maps $\mathcal{P}_X[\cdot]$ and $\mathcal{A}_X[\cdot]$, each indexed by finite name-sets X. These maps are defined for all arguments whose free names are in X, so each process or alternation has an image in many unary ground homsets.

Definition 6.6 (translation of finite CCS) The translations $\mathcal{P}_X[\cdot]$ for processes and $\mathcal{A}_X[\cdot]$ for alternations are defined by mutual recursion:

$$
\begin{array}{rcl|rcl}
 & & & \mathcal{A}_X[0] & = & X \mid 1 \\
\mathcal{P}_X[A] & = & \text{alt}.\mathcal{A}_X[A] & \mathcal{A}_X[\overline{x}.P] & = & \text{send}_x.\mathcal{P}_X[P] \ (x \in X) \\
\mathcal{P}_X[\nu x P] & = & /y \circ \mathcal{P}_{y \uplus X}[\{y/x\}P] & \mathcal{A}_X[x.P] & = & \text{get}_x.\mathcal{P}_X[P] \ (x \in X) \\
\mathcal{P}_X[P \mid Q] & = & \mathcal{P}_X[P] \mid \mathcal{P}_X[Q] & \mathcal{A}_X[A+B] & = & \mathcal{A}_X[A] \mid \mathcal{A}_X[B] .
\end{array}
$$
                                    □

In translating the prefix forms for input and output we have used the nesting operator $\text{K}_{\vec{x}}.G$ introduced in Chapter 3, permitting names to be shared between an ion and its contents. The term $\nu x P$ is first varied by alpha-equivalence, replacing x by some $y \notin X$. A substitution $\{y/x\}$ on CCS terms is metasyntactic, and not to be confused with the *bigraph* y/x.

Note that restriction and parallel composition are modelled directly by closure and merge product, and need no extra controls. It is perhaps surprising that summation '+' of CCS is also expressed as merge product. But merge product is a purely structural or static operation, with no commitment to any dynamic interpretation; the distinction between parallel composition and summation in our bigraphical encoding of CCS is achieved by its reaction rule, as we shall see in Chapter 10.

Our translation maps are surjective on unary ground homsets; that is, our place sorting excludes from $\text{BG}(\Sigma_{\text{ccs}})$ every bigraph that is not in the image of a translation map. They are not injective; instead, they induce upon CCS an equivalence $\equiv$ that corresponds exactly to our structural congruence, justifying the latter. We now express these results precisely; the proofs are the subject of Exercise 10.1.

Theorem 6.7 (bijective translation)

(1) The translations $\mathcal{P}_X[\cdot]$ and $\mathcal{A}_X[\cdot]$ are surjective on unary ground homsets.

(2) $P \equiv Q$ *iff* $\mathcal{P}_X[P] = \mathcal{P}_X[Q]$, *and* $A \equiv B$ *iff* $\mathcal{A}_X[A] = \mathcal{A}_X[B]$.

We shall take up the dynamics of CCS when we have introduced bigraphical reactive systems (BRSs) in general. For now, we wish to confirm that our sorting will be amenable to that general theory, so we shall prove our sorting to be safe. Let $\mathcal{U} : \text{`BG}(\Sigma_{\text{ccs}}) \to \text{`BG}(\mathcal{K}_{\text{ccs}})$ be its forgetful functor. Recall from Definition 4.6 that a sorting is safe if its forgetful functor $\mathcal{U}$ is safe, i.e. in particular it creates RPOs and reflects pushouts. Also recall from Proposition 4.10 that $\mathcal{U}$ reflects pushouts if every arrow in its domain is op-cartesian. So we first prove:

Lemma 6.8 *If Σ is a stratified sorting with forgetful functor $\mathcal{U}$, then every bigraph in `BG(Σ) is op-cartesian for $\mathcal{U}$.*

Proof   Let $F : I \to J$ and $H : I \to K$ be Σ-sorted, with $\mathcal{U}$-images $F' : I' \to J'$ and $H' : I' \to K'$ such that $H' = G' \circ F'$ for some $G' : J' \to K'$. (Refer to the diagram of Definition 4.9.) There can exist only one sorted $G : J \to K$ such that $H \circ G = F$, since its interfaces are already sorted and the sorts of its nodes in G are determined by those in H. It is routine to confirm that G is indeed well-sorted, with $\mathcal{U}(G) = G'$ and $G \circ F = H$. This completes the proof of the lemma.   □

We now claim:

Proposition 6.9 (safe stratified sorting) *Every stratified sorting is safe.*

Proof   Let Σ be stratified, with underlying basic signature $\mathcal{K}$ and forgetful functor $\mathcal{U}$. First we require that $\mathcal{U}$ creates RPOs. So let $\vec{D}$ be a bound for $\vec{A}$ in `BG($\Sigma$), with $\mathcal{U}$-images $\vec{D}'$ and $\vec{A}'$. Let $(\vec{B}', B')$ be an RPO for $\vec{A}'$ to $\vec{D}'$ in `BG($\mathcal{K}$). We seek first a preimage $(\vec{B}, B)$ which is a sorted bound for $\vec{A}$ to $\vec{D}$. There is only one possibility, since the sorts of the mediating interface of the triple and of its nodes are uniquely determined by stratified sorting, and it is easily shown to be a relative bound. Furthermore, by using the op-cartesian property of the existing arrows, we ensure a unique mediating arrow to any other sorted relative bound $(\vec{C}, C)$, thus establishing $(\vec{B}, B)$ as a sorted RPO.

Next, we require that $\mathcal{U}$ reflects pushouts; this follows by Proposition 4.10. Finally, the remaining three safety conditions are easily established.   □

EXERCISE 6.2 For the built environment of Chapter 1, design a place sorting that excludes control nestings not already used in the bigraph E. *Hint:* You probably need disjunctive sorts, e.g. $\hat{ar}$, allowing a building to contain both agents (a) and rooms (r).

What are the sorted interfaces of the bigraphs C, D and E, and of the redexes in rules B1–B3?   □

Before leaving place sorting, let us consider how it can be used to introduce controls of arbitrary *rank* k, a natural number. At present our atomic controls have rank 0, and the others have rank 1, i.e. their ions have a single site. We did not introduce controls with larger rank, since they can be encoded with the help of sorting. The diagram indicates, in terms of ions, how to encode a control M with rank k, using controls of rank 1.

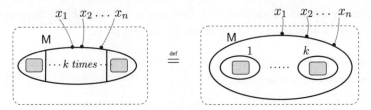

The encoding works by extending an existing $\Sigma = (\Theta, \mathcal{K}, \Phi)$ to Σ^*, as follows:

(i) Add a special sort 'cell' to Θ. Then, for each finite ordinal j, add to $\mathcal{K}$ a new non-atomic control j with sort 'cell'. Call a node with control j a j-*cell*.

(ii) For each control M of rank k, extend $\mathcal{K}$ by assigning M an arity, its rank, and a sort from Θ. Then refine Φ by requiring that if M has rank k then each M-node has exactly k children, namely a j-cell for each $j \in \{1, \ldots, k\}$; conversely, require that the parent of every cell is a node with ranked control.

(iii) Further refine Φ by imposing any required relationship between the sort assigned to a cell's parent and the sorts assigned to its children.

This characterises Σ^* in terms of Σ, allowing freedom for extra sorting constraints on ranked controls. Note that the refined sorting condition ensures that the sort 'cell' does not occur in interfaces; the encoding of a node with ranked control is never split by composition. We can see that the degenerate cases $k = 0$ and $k = 1$ correspond accurately to our present atomic and non-atomic controls. We may thus regard all controls as ranked.

This concludes the presentation of place sorting. It could have been done at first for place graphs only, and then extended to bigraphs. We were led to do it directly for bigraphs because our example, CCS, requires linking as well as placing.

6.2 Link sorting, arithmetic nets and Petri nets

We now turn to the classification of links. We start with the simple example of arithmetic nets, and continue by defining a particular class of link sortings illustrated by these nets. We then apply this class of sortings to Petri nets. We treat both examples using link graphs alone; the extension to bigraphs is trivial.

Since link graphs have no regions, their diagrams have no enclosing rectangles; port-blobs can also be omitted from these diagrams without risk of confusion.

Definition 6.10 (link sorting) A *link-sorting (discipline)* is a triple $\Sigma = (\Theta, \mathcal{K}, \Phi)$ where Θ is a non-empty set of *sorts*, and $\mathcal{K}$ is a *link-sorted signature*, a basic signature enriched with a sort assigned to each member of the arity of each control. Thus each port in a (link)-sorted link graph gets a sort. Furthermore, each link is given a sort. For an open link, this appears in an interface, taking the form $\{x_0 : \theta_0, \ldots, x_{n-1} : \theta_{n-1}\}$; also each edge (closed link) in a bigraph is given a sort.[1]

Finally, Φ is a rule on such enriched bigraphs that is satisfied by the identities and symmetries and preserved by composition and product.

The s-category and category of, respectively, concrete and abstract Σ-sorted link graphs are written `$\mathrm{LG}(\Sigma)$ and $\mathrm{LG}(\Sigma)$. When Σ is understood, these link graphs are often called *well-sorted*. □

Just as for place sorting, there is a forgetful functor for link sorting; it deletes link sorts from the points and links of both interfaces and bigraphs. And again, it commutes with the lean-support quotient functor. We need not repeat the details.

We are now ready to illustrate link sorting.

Example 6.11 (arithmetic nets) Adopt the basic signature

$$\mathcal{K}_{\mathsf{arith}} \overset{\text{def}}{=} \{\mathbf{0} : 1,\ \mathsf{S} : 2,\ + : 3,\ \rightarrow : 2\}$$

representing *zero*, *successor*, *plus* and *forwarding*. Here are the corresponding atoms, together with an example of an arithmetic net as a link graph in $\mathrm{LG}(\mathcal{K}_{\mathsf{arith}})$:

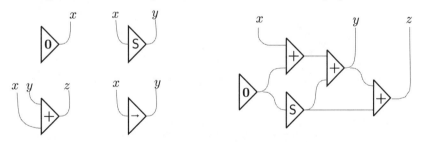

The nets resemble Lafont's interaction nets, but allow sharing of subexpressions. Their dynamics can be defined naturally in bigraphs, but here we confine ourselves to sorting. We can illustrate the need for sorting in terms of our example. The

---

[1] In previous work sorts were not assigned to edges; that is, they were assigned to open links but not to closed links. In examples it seems that assigning sorts to edges is often redundant; nonetheless, it may be necessary sometimes and it is also convenient for the theory. I am grateful to Mikkel Bundgaard for pointing this out.

illustrated net makes sense according to the interpretation suggested by the node-shapes: the 'output' of each constructor is fed into any number of other constructors as input. But some nets in LG($\mathcal{K}_{arith}$) make no sense; for example, there is nothing to exclude a net in which an input port receives input from no sources, or from two or more sources. As a first step towards a sorting to exclude such nets, we define the following class of link sortings:

Definition 6.12 (many–one sorting) A *many–one sorting* $\Sigma = (\Theta, \mathcal{K}, \Phi)$ has two sorts, i.e. $\Theta = \{s, t\}$. The signature $\mathcal{K}$ assigns sorts to control arities in some arbitrary way. The formation rule Φ is as follows:

no link has more than one s-point;
a link has sort s iff it has an s-point;
every closed link has sort s.

There is no constraint on the number of t-points in a link.   □

It is helpful to think of s and t as standing for 'source' and 'target'. Many–one sortings vary in their signature. Let us now define Σ_{arith} to be a many–one sorting whose link-sorted signature is $\mathcal{K}_{arith}$ extended by a sort-assignment as follows:

$$\mathcal{K}_{arith} \stackrel{\text{def}}{=} \{0 : s, \ S : ts, \ + : tts, \ \rightarrow : ts\} \,,$$

i.e. arities are refined to sort-sequences, with the convention that the last in each sequence pertains to 'output' ports. Taking into account also the sorting of interfaces, here are the sorts assigned to our illustrated net:

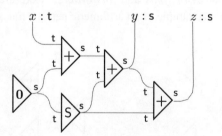

The sorts of edges are not shown; they are implied by the sorts of ports.

The reader can see that, in the link-sorted s-category LG(Σ_{arith}), many senseless nets have been excluded. It is an interesting exercise to check whether the sorting can be extended to exclude other doubtful nets; for example, nets with certain cycles. (The challenge is to find a sorting discipline that is preserved by the categorical operations.) At the end of this chapter we consider safety of many–one sorting.   □

Let us now turn to Petri nets. Recall that a Petri net has two kinds of node, usually called places and transitions, forming a directed bipartite graph. For each transition t, the places from which an arc enters t are its *pre-conditions*, and the places entered by an arc from t are its *post-conditions*. Places may hold *tokens*; if all the pre-conditions of t have a token then t can *fire* – meaning that each of its pre-conditions loses a token and each of its post-conditions gains one. Thus the net remains constant; only the tokens move.

We look at a particular Petri net regime, called *condition–event* nets. Their places are called *conditions*, and their transitions are called *events*. (This conveniently avoids a clash with bigraph terminology, where the terms 'place' and 'transition' are already in use!) In these nets a condition may hold at most a single token; thus we can represent conditions by two controls, one ('marked') for holding a token, the other ('unmarked') for holding no token. As with arithmetic nets, the dynamics of Petri nets can be well represented in bigraphs, and this has been studied in detail elsewhere. Here we consider only the sorting of condition–event nets.

Example 6.13 (condition–event Petri nets) Adopt the basic signature

$$\mathcal{K}_{\text{petri}} \stackrel{\text{def}}{=} \{\mathsf{M}:1, \ \mathsf{U}:1, \ \mathsf{E}_{hk}:h+k\}$$

representing a *marked condition*, an *unmarked condition*, and an *event* with h pre-conditions and k post-conditions ($h, k \geq 0$). Here are the corresponding atoms, together with an example of a condition–event (c/e) net:

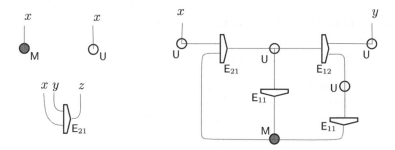

We depict the only port of a condition node as lying at its centre; thus the net has just three closed links (edges) and two open links. The marked condition node represents the presence of a *token* on the node, saying that this condition 'holds'; an unmarked condition node has no token, so it does not 'hold'. Two conditions have been made accessible by the names x and y, allowing the environment to 'observe' the net.

Our illustrated net makes sense; but, as with arithmetic nets, certain link graphs in $\text{LG}(\mathcal{K}_{\text{petri}})$ make no sense. For example, two event nodes should not be linked by an edge that contains no condition. To exclude senseless nets, we can again use a many–one sorting Σ_{petri}. But when we modify $\mathcal{K}_{\text{petri}}$ to assign sorts to control arities we see a striking difference from $\mathcal{K}_{\text{arith}}$:

$$\mathcal{K}_{\text{petri}} \stackrel{\text{def}}{=} \{\mathsf{M}:\mathsf{s},\ \mathsf{U}:\mathsf{s},\ \mathsf{E}_{hk}:\mathsf{t}^{h+k}\}\ .$$

That is, we assign t to all event ports and s to all condition ports. Taking into account also the sorting of interfaces, here are the sorts assigned to our illustrated net:

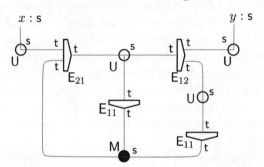

Again, the sorts of edges are not shown, but can be deduced. The reader may like to identify which senseless configurations have been excluded by the sorting. □

Having used two members of the family of many–one link sortings, we now establish that these sortings are all safe, in the sense of Definition 4.6.

Lemma 6.14 *Let* $\mathcal{U}:\mathrm{LG}(\Sigma)\to\mathrm{LG}(\mathcal{K})$ *be the forgetful functor for link graphs with a many–one sorting* Σ*; similarly for bigraphs. Then every link graph in* $\mathrm{LG}(\Sigma)$ *and bigraph in* $\mathrm{BG}(\Sigma)$ *is op-cartesian for* $\mathcal{U}$*.*

Proof   Consult the diagram of Definition 4.9, with $\mathcal{U}$ for $\mathcal{F}$, and use capital letters for arrows (since we are dealing with link graphs). Assume $F:I\to J$ and $H:I\to K$ to be many–one sorted; assume F' and G' unsorted such that $\mathcal{U}(F)=F'$ and $\mathcal{U}(H)=G'\circ F'$. We require unique G such that $\mathcal{U}(G)=G'$ and $H=G\circ F$.

Since the interfaces for G are fixed, and sorts of ports are determined by the sorted signature, there is exactly one $G:J\to K$ such that $\mathcal{U}(G)=G'$. It is then routine to check that G is well-sorted, and that $G\circ F=H$. □

We are now ready to prove

Theorem 6.15 (many–one sorting is safe)   *Every many–one link sorting is safe.*

Proof   It will be enough to prove this for link graphs. First, we establish that the forgetful functor $\mathcal{U} : \mathrm{LG}(\Sigma) \to \mathrm{LG}(\mathcal{K})$ of the sorting Σ creates RPOs. Let $\vec{D}$ bound $\vec{A}$ in $\mathrm{LG}(\mathcal{K})$, and let $\vec{D}'$ and $\vec{A}'$ be their unsorted images. Consider the construction of an unsorted RPO $(\vec{B}', B')$, with mediating interface I', for $\vec{A}'$ to $\vec{D}'$. Assign sorts to its ports and edges as dictated by the sorted signature of Σ. It can then be found that sorts can be assigned also to the names in I', creating a sorted interface I for a triple $(\vec{B}, B)$ that makes it a relative bound for $\vec{A}$ to $\vec{D}$.

To establish this as an RPO, consider any other sorted relative bound $(\vec{C}, C)$. Its $\mathcal{U}$-image $(\vec{C}', C')$ is a relative bound also for $\vec{A}'$ to $\vec{D}'$; so there is a unique mediating arrow from $(\vec{B}', B')$ to $(\vec{C}', C')$. Now, by the lemma, use the op-cartesian property of sorted link graphs such as $B_0 \circ A_0$ to ensure that a unique mediating arrow exists from $(\vec{B}, B)$ to $(\vec{C}, C)$. This establishes $(\vec{B}, B)$ as an RPO, as required.

Next, we have to show that $\mathcal{U}$ reflects pushouts. But this is immediate from the lemma combined with Proposition 4.10. Finally, as with stratified sorting, it is easy to establish the three remaining conditions of safety. $\quad\square$

Let us look briefly at another simple case of link sorting.

Definition 6.16 (plain sorting) Call a link sorting *plain* if its formation rule imposes only one constraint: namely, that all points in a link have the same sort as the link. $\quad\square$

For example, this provides a sorting to represent a version of CCS with several sorts of channel. Each channel may be shared by many senders and many receivers. To make communications respect the sorting, we represent the channel by a link of sort θ, say, and require all points in this link (e.g. 'send' and 'get' nodes) also to have sort θ. This example gets more interesting in the π-calculus, where such nodes have extra ports used to pass links as messages.

EXERCISE 6.3 (1) Show that the forgetful functor $\mathcal{U}$ for plain sorting is in general not op-cartesian. *Hint:* Consider two sorts θ, θ'. In the notation of Definition 4.9, show how f may have an idle name $x : \theta$ preventing the existence of a suitable g.

(2) In contrast, prove that every plain sorting is safe (see Definition 4.6). *Hint:* If $\vec{B}$ is an IPO for $\vec{A}$, then no name in the codomain of $\vec{B}$ is idle in *both* B_0 and B_1. $\quad\square$

6.3 The impact of sorting

To a considerable extent, the power of sorting lies in the variety of possible formation rules. This is true even for place sorting and link sorting independently, and doubly true when they are combined. We illustrated this combination when we considered adding plain link sorting to CCS, which is already place sorted. It is remarkable that the notion of *binding* or *locality* of links can be expressed by such a combination; the formation rule naturally involves both places and links. One approach to binding is outlined in Section 11.3. It has been adopted to encode the π-calculus in bigraphs.

There is a price to pay; we must be sure that other features harmonise with sorting. We have already insisted that composition and tensor product respect sorting. Now let us look briefly at the derived products and nesting. First, for the parallel product $F_0 \parallel F_1$ and merge product $F_0 \mid F_1$ with $F_i : I_i \to J_i$, we insist that whenever a name x is shared between I_0 and I_1 then it has the same link sort in both; similarly for J_0 and J_1. In addition, for merge product we insist that all roots of F_0 and F_1 have the same place sort. Next, for the nesting $F.G$ with $F : I \to \langle m, X \rangle$ and $G : m \to \langle n, Y \rangle$, we insist that each place in m has the same place sort in the outer face of F as in the inner face of G, and that a name x shared between X and Y has the same sort in each.

Even when these conditions are met, the product $F_0 \parallel F_1$ may violate the formation rule. For example, with many–one sorting, if x : s is a shared outer name then the link x in the product may have two s-points, which is not allowed.

In what follows, whenever we use these derived operators, we assume that the relevant formation rule is indeed respected.

Part II : Motion

7

Reactions and transitions

In this chapter we study dynamics at the general level of s-categories. It is based upon Section 2.2 and Chapter 4, and is independent of the intervening work on bigraphs.

Recall from Chapter 2 the distinction between concrete and abstract bigraphs; the former have their nodes and edges as support, while the latter have no support. In s-categories, this distinction is less sharp; an spm category is just an s-category with empty supports. Much of the work of this chapter therefore applies to both. However, when we introduce behavioural equivalence in Section 7.2, we first make sure it is robust (i.e. that the equivalence is preserved by context) in the case where the s-category possesses RPOs; we are then able to retain this robust quality when the s-category is quotiented, or abstracted, in a certain way – even if RPOs are thereby lost.

We begin in Section 7.1 with a notion of a basic *reactive system*, based upon an s-category equipped with *reaction rules*. This determines a basic *reaction relation* which describes how agents may reconfigure themselves. We refine this definition to a *wide* reactive system, with a notion of locality based on the width of objects in a wide s-category, introduced in Definition 2.14. We are then able to describe where each reaction occurs in an agent, and thus to define a *wide* reaction relation that permits reactions to occur only in certain places.

In Section 7.2 we introduce *labelled transition systems*, which refine reactive systems by describing the reactions that an agent may perform, possibly with assistance from its environment. These potential reactions are called (labelled) transitions; the label of a transition indicates how the environment contributes to it. In terms of them we define *bisimilarity*, a behavioural equivalence which captures the idea that two agents behave the same if and only if they 'react alike in all contexts', i.e. they have the same transitions. In a basic reactive system, bisimilarity may not be a *congruence*, i.e. it may not be preserved by context; but we show that it is so in a wide reactive system, for a tractable notion of transition system based upon RPOs (Definition 4.3). This prepares for the dynamic theory of bigraphs in Chapter 8.

In Section 7.3 we introduce a natural notion of *sub transition system*, in which the set of labels is reduced. Under certain conditions we show that this can only increase the bisimilarity relation between agents in the smaller system. We also recognise the possibility that it preserves the relation exactly. This indeed occurs, as we illustrate in terms of CCS in a later chapter.

In Section 7.4, via a quotient functor, we transfer transition systems and their bisimilarities to abstract reactive systems. Finally, on this basis, we outline the general procedure by which we shall derive a robust behavioural theory for abstract bigraphs from concrete ones.

Notation We here revert to the convention of Section 2.2 and Chapter 4, in using lower case letters to denote arrows in an s-category. Recall that a ground arrow or agent is one with domain ϵ, the origin. The letters a, b will always denote agents, and r, s will always denote agents that are redexes or reacta of reaction rules (Definition 7.1). We often call an arrow c a *context* if it is used in composition $c \circ a$ with an agent.   □

7.1 Reactive systems

In process calculi it is common to present the dynamics of processes by means of *reactions* of the form $a \longrightarrow a'$, where a and a' are agents. These reactions define all the possible changes of state. We generalise this to s-categories, as follows:

Definition 7.1 (basic reactive system) A *basic reactive system*, written ˋ$\mathbf{C}$(ˋ$\mathcal{R}$), consists of an s-category ˋ$\mathbf{C}$ equipped with a set ˋ$\mathcal{R}$ of *reaction rules*. An arrow $a : \epsilon \to I$ in ˋ$\mathbf{C}$ with domain ϵ is a *ground arrow* or *agent*, often written $a : I$.

Each reaction rule consists of a pair $(r : I, \ r' : I)$ of ground arrows, a *redex* and a *reactum*. The set ˋ$\mathcal{R}$ must be closed under support translation, i.e. if (r, r') is a rule then so is (s, s') whenever $r \simeq s$ and $r' \simeq s'$.[1]

The *reaction relation* $\longrightarrow$ over agents is the smallest such that $a \longrightarrow a'$ whenever $a \simeq c \circ r$ and $a' \simeq c \circ r'$ for some reaction rule (r, r') and context c for r and r'.   □

---

[1] A stricter requirement would be: if (r, r') is a rule then so is $(\rho \cdot r, \rho \cdot r')$, for any support translation ρ. This prevents the redex and reactum from being support-translated independently; thus it allows us to track the identity of nodes through reaction, and thereby get a grip on causality in a bigraphical reactive system. This stricter approach is examined in Section 11.1, and is a promising topic for further research. We have not pursued it far in this book, since our more liberal approach still yields enough control of identity to recover theory for existing process models.

In Chapter 8 we shall work with reactions in bigraphs, which possess a strong notion of *place*, allowing us to describe *where* a reaction occurs. Basic reactive systems have no notion of place. In Definition 2.14 we introduced it with the concept of width; recall that an s-category $`C$ is wide if it is equipped with a functor width : $`C \to$ NAT. We now exploit that definition to define a notion of activity, which describes the places in a wide agent where reactions are permitted.

Definition 7.2 (wide reactive system (WRS)) We define a *wide reactive system (WRS)* $`C(`R)$ to be a wide s-category $`C$ equipped with a set $`R$ of reaction rules, and also an *activity* relation

$$\text{act} \subseteq `C(I \to J) \times \text{width}(I)$$

for each homset. If f has domain I and $(f, i) \in$ act then we say f is *active* at i; if this holds for all $i \in \text{width}(I)$ then f is *active*. We impose conditions on activity as follows, denoting the widths of the domains of f and g by m and n:

- the identities and symmetries are active;
- $g \circ f$ is active at $i \in m$ iff f is active at i and g is active at $\text{width}(f)(i) \in n$;
- $f \otimes g$ is active at $i \in m+n$ iff f is active at $i \in m$ or g is active at $i-m \in n$;
- if $f \asymp f'$ and f is active at i then f' is active at i .

Now define a *location* $\tilde{i}$ of an object I to be a subset of $\text{width}(I)$. The reaction relation $\longrightarrow_{\tilde{j}}$ between agents is defined as follows: $a \longrightarrow_{\tilde{j}} a'$ whenever $a \asymp c \circ r$ and $a' \asymp c \circ r'$ for some reaction rule (r, r') and active context $c : I \to J$ such that $\tilde{j} \subseteq \text{width}(J)$ is the location given by $\tilde{j} = \{\text{width}(c)(i) \mid i \in \text{width}(I)\}$. □

Thus $\tilde{j}$ records the regions of $d \circ r$ where the reaction occurs.

To test this definition, let us anticipate what activity will mean in bigraphs. There we shall designate certain controls as active, and 'f is active at i' will mean that every ancestor-node of the site i of f has an active control. With this interpretation, it is easy to check that the four conditions hold.

EXERCISE 7.1 In bigraphs, a non-atomic control can be either active or passive. We say that a node is active iff its control is active. Check that, with the above interpretation, bigraphs satisfy the condition on $g \circ f$ stated in Definition 7.2. You need only consider place graphs.

Suppose A is an active control and B passive, both with arity 0. Thus A, B : $1 \to 1$ are ions, with only A active. Using these, give an example of two bigraphs f and g such that $g \circ f$ is active but g is not active at every site. □

The notion of WRS, which enriches a basic reactive system with a width functor and an activity relation, allows us to develop a dynamic theory at the general level of s-categories. In general a WRS is *concrete*, since s-categories have support. A special case of a WRS is an abstract one based upon an spm category, since this is just an s-category with empty supports.

Definition 7.3 (abstract WRS) A WRS is *abstract* if its underlying s-category is an spm category. □

We created an spm category of abstract bigraphs in Definition 2.20, by means of the lean-support quotient functor $\llbracket \cdot \rrbracket$ which forgets both supports and idle edges. This functor was the quotient of a bigraphical s-category by lean-support equivalence $\hat{\Rightarrow}$ (Definition 2.19), which includes support equivalence $\hat{=}$.

We wish similarly to quotient a concrete WRS to form an abstract one. At this general level we have no notion of leanness, so there is no lean-support quotient functor. We can indeed quotient by support equivalence $\hat{=}$, but we can do better, and find a family of quotients of which lean-support equivalence is an instance specific to bigraphs.

Definition 7.4 (structural congruence) An equivalence relation $\equiv$ on each homset of a wide s-category $\grave{}\mathbf{C}$ is a *structural congruence* if it is preserved by composition and tensor product and preserves width, i.e. if $f \equiv g$ then $\mathrm{width}(f) = \mathrm{width}(g)$. It is called an *abstraction* if it includes support equivalence. We denote the $\equiv$-equivalence class of f by $\llbracket f \rrbracket$.

In a WRS $\grave{}\mathbf{C}(\grave{}\mathcal{R})$ an abstraction is *dynamic* if in addition it respects reaction and activity; that is,

- if $f \longrightarrow_{\bar{\imath}} f'$ and $g \equiv f$ then $g \longrightarrow_{\bar{\imath}} g'$ for some $g' \equiv f'$;
- if f is active at i and $f \equiv g$ then g is active at i. □

Structural congruences should not be confused with behavioural congruences such as bisimilarity; in particular, we define the latter only over ground arrows, while structural congruences apply to all arrows.

EXERCISE 7.2 Check that, in bigraphs, both $\hat{=}$ and $\hat{\Rightarrow}$ are abstractions. □

Definition 7.5 (quotient wide s-category) Let $\grave{}\mathbf{C}$ be a wide s-category, and let $\equiv$ be an abstraction on $\grave{}\mathbf{C}$. Then

$$\mathbf{C} \stackrel{\mathrm{def}}{=} \grave{}\mathbf{C}/\equiv$$

is the wide spm category whose objects are those of $\mathbf{C}$, and whose arrows $\llbracket f \rrbracket : I \to J$ are $\equiv$-equivalence classes of the homset $I \to J$ in $\mathbf{C}$. Composition, tensor product, identities and symmetries are defined just as for support quotient in Definition 2.15, and in $\mathbf{C}$ we define $\mathrm{width}(\llbracket f \rrbracket) \stackrel{\mathrm{def}}{=} \mathrm{width}(f)$. □

To form an abstract WRS we can quotient a concrete WRS by a dynamic abstraction:

Definition 7.6 (quotient WRS) Let $`\mathbf{C}(`\mathcal{R})$ be a WRS, and $\equiv$ a dynamic abstraction on $`\mathbf{C}$. Then define $\mathbf{C}(\mathcal{R})$, the quotient of $`\mathbf{C}(`\mathcal{R})$ by $\equiv$, as follows:

- $\mathbf{C} = `\mathbf{C}/\equiv$, and $\mathcal{R} = \{([\![r]\!], [\![r']\!]) \mid (r, r') \in `\mathcal{R}\}$;
- $[\![f]\!]$ is active at i iff f is active at i. $\hfill\square$

An abstract WRS has its own reaction relation $\longrightarrow_{\tilde{i}}$ indexed by locations. How does the reaction relation in a concrete WRS relate to that of its abstract quotient? The answer is simple, and included in the following theorem that justifies the above constructions.

Theorem 7.7 (abstract WRS) *The construction of Definitions 7.5 and 7.6, applied to a concrete WRS* $`\mathbf{C}(`\mathcal{R})$, *yields an abstract WRS* $\mathbf{C}(\mathcal{R})$, *whose underlying wide spm category* $\mathbf{C}$ *is the codomain of a functor of wide s-categories*

$$[\![\cdot]\!] : `\mathbf{C} \to \mathbf{C} .$$

Moreover the construction preserves the reaction relation, in the following sense:

(1) if $f \longrightarrow_{\tilde{i}} f'$ *in* $`\mathbf{C}(`\mathcal{R})$ *then* $[\![f]\!] \longrightarrow_{\tilde{i}} [\![f']\!]$ *in* $\mathbf{C}(\mathcal{R})$
(2) if $[\![f]\!] \longrightarrow_{\tilde{i}} g'$ *in* $\mathbf{C}(\mathcal{R})$ *then* $f \longrightarrow_{\tilde{i}} f'$ *in* $`\mathbf{C}(`\mathcal{R})$ *for some* f' *with* $[\![f']\!] = g'$.

In this sense, abstraction of a WRS preserves its behaviour. We now turn to a more refined notion of behaviour, and we shall find that it, too, is preserved by abstraction.

7.2 Transition systems

As we have seen, neither the basic nor the wide reaction relation, i.e. neither $\longrightarrow$ nor $\longrightarrow_{\tilde{i}}$, takes account of the reactions arising from cooperation between an agent and its environment. For this purpose we introduce labelled transition systems.

A *labelled transition* between agents takes the form $a \xrightarrow{\ell} a'$, where the *label* ℓ is drawn from some vocabulary expressing the possible interactions between an agent and its environment. This is more refined than a reactive system, since ℓ can witness the possibility that a contains only part of a redex, relying on the context or environment to supply the rest. Thus a may have exactly the same unaided reactions as another agent b, but may contain a part of a redex that b does not; then, when we place it in a context, a may behave differently from b.

Henceforward we shall use 'transition' to mean 'labelled transition'. In general, transitions do not presuppose reaction rules; it is possible to *define* the dynamics of bigraphs by transitions, as indeed has been done for various process calculi. But later we shall find that we can derive transitions from reaction rules.

We seek notions of behavioural equivalence of agents such that, whenever a and b are equivalent, they are also equivalent in all contexts; that is, $c \circ a$ and $c \circ b$ are equivalent for all contexts c. Transitions are important for this purpose, since they represent not only the *actual* behaviour of agents, but also their *potential* behaviour in collaboration with a context.

We now define transition systems formally.

Definition 7.8 (transition system)   A *transition system (TS)* for a wide s-category is a quadruple[2]

$$\mathcal{L} = (\mathsf{Agt}, \mathsf{Lab}, \mathsf{Apl}, \mathsf{Tra})$$

where Agt is a set of agents, Lab is a set of *labels*, $\mathsf{Apl} \subseteq \mathsf{Agt} \times \mathsf{Lab}$ is the *applicability relation*, and $\mathsf{Tra} \subseteq \mathsf{Apl} \times \mathsf{Agt}$ is the *transition relation*.

When $(a, \ell) \in \mathsf{Apl}$ we say that ℓ *applies to* a. A triple $(a, \ell, a') \in \mathsf{Tra}$ is called a *transition*; we write it $a \xrightarrow{\ell} a'$. We sometimes call a the *source* and a' the *target* of the transition. If c is an arrow such that $a \in \mathsf{Agt}$ implies $c \circ a \in \mathsf{Agt}$ whenever defined, then we call c an $\mathcal{L}$-*context*.

A transition system is *raw* if its labels contain no graphical structure.   □

Many behavioural equivalences or preorders can be built upon transition systems. For example, two agents are said to be *trace equivalent* if, starting from each one, the same sequences of transition labels can be observed. Another example is the *failures ordering* of CSP; an agent a is said to *refine* another, b, if the 'failures' of a are included in those of b. The theory of these can be developed in the same way as that of bisimilarity, which we now define:

Definition 7.9 (bisimilarity, congruence)   Let `C be equipped with a transition system $\mathcal{L}$. A *simulation* for $\mathcal{L}$ is a binary relation $\mathcal{S}$ between agents such that if $a\mathcal{S}b$ and $a \xrightarrow{\ell} a'$, and also ℓ applies to b, then there exists b' such that $b \xrightarrow{\ell} b'$ and $a'\mathcal{S}b'$. A *bisimulation* is a symmetric simulation.

Bisimilarity for $\mathcal{L}$, denoted by $\sim_{\mathcal{L}}$, is the largest bisimulation. It is a *congruence* if $a \sim_{\mathcal{L}} b$ implies $c \circ a \sim_{\mathcal{L}} c \circ b$ for every $\mathcal{L}$-context c.   □

When the transition system $\mathcal{L}$ is understood we shall often write $\sim$ instead of $\sim_{\mathcal{L}}$.

The above definition is standard, except for the extra condition that ℓ applies to b. Note that the largest bisimulation is well-defined; it is simply the union of all bisimulations. So another way to describe bisimilarity is to say that a and b are bisimilar, $a \sim_{\mathcal{L}} b$, if there exists a bisimulation containing the pair (a, b).

---

[2] This formulation of transition systems is due to O.H. Jensen [46].

Our definition of a transition system constrains neither its labels nor its transitions. In particular, it leaves open whether these are raw or not. For example, in the π-calculus a raw TS was defined first, and later a reactive system was defined and shown consistent with it. The TS was also found to yield a congruential bisimilarity.

Here, by contrast, we have two aims. First, we wish to *derive* a TS from a given set of reaction rules, since we wish to have only a single notion of dynamics for a reactive system. Second, we wish to prove the bisimilarity of this derived TS to be a congruence. We first achieve these aims in a way that is simple and informative, though unsatisfactory. It relies on declaring the label of a transition to be a bigraphical context for its source agent. Later we shall need to refine this approach.

Definition 7.10 (full transition system) In a WRS with rules $\grave{\mathcal{R}}$, a transition system is *full* if each label f is a bigraph, and f applies to an agent a iff it is a context for a. Moreover, each transition $a \stackrel{f}{\longrightarrow} a'$ is such that, for some reaction rule $(r, r') \in \grave{\mathcal{R}}$ and active context d for r and r', the following diagram commutes and $a' \simeq d \circ r'$.

The *full transition system* FT has all ground arrows as agents, all arrows as labels, and all transitions $a \stackrel{f}{\longrightarrow} a'$ that satisfy the above conditions for some rule $(r, r') \in \grave{\mathcal{R}}$. □

In the diagram we may think of a containing part of a redex r, and f supplying the remainder of that redex.

We now give the simple proof that bisimilarity for FT is a congruence. This is hardly surprising, because by allowing any context to be a label we have allowed our transitions to 'observe' an agent in any context.

Proposition 7.11 (congruence of full bisimilarity) *In any WRS, bisimilarity for* FT *is a congruence.*

Proof Assuming that $a \sim_{\text{FT}} b$, we wish to show that $c \circ a \sim_{\text{FT}} c \circ b$, where c is any context for a and b. For this purpose, suppose that $c \circ a \stackrel{f}{\longrightarrow} a'$; then we seek b' such that $c \circ b \stackrel{f}{\longrightarrow} b'$ and $a' \sim_{\text{FT}} b'$.

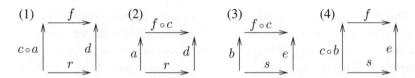

For some reaction rule (r, r') the diagram (1) commutes, d is active and $a' \simeq d \circ r'$. Then (2) also commutes; hence there is a transition $a \xrightarrow{f \circ c} a'$. Since $a \sim_{_{FT}} b$, for some b' we have the transition $b \xrightarrow{f \circ c} b'$ and $a' \sim_{_{FT}} b'$. So, for some rule (s, s') and active context e, (3) commutes and $b' \simeq e \circ s'$. Then (4) commutes, so $c \circ b \xrightarrow{f} b'$ and we are done.   □

This result is pleasant, but needs to be refined. The defect of FT is that it allows arbitrary contexts as labels. Labels will be arbitrarily large – much larger than needed to represent the cooperation between an agent and its environment in creating a redex. Furthermore, since $f \circ a = d \circ r$, the context d may contain much of this environment; it follows that the target $a' \simeq d \circ r'$ of the transition will also be large. If labels are to be contexts, then we would like to restrict them to be small in some sense. We shall shortly define a notion of minimal label. But there is another difficulty, as follows.

A weakness of taking labels to be contexts is that such a label f in a transition $a \xrightarrow{f} a'$ does not record *where*, within $f \circ a$, the redex of a possible reaction occurs. It then turns out that, if we limit the class of contexts permitted as labels, we lose the congruence of bisimilarity. This is best seen with the help of an example, showing that if we limit label contexts to those that are minimal (to be defined shortly) then two agents that have the same transitions – and are therefore bisimilar – can be distinguished by placing them in a larger context which only permits reaction in certain places.

Example 7.12 (non-congruence) This example shows that bisimilarity based upon unlocated transitions is not in general a congruence for bigraphs. Take the basic signature $\mathcal{K} = \{K, L, M\}$, each with arity zero, and declare K and L to be *atomic*, and M to be *passive* – i.e. it can contain no reaction. Let (K, L) be the only reaction rule, where K means the atom K.1. It can then be shown that $a \sim b$ in the TS which has only minimal contexts as labels, where $a = K \otimes L$ and $b = L \otimes K$.

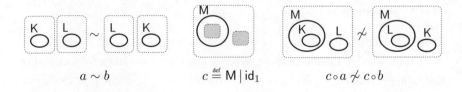

$$a \sim b \qquad\qquad c \stackrel{\text{def}}{=} M \mid id_1 \qquad\qquad c \circ a \not\sim c \circ b$$

But for the context c as shown we have $c \circ a \not\sim c \circ b$. For in b the redex K lies in an active context, so there is a transition $c \circ b \xrightarrow{\text{id}} ;$ but $c \circ a$ has no id-labelled transition, since its redex K lies in a passive context, the M-ion. □

Returning now to WRSs with their wide reaction relations $\longrightarrow_{\tilde{i}}$, we shall refine the notion of contexts-as-labels to take account of location of the underlying re-action, and thus refine bisimilarity so as to make it a congruence. If we add this quantum of information to a transition, then we are able to limit the transitions of a TS to those that are minimal in a precise sense.

Definition 7.13 (contextual transition) In a WRS, a transition $a \xrightarrow{\ell} a'$ is *contextual* if its label ℓ takes the form $(f, \tilde{j})$, where $f : I \to J$ is a context for a and $\tilde{j}$ a location of J. The label applies to an agent a iff $f \circ a$ is defined.

A contextual transition $(a, (f, \tilde{j}), a')$ is written $a \xrightarrow{f}_{\tilde{j}} a'$. It has an underlying reaction rule (r, r') with width m such that for some active $d : I \to J$ the diagram commutes, $\tilde{j} = \{\text{width}(d)(i) \mid i \in \text{width}(I)\}$ and $a' \asymp d \circ r'$. A contextual transition $a \xrightarrow{f}_{\tilde{j}} a'$ is *minimal* if its diagram is an IPO.

A transition system is *contextual* if its transitions are contextual, and its agents and labels are closed under $\asymp$. It is *minimal* if its transitions are minimal. □

In the transition $a \xrightarrow{f}_{\tilde{j}} a'$ we are justified in calling the label $(f, \tilde{j})$ *contextual*, not only because f is a context for a, but also because $\tilde{j}$ is the range of width(d), where d is the context in which the underlying redex lies. Note that this redex itself cannot be recovered from the information recorded in the transition; this opens the possibility that two agents may be behaviourally equivalent even though their transitions are based upon different reaction rules.

There are many minimal TSs. (The term 'minimal' applies to the transitions, not to the system.) We now distinguish a family of them.

Definition 7.14 (largest minimal TS) Given a WRS and a set $\mathcal{I}$ of its objects, the minimal TS $\text{MT}_\mathcal{I} = (\text{Agt}, \text{Lab}, \text{Apl}, \text{Tra})$ is defined as follows:

- Agt has all agents $a : I$ for $I \in \mathcal{I}$;
- Lab has all labels occurring in Tra;
- Apl has all pairs (a, ℓ) where $\ell = (f, \tilde{i})$ is a transition label with $f \circ a$ defined;
- Tra has all minimal transitions $a \xrightarrow{f}_{\tilde{i}} a'$ for $a, a' \in \text{Agt}$.

We shall write MT for $\text{MT}_\mathcal{I}$ when $\mathcal{I}$ is understood. □

Thus we are mainly interested in two species of transition system: raw and mini-mal. Minimal TSs are the ones that we shall derive uniformly for any WRS. But we shall also consider raw TSs that are specific to particular process calculi, including some that have been studied in depth, in order that the bisimilarities they induce can be compared with those induced by derived TSs.

To clarify the relationship between reactions and contextual transitions, it is helpful to compare them with diagrams. Here are the reaction $a \longrightarrow_{\tilde{\jmath}} a'$ and the transition $a \xrightarrow{f}_{\tilde{\jmath}} a'$, both based upon a reaction rule (r, r'). Like-named entities in the two diagrams are unrelated. In each case d is active, and $\tilde{\jmath} \subseteq \text{width}(J)$ is given by $\tilde{\jmath} = \{\text{width}(d)(i) \mid i \in \text{width}(I)\}$. The reaction can also be seen as a contextual transition $a \xrightarrow{\text{id}_J}_{\tilde{\jmath}} a'$ whose label has an identity context. Conversely, underlying the transition there is a reaction $f \circ a \longrightarrow_{\tilde{\jmath}} a'$. The transition is minimal if its square is an IPO.

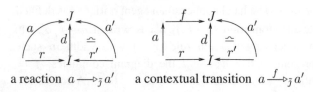

a reaction $a \longrightarrow_{\tilde{\jmath}} a'$ a contextual transition $a \xrightarrow{f}_{\tilde{\jmath}} a'$

Width plays two roles in Definition 7.13. It takes part in the assertion that d is active, i.e. active everywhere in the width m of its domain; it also defines the location $\tilde{\jmath}$ in terms of m. Note that, since $\tilde{\jmath}$ is a location in the codomain of f, another transition $b \xrightarrow{f}_{\tilde{\jmath}} b'$ may have the same label $(f, \tilde{\jmath})$, even if its underlying reaction rule has width different from m.

EXERCISE 7.3 Prove that in a concrete WRS the transition relation is consistent with reaction, i.e. that $a \xrightarrow{f}_{\tilde{\imath}} a'$ implies $f \circ a \longrightarrow_{\tilde{\imath}} a'$. *Hint:* Very easy!   □

Let us revisit Example 7.12, to see why it does not contradict the congruence of bisimilarity for MT. The reason is that we no longer have $a \sim b$, since their transitions have different locations; in fact, $a \xrightarrow{\text{id}}_{\tilde{\imath}} a'$ and $b \xrightarrow{\text{id}}_{\tilde{\jmath}} b'$, where $\tilde{\imath} = \{0\}$ and $\tilde{\jmath} = \{1\}$.

We are now ready for our main result that applies to all wide reactive systems: that bisimilarity for MT is indeed a congruence. The importance of this is that the labels of this TS are tractable, since each one is part of the cospan of an IPO.

We begin by recalling the standard technique of 'bisimulation up to ...'. It is well known[3] that if an equivalence $\equiv$ is included in bisimilarity, then to establish bisimilarity it is enough to exhibit a *bisimulation up to* $\equiv$; that is, a symmetric relation S such that whenever aSb then each transition of a is matched by b in $S^{\equiv}$, the closure of S under $\equiv$. It is easy now to prove the following:

---

[3] This property is valid for *strong* bisimilarity, which is what concerns us here.

Proposition 7.15 (bisimulation up to support equivalence)

(1) Support equivalence $\asymp$ is a bisimulation for MT.

(2) To prove $a \sim_{\mathcal{M}} b$ it is enough to show that $(a, b) \in \mathcal{S}$ for some $\mathcal{S}$ which is a bisimulation up to $\asymp$.

EXERCISE 7.4 Prove this. *Hint:* For the first part, use Proposition 4.5(5), concerning support translation of RPOs (and hence for IPOs). □

We may now prove the congruence theorem.[4]

Theorem 7.16 (congruence of minimal bisimilarity) *In a wide reactive system with RPOs, equipped with* MT, *bisimilarity of agents is a congruence; that is, if $a_0 \sim a_1$ then $c \circ a_0 \sim c \circ a_1$, where c is any context for a_0 and a_1.*

Proof   We establish the following as a bisimulation up to $\asymp$:

$$\mathcal{S} \stackrel{\text{def}}{=} \{(c \circ a_0, c \circ a_1) \mid a_0 \sim a_1, c \text{ any context}\} .$$

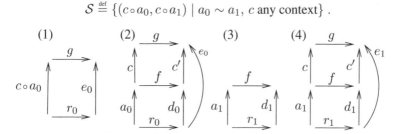

Suppose that $a_0 \sim a_1$, and that $c \circ a_0 \xrightarrow{g}_{\tilde{\jmath}} b'_0$, for some label g that applies to $c \circ a_1$. It is enough to find b'_1 such that $c \circ a_1 \xrightarrow{g}_{\tilde{\jmath}} b'_1$ and $(b'_0, b'_1) \in \mathcal{S}^{\asymp}$.

There exist a ground reaction rule (r_0, r'_0) with codomain H_0, and an active context e_0 such that $b'_0 \asymp e_0 \circ r'_0$ and $\tilde{\jmath} = \{\text{width}(e_0)(h) \mid h \in \text{width}(H_0)\}$, and moreover diagram (1) is an IPO. There exists an RPO (f, d_0, c') for (a_0, r_0) relative to the bound $(g \circ c, e_0)$, so by RPO theory each square in diagram (2) is an IPO, with d_0 active, and c' active at $\tilde{\imath} = \{\text{width}(d_0)(h) \mid h \in \text{width}(H_0)\}$.

So the lower square underlies a transition $a_0 \xrightarrow{f}_{\tilde{\imath}} a'_0$, where $a'_0 = d_0 \circ r'_0$. Now $f \circ a_1$ is defined (since $g \circ c \circ a_1$ is defined and $g \circ c = c' \circ f$) and $a_0 \sim a_1$, so there is a transition $a_1 \xrightarrow{f}_{\tilde{\imath}} a'_1$ with $a'_0 \sim a'_1$. But support translation of a'_1 preserves both of these properties; so we may assume a rule (r_1, r'_1) with codomain H_1 and an active d_1 such that $a'_1 = d_1 \circ r'_1$, $|c'| \cap |a'_1| = \emptyset$ and $\tilde{\imath} = \{\text{width}(d_1)(h) \mid h \in \text{width}(H_1)\}$, and moreover diagram (3) is an IPO.

Now replace the lower square of (2) by diagram (3), obtaining diagram (4) in which, by RPO theory, the large rectangle is an IPO. Moreover $e_1 \stackrel{\text{def}}{=} c' \circ d_1$ is

---

[4] There are many behavioural equivalences for transition systems other than bisimilarity. It has been shown [54] that some of them, e.g. the failures equivalence [44], are also congruences for derived TSs.

active, since c' is active at $\tilde{i}$. Hence $c \circ a_1 \xrightarrow{g}_{\tilde{j}} b_1'$ where $b_1' \overset{\text{def}}{=} e_1 \circ r_1'$. Finally $(b_0', b_1') \in \mathcal{S}^{\rightleftharpoons}$ as required, because $b_0' \rightleftharpoons c' \circ a_0'$ and $b_1' \rightleftharpoons c' \circ a_1'$ with $a_0' \sim a_1'$. $\square$

Having understood how a contextual transition system can be derived for a WRS, and in particular how its bisimilarity may be a congruence, we can consider the TS as weaned from the reaction rules that gave birth to it. But the reaction rules remain important for many applications.

7.3 Sub transition systems

Consider a wide s-category equipped with a TS, either raw or contextual. It can happen that bisimilarity is unaffected if we reduce the transition system itself, i.e. discard some of the transitions. To set the scene, let us define what it means to reduce an arbitrary transition system.

Definition 7.17 (sub transition system) A transition system $\mathcal{M}$ is a *sub transition system* of $\mathcal{L}$, written $\mathcal{M} \prec \mathcal{L}$, if each of the four components of $\mathcal{M}$ is a subset of the corresponding component of $\mathcal{L}$. $\square$

In general, the bisimilarity of the sub-TS $\mathcal{M}$ is incomparable with that of $\mathcal{L}$. For example, if $\mathcal{M}$ has no labels then all its agents are bisimilar; on the other hand if $a \sim b$ in $\mathcal{L}$, and each has transitions in $\mathcal{L}$, then by keeping in $\mathcal{M}$ the transitions of a but omitting those of b we find that $a \not\sim b$ in $\mathcal{M}$.

Let us now consider a natural class of sub-TSs:

Definition 7.18 (definite sub transition system) Let $\mathcal{M} \prec \mathcal{L}$. Then $\mathcal{M}$ is a *definite* sub transition system if $\mathsf{Agt}_{\mathcal{M}}$ and $\mathsf{Lab}_{\mathcal{M}}$ define the other two components of $\mathcal{M}$, in this sense: for all $a, a' \in \mathsf{Agt}_{\mathcal{M}}$ and $\ell \in \mathsf{Lab}_{\mathcal{M}}$

– if ℓ applies to a in $\mathcal{L}$ then it applies to a in $\mathcal{M}$;
– if $a \xrightarrow{\ell}_{\tilde{i}} a'$ is a transition in $\mathcal{L}$ then it is a transition in $\mathcal{M}$. $\square$

Proposition 7.19 (definite sub-TS) *Let $\mathcal{M}$ be a definite sub-TS of $\mathcal{L}$, and let $a \sim_{\mathcal{L}} b$. Then also $a \sim_{\mathcal{M}} b$.*

Proof   It is easy to show that $\sim_{\mathcal{L}}$ is a bisimulation for $\mathcal{M}$. $\square$

So by restricting attention to a definite sub transition system we can only increase its bisimilarity relation. This raises an important question: are there situations in which the relation remains unchanged? For now, let us only make a definition:

Definition 7.20 (faithful sub transition system) $\mathcal{M}$ is a *faithful* sub transition system of $\mathcal{L}$ if, restricted to the agents of $\mathcal{M}$, we have $\sim_{\mathcal{M}} = \sim_{\mathcal{L}}$. $\square$

Thus, by reducing $\mathcal{L}$ to a definite and faithful sub transition system, we show that the omitted labels contribute nothing to distinguishing agents by their behaviour. This both clarifies our understanding and lightens the task of establishing bisimilarity. In Chapter 8 we shall achieve this for bigraphs under certain conditions.

7.4 Abstract transition systems

We now wish to see how both raw and contextual transition systems behave under a quotient of a wide s-category that yields a wide spm category equipped with an abstract TS. We shall be interested in TSs that harmonise with a structural congruence, in this sense:

Definition 7.21 (respect)   A dynamic abstraction $\equiv$ *respects* a raw transition system if, whenever $a \overset{\ell}{\longrightarrow} a'$ and $b \equiv a$, then $b \overset{\ell}{\longrightarrow} b'$ for some $b' \equiv a'$.

It *respects* a contextual transition system $\mathcal{L}$ if, whenever $a \overset{f}{\longrightarrow}_{\tilde{i}} a'$ and $b \equiv a$ and $g \equiv f$, where $(g, \tilde{i}) \in \mathsf{Lab}_{\mathcal{L}}$ with $g \circ b$ defined, then $b \overset{g}{\longrightarrow}_{\tilde{i}} b'$ for some $b' \equiv a'$.   □

There are many possible dynamic abstractions on bigraphs. They do not necessarily respect a transition system.

EXERCISE 7.5 Answer the following informally for bigraphs:

(1) Let $A : 1$ and $B : 1$ be atomic controls. For two arbitrary bigraphs F and G in the same homset, define $F \equiv G$ to mean that they are identical when every B-node linked to an A-node is deleted. Let $\overline{F}$ denote the result of deleting every B-node linked to an A-node. Is it true that $\overline{G \circ F} = \overline{G} \circ \overline{F}$? Is $\equiv$ a structural congruence, or even an abstraction? Does it respect MT?

(2) Let A and B be non-atomic controls with equal arity. Define $F \equiv G$ to mean that they are identical when every B-node is replaced by an A-node. Is $\equiv$ a structural congruence, or even an abstraction? Does it respect MT, provided that no parametric redex contains an A- or B-node?   □

Let us now return to the transition systems induced by quotient. Given a transition system $\mathcal{L}$ and an abstraction $\equiv$ for a concrete WRS, the $\equiv$-quotient functor induces a TS for the quotient abstract WRS by simply applying the functor to every bigraph in each of the four components of $\mathcal{L}$. The main difference between raw and contextual TSs is that, in the former, the labels are left unchanged. To be precise:

Definition 7.22 (transitions for a quotient)   Let $`\mathbf{C}$ be a wide s-category equipped with a raw or contextual transition system $\mathcal{L} = (\mathsf{Agt}, \mathsf{Lab}, \mathsf{Apl}, \mathsf{Tra})$, and let $\equiv$ be an abstraction on $`\mathbf{C}$. Denote the $\equiv$-quotient of $`\mathbf{C}$ by $\mathbf{C}$, an spm category. Then the contextual transition system $[\![\mathcal{L}]\!] = (\mathsf{Agt}', \mathsf{Lab}', \mathsf{Apl}', \mathsf{Tra}')$ *induced* by $\equiv$ on $\mathbf{C}$ has components generated as follows:

For $\mathcal{L}$ raw:
- if $a \in \mathsf{Agt}$ then $[\![a]\!] \in \mathsf{Agt}'$
- $\mathsf{Lab}' = \mathsf{Lab}$
- if $(a, \ell) \in \mathsf{Apl}$ then $([\![a]\!], \ell) \in \mathsf{Apl}'$
- if $a \xrightarrow{\ell} a'$ in Tra then $[\![a]\!] \xrightarrow{\ell} [\![a']\!]$ in Tra' .

For $\mathcal{L}$ contextual:
- if $a \in \mathsf{Agt}$ then $[\![a]\!] \in \mathsf{Agt}'$
- if $(f, \tilde{\imath}) \in \mathsf{Lab}$ then $([\![f]\!], \tilde{\imath}) \in \mathsf{Lab}'$
- if $(a, (f, \tilde{\imath})) \in \mathsf{Apl}$ then $([\![a]\!], ([\![f]\!], \tilde{\imath})) \in \mathsf{Apl}'$
- if $a \xrightarrow{f}_{\tilde{\imath}} a'$ in Tra then $[\![a]\!] \xrightarrow{[\![f]\!]}_{\tilde{\imath}} [\![a']\!]$ in Tra' . $\square$

This may not make bisimilarity a congruence in $\mathbf{C}$, even if it is so in $`\mathbf{C}$. However the next theorem, proved in Appendix A.4, ensures this in the presence of respect.

Theorem 7.23 (bisimilarity induced by quotient) *Let* $`\mathbf{C}$ *be a wide s-category that is equipped with a raw or contextual transition system* $\mathcal{L}$. *Let* $\equiv$ *be an abstraction on* $`\mathbf{C}$ *that respects* $\mathcal{L}$. *Denote the* $\equiv$-*quotient of* $`\mathbf{C}$ *by* $\mathbf{C}$, *an spm category. Then the following hold for* $[\![\mathcal{L}]\!]$:

(1) $a \sim b$ *in* $`\mathbf{C}$ *iff* $[\![a]\!] \sim [\![b]\!]$ *in* $\mathbf{C}$.
(2) *If bisimilarity is a congruence in* $`\mathbf{C}$ *then it is a congruence in* $\mathbf{C}$.

Thus, a transition system and its bisimilarity are treated well by a suitable quotient of a wide s-category. We can harmonise this treatment with a suitable quotient of a WRS $`\mathbf{C}(`\mathcal{R})$ (Definition 7.6), as follows:

Proposition 7.24 (quotient reaction and transition) *Let* $`\mathbf{C}(`\mathcal{R})$ *be a concrete WRS equipped with a contextual TS* $\mathcal{L}$ *based upon* $`\mathcal{R}$, *and let* $\equiv$ *be a dynamic abstraction for the WRS.*

Then in the quotient WRS (Definition 7.6), equipped with the transition system induced from $\mathcal{L}$ *as in Definition 7.22, transition is consistent with reaction:*

$$p \xrightarrow{g}_{\tilde{\imath}} p' \text{ implies } g \circ p \longrightarrow_{\tilde{\imath}} p' .$$

EXERCISE 7.6 Prove this. *Hint:* You need Exercise 7.3 and Theorem 7.7. $\square$

These results prepare for a uniform procedure that yields a behavioural congruence for an abstract WRS. The procedure moves to a concrete WRS and back again. It is justified because support is necessary for deriving a tractable behaviour model based upon a transition system. Given an abstract WRS $\mathbf{C}(\mathcal{R})$, the procedure has three steps: move to a concrete WRS; construct a concrete transition system there; then bring it back to the abstract WRS. Here are the steps in more detail:

(A) Define a concrete WRS $`C(`R)$ such that $\mathbf{C}$ and $\mathcal{R}$ are the quotients of $`C$ and $`R$ by some dynamic abstraction $\equiv$.
(B) Derive a contextual transition system $\mathcal{L}$ for $`C(`R)$ with an associated behavioural congruence $\sim_{\mathcal{L}}$, and ensure that $\equiv$ respects $\mathcal{L}$.
(C) Use Definition 7.22 to transfer $\mathcal{L}$ to the abstract WRS $\mathbf{C}(\mathcal{R})$, and Theorem 7.23 to ensure a behavioural congruence in $\mathbf{C}(\mathcal{R})$.

In Chapter 8 we shall find that this can be done for any bigraphical reactive system (BRS), as defined in Definition 8.6, satisfying very general conditions. In that case the chosen abstraction $\equiv$ will be lean-support equivalence, the transition system $\mathcal{L}$ will be derived using the RPOs of Chapter 4, and the behavioural congruence $\sim_{\mathcal{L}}$ will be bisimilarity (though other behavioural congruences are likely to work also).

Thus contextual reactive systems yield a generic behavioural theory. Its importance is not only that it specialises to bigraphs, but also that it provides insight for reactive systems in general. Indeed the special case of bigraphs is itself generic, since – as cited in Chapter 12 – many different process calculi can be faithfully encoded in bigraphs. Our three-step procedure will be illustrated for a class of Petri nets in Chapter 9 and for finite CCS in Chapter 10.

8

Bigraphical reactive systems

As a first step in defining the dynamics of bigraphs, we refine the notion of a reaction rule to make it *parametric*. This leads to the formal definition of a bigraphical reactive system (BRS), and then to a taxonomy of BRSs, followed by their behavioural theory.

We begin by illustrating the notion of parametric reaction:

Example 8.1 (CCS reaction in bigraphs) In Example 3.18 we gave the redex of the usual CCS reaction rule as an example of a bigraphical algebraic expression; we now look at the whole rule.

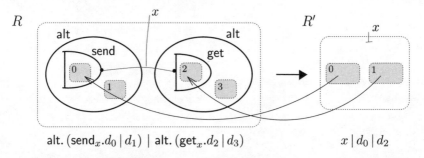

$$\mathsf{alt}. (\mathsf{send}_x.d_0 \mid d_1) \mid \mathsf{alt}. (\mathsf{get}_x.d_2 \mid d_3) \qquad\qquad x \mid d_0 \mid d_2$$

The rule is parametric. The parametric redex $R = \mathsf{alt}. (\mathsf{send}_x \mid \mathsf{id}) \mid \mathsf{alt}. (\mathsf{get}_x \mid \mathsf{id})$ has four sites, to be filled by arbitrary parameters $d_0, \ldots, d_3$. Sites 0 and 2 are for processes, and sites 1 and 3 are for alternations (summations). The reactum $R' = x \mid \mathsf{id} \mid \mathsf{id}$ has two sites, to be filled by parameters as indicated by the back-pointing arrows. The placing of parameters is also shown by the algebraic expression. This rule discards parameters 1 and 3.

Recall that in CCS the input and output prefixes are guarding; they prevent internal reaction. To capture this we have to define *activity* for bigraphs, and to declare all CCS controls *passive*, in the sense that we now define. □

88

Definition 8.2 (dynamic signature, activity) A signature is *dynamic* if it assigns to each control K a *status* in the set {atomic, passive, active}. We say that a K-node is atomic if its control is assigned the status atomic, and so on.

A bigraph $G : \langle m, X \rangle \to \langle n, Y \rangle$ is *active at a site* at $i \in m$ if every ancestor node of site i is active. G is *active* if it is active at every site (see Definition 7.2).   □

In the CCS signature we declare the controls 'alt', 'send' and 'get' all to be passive, ensuring that reaction only occurs at the top level. In contrast, for the calculus of mobile ambients (see Figure 1.1) we declare the ambient control 'amb' to be active, to allow reactions inside an ambient.

The initial purpose of this chapter is to explain how parametric reaction rules generate the reaction relation of a BRS, as the basis for the dynamic theory of BRSs. We then specialise to BRSs the theory of transition systems and behavioural equivalence developed for WRSs in Chapter 7. That theory was first developed for a concrete WRS, based upon an s-category, and transferred at the end to its quotient abstract WRSs based upon an spm category. Similarly, much of the present chapter is devoted to answering the question: What conditions on a concrete BRS allow us to obtain a tractable minimal TS whose behavioural equivalence is a congruence? Recall that in a minimal TS every transition is based upon an IPO, and that MT is the largest such TS, having all possible agents and all possible minimal transitions between them.

In Section 8.1 we define parametric reaction formally, and then deduce from Chapter 7 that, in a *safe* concrete BRS equipped with the minimal transition system MT, bisimilarity is always a congruence; this is because safeness ensures that RPOs exist. In Section 8.2 we identify conditions under which MT can be reduced to more tractable transition systems, while preserving the bisimilarity equivalence – hence also preserving its congruence.

Finally, we transfer this transition system to the quotient abstract BRS, via the lean-support quotient functor. It turns out that the same conditions ensure that the behavioural congruence is preserved for this abstract BRS.

Notation We now resume the convention that arbitrary bigraphs are denoted by upper case italic letters, and ground bigraphs by lower case. However, I, J, K denote interfaces, and X, Y, Z denote name-sets. We use sans-serif letters A, B, C, K, L, M, N for arbitrary controls. We use R, S for parametric redexes (Definition 8.5), r, s for ground redexes, and L, M for arbitrary contexts used as labels.   □

8.1 Dynamics for a BRS

The CCS rule shown above illustrates how the parameter of a redex R is *instantiated* for the reactum R'. In general we shall have a redex $R : m \to J$ and reactum

$R' : m' \to J$, both parametric, and the reaction rule will specify an *instantiation map* $\eta : m' \to m$ which determines, for each $j \in m'$, which factor of the parameter of R should occupy the jth site of R'. Care is needed to define instantiation precisely. Consider a simple example that duplicates its parameter:

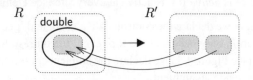

We might expect this rule to generate reactions of the form $\text{double}.a \longrightarrow a \mid a$, where a is any ground prime. So if a has a closed link, say $a = /x \circ \mathsf{A}_x$ (with A atomic), there would be a reaction

$$a \longrightarrow (/x \circ \mathsf{A}_x) \mid (/x \circ \mathsf{A}_x) .$$

But we have $\text{double}.a = /x \circ (\text{double}.\mathsf{A}_x)$, so there exists also a reaction

$$a \longrightarrow /x \circ (\mathsf{A}_x \mid \mathsf{A}_x) .$$

This shows that – since closure is not located – it is unclear whether or not the closed link is itself duplicated.

To settle this issue, we shall define *instantiation* of a parameter in terms of its discrete normal form, established uniquely in Definition 3.10. The effect is that all replicated closed links will be shared, as in the second alternative above. To avoid sharing such a link, under a replicating reaction, one must express it instead as a *bound* link as explored in Section 11.3. This has already been carried out in a translation of the π-calculus into bigraphs,[1] but it lies beyond the main scope of this book.

Definition 8.3 (instantiation) In a bigraphical s-category $\mathbf{`C} = \mathbf{`BG}(\Sigma)$, let $\langle m, X \rangle$ and $\langle n, X \rangle$ be two sorted interfaces (sorts not shown), and let $\eta : n \to m$ be a map of finite ordinals that preserves place sorts. Define the *instance* function $\overline{\eta} : \mathbf{`C}\langle m, X \rangle \to \mathbf{`C}\langle n, X \rangle$ on agents as follows: Given an agent $g : \langle m, X \rangle$, find its DNF $g = \lambda \circ (d_0 \otimes \cdots \otimes d_{m-1})$ (Proposition 3.9). Then

$$\overline{\eta}(g) \stackrel{\text{def}}{=} \lambda \circ (d_0' \parallel \cdots \parallel d_{n-1}'),$$

where $d_j' \mathbin{\hat{=}} d_{\eta(j)}$ for each $j \in n$. The function is defined up to $\hat{=}$. $\qquad\square$

---

[1] See [47].

We use the parallel product $d'_0 \parallel \cdots \parallel d'_{n-1}$, rather than the tensor product, because any replicated factors in the product – as will occur if η is non-injective – will share names. Note also that $\overline{\eta}(g)$ has the same outer names X as g.[2]

Linking commutes with instantiation. For if $g = \lambda \circ d$ and we wish to instantiate $f = \mu \circ g$, then we first find the DNF $f = \mu \circ \lambda \circ d$; so we may apply μ before or after instantiation, with no difference of result. Formally:

Proposition 8.4 (linking an instance) *Linking commutes with instantiation; that is, $\mu \circ \overline{\eta}(g) \simeq \overline{\eta}(\mu \circ g)$.*

Proof Let $g : \langle m, X \rangle$, with $\eta : m' \to m$. Take the DNF $g = \lambda \circ d$, where $\lambda : Y \to X$. Then $\overline{\eta}(g) = \lambda \circ d'$, where $d' = d'_0 \parallel \cdots \parallel d'_{m'-1}$ with each $d'_i \simeq d_{\eta(i)}$. So

$$\begin{aligned}
\overline{\eta}(\mu \circ g) &= \overline{\eta}(\mu \circ (\lambda \circ d)) = \overline{\eta}((\mu \circ \lambda) \circ d) \\
&\simeq (\mu \circ \lambda) \circ d' = \mu \circ (\lambda \circ d') \simeq \mu \circ \overline{\eta}(g) .
\end{aligned}$$
$\square$

Before going further, we must take account of the fact that we are working in `BG($\Sigma$), where $\Sigma$ is an arbitrary sorting. Although `BG(Σ) is required to be an s-category (Definitions 6.1 and 6.10), it does not require all our elements – in particular *join*, substitution and closure – and the derived operators of parallel and merge product and nesting to exist at all sorts. For example, many–one sorting demands that each s-link contain exactly one s-point, and this excludes non-trivial substitution at sort s (though it admits them at sort t). This also means that some uses of parallel product ($\parallel$) violate many–one sorting.

Since we are developing a dynamical theory based upon reaction rules we shall make the following assumption: if, in a BRS, a reaction rule allows a parameter to have a name of sort θ, then the BRS must admit substitutions and closures at sort θ.[3]

From now on in this chapter we are involved with an arbitrary sorting, possibly under some constraints. To avoid heavy notation we continue to write an interface as $\langle m, X \rangle$, even though the roots in m and the names in X may carry place sorts or link sorts respectively.

We are now able to define the dynamics of bigraphs, relying on Definition 7.1 for the way the reaction relation is determined by a set of ground reaction rules.

Definition 8.5 (parametric reaction rules) A *parametric reaction rule* for bigraphs is a triple of the form

$$(R : m \to J, \ R' : m' \to J, \ \eta)$$

---

[2] This is implied by the convention stated at the start of Section 3.2: for $\lambda : Y \to X$, the composition $\lambda \circ f$ still has outer names X (though some may be idle) even when f has fewer outer names than Y.

[3] This question does not arise for our application of many–one sorting to Petri nets, since its reaction rules are not parametric.

where R is the *parametric redex*, R' the *parametric reactum*, and $\eta : m' \to m$ a map of finite ordinals. R and R' must be lean, and R must have no idle roots or names. The rule generates all ground reaction rules (r, r'), where

$$r \simeq R.d \,, \quad r' \simeq R'.\overline{\eta}(d)$$

and $d : \langle m, Y \rangle$ is discrete. □

In Example 8.1 we may think of R either as taking a parameter of width 4, or as taking four prime parameters. The definition of ground rules, using nesting, ensures that the names of the parameter are exported to the context in which the redex resides.

EXERCISE 8.1 Assume the place sorting for CCS introduced in Definition 6.5. In the parameter $d = d_0 \otimes \cdots \otimes d_3$ shown in Example 8.1, assume that d_i has outer names Y_i ($i \in 4$) and $Y = \biguplus_i Y_i$. Write down the sorted interfaces of R, R', r, r' and each d_i. □

Our present definition of parametric rules is rather simple, but the reader may think of ways to vary it. Here are two features that could be varied:

(i) Why do we make parameters discrete? In fact the reaction relation would be unchanged if we allowed arbitrary agents as parameters, since instantiation of an agent is defined in terms of its underlying discrete bigraph. But discrete parameters simplify analysis, especially for transitions and bisimilarity.

(ii) Can we track the identity of nodes through a reaction? Our definition does not allow this, but it would be useful in some applications. Look again at the rules **B1–B3** for the built environment in Chapter 1; we may well wish to stipulate that the agent involved is the same, before and after the reaction. It is not difficult to alter the definition to admit such tracking, by means of *support*; this allows properties of a system's history to be expressed, such as 'agent u has never visited room v'. Thus support has broader usage than ensuring the existence of RPOs (and hence the derivation of transition systems). Tracking is examined further in Section 11.1.

We are now ready to define our central concept:

Definition 8.6 (bigraphical reactive system (BRS)) A *(concrete) bigraphical reactive system (BRS)* over Σ consists of `BG($\Sigma$) equipped with a set `$\mathcal{R}$ of parametric reaction rules closed under support equivalence; that is, if $R \simeq S$ and $R' \simeq S'$ and `$\mathcal{R}$ contains $(R, R', \eta)$, then it also contains $(S, S', \eta)$. We denote the BRS by `BG(Σ, `$\mathcal{R}$). It is *safe* if its sorting Σ is safe. □

Having seen how parametric rules generate ground rules, it is easy to check that each BRS is a reactive system. Moreover there is an obvious width functor for bigraphs; for an interface $I = \langle m, X \rangle$ define width(I) to be m, and for a bigraph $G : I \to J$ define width(G)(i), for all $i \in$ width(I), to be the unique $j \in$ width(J) such that $j = prnt_G^k(i)$ for some k. Without further proof we can now assert:

Proposition 8.7 (BRSs are wide) *Every BRS is a wide reactive system.*

Recall that in Chapter 7 we equipped a WRS only with ground reaction rules, not with parametric rules. We could indeed have defined parametric rules for a WRS, but we have more reason to do so for a BRS. This is because bigraphs have a rich structure that permits us to classify BRSs according to the structural properties of their parametric rules, such as those mentioned at the end of Definition 8.6.

All the work in Chapter 7 on transition systems and bisimilarity – especially on contextual transition systems – can be applied to BRSs, provided they are safe (ensuring RPOs). Most importantly, from Theorem 7.16 we deduce:

Corollary 8.8 (congruence of bisimilarity) *In any safe concrete BRS equipped with* MT, *the transition system with all minimal transitions, bisimilarity $\sim$ is a congruence.*

Now let us transfer this congruence to an abstract BRS BG($\Sigma,\mathcal{R}$), where BG(Σ) and $\mathcal{R}$ are obtained by the lean-support quotient functor $[\![\cdot]\!]$ of Definition 2.19 and Theorem 2.20. We must first prove that the minimal transition system MT respects $\eqcirc$:

Proposition 8.9 (abstraction respects transitions) *In a concrete BRS with* MT:

(1) Every label context is lean.

(2) Lean-support equivalence respects the transitions. In other words, whenever $a \xrightarrow{L}_{\bar{\imath}} a'$, if $a \eqcirc b$ and $L \eqcirc M$ where $(M, \bar{\imath})$ is a label with $M \circ b$ defined, then $b \xrightarrow{M}_{\bar{\imath}} b'$ for some b' such that $a' \eqcirc b'$.

(3) Lean-support equivalence is a bisimulation.

Proof For (1), use Proposition 5.24(1) and the fact that every discrete agent is lean. For (2), use Proposition 5.24(2); the fact that each redex is lean ensures that it cannot share an idle edge with the agent a. Then (3) follows directly from (2). $\square$

We are now ready to transfer the congruence results of Corollary 8.8 from concrete to abstract BRSs. The following is immediate from Theorem 7.23:

Corollary 8.10 (behavioural congruence in a safe abstract BRS) *Assume that `BG($\Sigma,`\mathcal{R}$) is a safe concrete BRS, and let BG($\Sigma,\mathcal{R}$) be its lean-support quotient.*

Let $\sim$ denote bisimilarity both for the transition system MT *in* `BG($\Sigma$,`$\mathcal{R}$) *and for the transition system it induces in* BG(Σ,$\mathcal{R}$). *Then*

   (1) $a \sim b$ iff $[\![a]\!] \sim [\![b]\!]$.
   (2) Bisimilarity $\sim$ is a congruence in BG(Σ,$\mathcal{R}$).

Thus we have assured a congruential behavioural equivalence for a broad class of BRSs characterised by only one condition: that they are safe. But the results of this section apply more widely; they apply to any BRS that has RPOs. As we have seen, safeness is an easily-checked sufficient condition for RPOs to exist.

Let us now see how this enables us to specialise the three-step procedure defined at the end of Chapter 7, in order to develop the behavioural theory of a given safe abstract BRS BG(Σ,$\mathcal{R}$), as follows:

   (A) Take the structural congruence $\equiv$ to be lean-support equivalence $\eqcirc$. Equip the (concrete) bigraphical s-category `BG($\Sigma$) with concrete reaction rules `$\mathcal{R}$ which consists of all lean preimages of $\mathcal{R}$ by the lean-support quotient functor $[\![\cdot]\!]$, yielding the concrete BRS `BG($\Sigma$,`$\mathcal{R}$). This automatically satisfies the sorting discipline of Σ, and also the constraints (no idle names or roots) on redexes, since these conditions are unaffected by the lean-support quotient.

   (B) Since the concrete BRS is safe, it has RPOs; hence we can equip it with the minimal transition system MT, and this yields a congruential bisimilarity $\sim_{\text{MT}}$, which is respected by $\eqcirc$.

   (C) Finally, taking the quotient of the transition system MT by $[\![\cdot]\!]$, we arrive back in the abstract BRS BG(Σ,$\mathcal{R}$) equipped with a transition system $[\![\text{MT}]\!]$ having a congruential bisimilarity.

We now turn to additional conditions that can make a BRS easier to handle. The most prominent of these are conditions on the rule-set $\mathcal{R}$; they have the effect of further reducing the transition system MT, making it more tractable. Apart from this, the three-step procedure remains unchanged; the reader will find it helpful to bear this procedure in mind as a background for understanding the behavioural theories of Petri nets and CCS, developed in Section 9.2 and Chapter 10 respectively.

8.2 Dynamics for a nice BRS

The minimal transition system is quite tractable, since each support element of a label lies either in the agent or in the underlying redex. As we shall now see, for certain classes of BRS our derived transition systems become still more tractable, and indeed – for BRSs that encode known process models such as Petri nets – closer to known semantic treatments. In Definition 8.18 we shall use the adjective 'nice' to denote a class of BRSs with several pleasant attributes, and then prove a theorem to show how this eases the theory of their transition systems.

We begin by asking: Having limited MT to contain only minimal transitions, can we even remove some of these without affecting bisimilarity – and hence without losing behavioural congruence? We may try including only those transitions whose agents make a non-trivial contribution to the underlying reaction. Also the agents that arise in our applications are often prime – indeed this will be true for CCS – so we may try restricting ourselves to prime agents. To be precise:

Definition 8.11 (engaged transition, prime transition) A transition $a \xrightarrow{L} _{\tilde{\imath}} a'$ based on a reaction with parametric redex R is *engaged* if $|a| \cap |R| \neq \emptyset$. A transition is *prime* if both a and a' are prime. $\square$

We might expect a disengaged transition $a \xrightarrow{L} _{\tilde{\imath}} a'$ to be redundant. If the agent a shares no node or edge with the parametric redex R then surely any other agent b should be able to make a transition with the same label, to some suitable b'? If so, then we could ignore such transitions without affecting the bisimilarity. But this argument needs to be made precise, and depends upon constraints that we define below.

Another incentive to include only the engaged transitions is that we are more likely to be able to confine attention to prime transitions. For suppose that an agent a is prime, and also that a parametric redex R has prime outer face; then in an engaged transition $a \xrightarrow{L} _{\tilde{\imath}} a'$ based on R, the ground redex r will also be prime, with $|a| \cap |r| \neq \emptyset$. It follows that any IPO (L, D) for the span (a, r) will have prime outer face, hence a' – and indeed the transition – will be prime. On the other hand, if the transition is disengaged then – by Corollary 5.21 – even if a is prime a' will *not* be so.

Note that if a transition $a \xrightarrow{L} _{\tilde{\imath}} a'$ is prime then its location $\tilde{\imath}$ must be the singleton $\{0\}$; we therefore write simply $a \xrightarrow{L} a'$.

It will turn out that we can often exclude disengaged transitions without affecting bisimilarity. We shall show this for any BRS that is *simple, unary, unambiguous* and *affine*. We now define the first three of these properties (we come to 'affine' later); they are satisfied by a wide range of BRSs, including finite CCS.

Recall that a link is *open* if it is a name, otherwise *closed*. Also recall from Definition 8.5 that a parametric redex is lean and has no idle names or roots. We now submit it to further constraints:

Definition 8.12 (simple, unary) A parametric redex is *simple* if it is

- *open*: every link is open
- *guarding*: no site has a root as parent
- *inner-injective*: no two sites are siblings.

A parametric redex is *unary* if its outer face is. A reaction rule is *simple*, or *unary*, if its redex is so. A BRS is *simple*, or *unary*, if all its reaction rules are so. □

Simpleness is not a severe constraint. For 'guarding' and 'inner-injective' one can argue convincingly that they only exclude redexes that are either unnecessary because their work can be done by other rules, or over-permissive because they allow wild reconfigurations. The 'open' constraint limits expressive power somewhat, but greatly eases analysis; and it is remarkable that the rules required to model CSP, CCS, π-calculus, Petri nets and mobile ambients are all open.

All the conditions in Definition 8.12 pertain to individual reaction rules. But there is an important condition that pertains to a set $\grave{\mathcal{R}}$ of rules, and is concerned with how they relate to each other. Recall that an engaged transition $a \xrightarrow{L}_{\widetilde{\imath}} a'$ based on a parametric redex R is one in which $|a| \cap |R| \neq \emptyset$. Thus 'engaged' is a property of a transition together with its underlying redex. Indeed, a transition may be engaged if it arises from a redex R, but disengaged if it arises from another redex S:

Definition 8.13 (ambiguity) A label of a transition system $\mathcal{L}$ is *ambiguous* if it occurs both in an engaged and in a disengaged transition. A transition system is *ambiguous* if it has an ambiguous label. □

EXERCISE 8.2 This exercise deals with place graphs. Take two controls $A, B : 0$, with B atomic. Let $R = A \circ (\mathrm{id}_1 \mid B)$ and $R' = B$ be the redex and reactum of a parametric rule. Note that R has one site; R' has none.

Prove that the prime transition $a \xrightarrow{L} a'$ is ambiguous, where $a = a' = B^v$ and $L = A^w \circ (\mathrm{id}_1 \mid B^u)$. (The superscripts on ions denote their nodes.) □

Under certain conditions, one of which excludes ambiguity, we shall be able to reduce the transition system MT to one containing only engaged transitions. Our sub-TS will be restricted to prime agents, and we constrain every label L in a prime transition to be unambiguous, i.e. the L-transitions are either all engaged or all disengaged.

Recall from Definition 3.19 the notion of a *tight* bigraph. Roughly speaking (the definition is precise) a bigraph R is tight if, when it occurs within some prime agent g, and g is 'split' into two parts each containing a non-empty part of R, then these two parts must be non-trivially linked. The instance that concerns us is when $g = L \circ a$, where a and L are the source and label of a transition, and R is a parametric redex. The following is proved in Appendix A.5:

Proposition 8.14 (unambiguous label) *Let L be the label of a prime transition in* MT, *in a safe BRS where every redex is simple, unary and tight. Then the label L is unambiguous.*

We now define a sub transition system of MT with unambiguous labels and engaged transitions:

Definition 8.15 (prime engaged transition system) In a safe concrete BRS, assume that every parametric redex is simple, unary and tight. Let PE be the sub-TS of MT consisting of

$\mathsf{Agt}_{\mathsf{PE}}$ – all prime agents at certain interfaces
$\mathsf{Lab}_{\mathsf{PE}}$ – the labels of all prime engaged transitions with $a, a' \in \mathsf{Agt}_{\mathsf{PE}}$
$\mathsf{Apl}_{\mathsf{PE}}$ – the restriction of $\mathsf{Apl}_{\mathsf{MT}}$ to $\mathsf{Agt}_{\mathsf{PE}} \times \mathsf{Lab}_{\mathsf{PE}}$
$\mathsf{Tra}_{\mathsf{PE}}$ – the restriction of $\mathsf{Tra}_{\mathsf{MT}}$ to $\mathsf{Apl}_{\mathsf{PE}} \times \mathsf{Agt}_{\mathsf{PE}}$. $\qquad\square$

The agent interfaces are typically determined in terms of the sorting of the BRS.

We now summarise as a theorem what we have established so far. The main result is that, under certain conditions, tightness ensures that PE is definite.[4] It appears that tightness holds for a wide range of calculi, including CCS, Petri nets and the calculus of mobile ambients.[5]

Theorem 8.16 (prime engaged transitions are definite) *In a safe concrete BRS where every parametric redex is simple, unary and tight:*

(1) Every label of PE *is unambiguous.*

(2) Every transition of PE *is engaged.*

(3) PE *is a definite sub transition system of* MT.

(4) $\sim_{\mathsf{MT}} \subseteq \sim_{\mathsf{PE}}$ restricted to prime agents.

Proof (1) follows from Proposition 8.14, since for every $L \in \mathsf{Lab}_{\mathsf{PE}}$ there is some engaged L-transition in $\mathsf{Tra}_{\mathsf{PE}}$. (2) follows directly from the definition of PE, Definition 8.15. (3) follows from the definition of 'definite', Definition 7.18. (4) is a direct corollary of Proposition 7.19. $\qquad\square$

Clause (4) of the theorem prompts us to ask whether PE is faithful to MT, i.e. whether the bisimilarities coincide on the agents of PE. The following example, due to Ole Jensen, shows that sometimes they do not:

---

[4] In [65], Corollary 9.14, it was wrongly stated that another condition fulfils this purpose – namely that the BRS should lack *subsumption*, in a precise sense. The theory was applied there only to CCS and to a class of Petri nets, whose rules are in fact tight, so nothing false was deduced.
It must be emphasised that tightness is just one condition that excludes ambiguity, and suffices for our present purpose. Other conditions, possibly weaker, may well exist.
[5] See Jensen [46].

Example 8.17 (unfaithful engaged transitions) Let L : 0 be a non-atomic control, and let M : 1 and N : 0 be atomic. For the atomic controls, adopt the convention that M_x means $M_x.1$ and N means N.1. Consider the following two reaction rules:

$$L.d \longrightarrow d \mid d$$
$$M_x \mid M_x \longrightarrow M_x .$$

This defines a BRS that is safe, simple and unary. However, we can exhibit two agents a and b such that $a \sim_{\mathrm{PE}} b$ but $a \not\sim_{\mathrm{MT}} b$. Let $a = /x \circ M_x$ and $b = N$. Neither has an engaged transition, hence $/x \circ M_x \sim_{\mathrm{PE}} N$. (The closure $/x$ prevents an engaged transition by a.) But each can do a unique L-transition, distinguishing them as follows:

$$/x \circ M_x \xrightarrow{\;L\;} /x \circ (M_x \mid M_x) \xrightarrow{\;\mathrm{id}\;} /x \circ M_x$$
$$N \xrightarrow{\;L\;} N \mid N \xrightarrow{\;\mathrm{id}\;} .$$

Thus PE is not faithful to MT.   □

The unfaithfulness in this example depends upon the interaction between closure and the replication caused by the rule $L.d \longrightarrow d \mid d$. We shall therefore be content to prove faithfulness of prime engaged transitions for BRSs that lack replication, i.e. the instantiation map η in every reaction rule is injective.

Definition 8.18 (affine, tight, nice) A reaction rule is *affine* if its instantiation map η is injective, and *tight* if its redex is tight (see Definition 3.19).

A reaction rule is *nice* if it is safe, simple, unary, affine and tight. A BRS `BG($\Sigma$,`$\mathcal{R}$) is *nice* if all its reaction rules are nice. Similarly for an abstract BRS BG(Σ,$\mathcal{R}$).   □

We have adopted the term 'nice' to avoid repeated adjectives. The following results are for nice BRSs, though they may well hold under more relaxed conditions.

We now assert the faithfulness theorem. It depends on one further condition, namely that the interfaces of prime agents are chosen so that they are all *hard*, as defined in Definition 6.2. The full proof is in Appendix A.6.

Theorem 8.19 (engaged transitions are faithful) *In a nice BRS, let* PE *be a prime engaged transition system whose agents are hard. Then*

(1) PE *is faithful to the minimal transition system* MT.

(2) $\sim_{\mathrm{PE}}$ *is a congruence.*

We are now ready to transfer the congruence results of Corollary 8.8 to nice abstract BRSs, just as we did for safe abstract BRSs in the previous section. Note that niceness is independent of the concrete/abstract distinction; a concrete BRS is nice if and only if its lean-support quotient is nice.

Corollary 8.20 (behavioural congruence in a nice abstract BRS) *Assume that* `BG(Σ,`R) *is a nice concrete BRS, and let* BG(Σ,R) *be its lean-support quotient. Assume that the agents of the prime engaged transition system* PE *are hard. Let* $\sim_{PE}$ *denote bisimilarity both for* PE *in* `BG(Σ,`R) *and for the corresponding bisimilarity induced in* **C**. *Then*

(1) $a \sim_{PE} b$ *iff* $[\![a]\!] \sim_{PE} [\![b]\!]$.
(2) Bisimilarity $\sim_{PE}$ *is a congruence in* BG(Σ,R).

Proof It is routine to check that PE respects lean-support equivalence. The result then follows from the faithfulness theorem, Theorem 8.19, together with Theorem 7.23. □

The reader's patience may be taxed by the various conditions we have imposed in this chapter, to achieve reasonable properties of behaviour. The bigraph model may be considered too permissive! But a broad framework has seemed necessary, to embrace a variety of existing process calculi; and something is learned from discovering, within such a framework, properties which those calculi share and which explain why they work well. This knowledge will be useful for the invention of new specific calculi.

On a broader frontier, there are applications whose structure and reactions can be formulated as BRSs, but where the concepts of labelled transition systems and behavioural equivalence are less relevant. Such applications are likely to arise in biological systems and in ubiquitous computing.

9

Behaviour in link graphs

In this chapter we explore the behaviour of our two examples in link graphs: arithmetic nets and Petri nets. These were both introduced in Chapter 6, as applications of many–one sorting. The simple algebraic manipulations of link graphs in this chapter are analogous to the algebra developed for bigraphs in Chapter 3.[1]

9.1 Arithmetic nets

In Example 6.11 we introduced arithmetic nets as a simple example of link graphs. With the many–one sorting discipline they constitute $\text{LG}(\Sigma_{\text{arith}})$, with signature

$$\mathcal{K}_{\text{arith}} \overset{\text{def}}{=} \{0:\text{s},\ \text{S}:\text{ts},\ +:\text{tts},\ \rightarrow:\text{ts}\}\ .$$

Here again are the atoms, and the typical net, that were shown in Example 6.11:

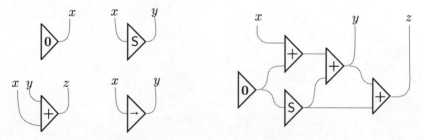

The net represents the equations $y = S0 + (0 + x)$ and $z = S0 + (S0 + (0 + x))$, with many shared subexpressions. Here we bring $\text{LG}(\Sigma_{\text{arith}})$ to life with a set $\mathcal{R}_{\text{arith}}$ of reaction rules, shown in the following diagrams. They use the *forwarder* '$\rightarrow$' to avoid links containing more than one outer name. The question mark '**?**' denotes any node (with zero or more target ports). The rules define a link-graphical reactive system $\text{LG}(\Sigma_{\text{arith}}, \mathcal{R}_{\text{arith}})$.

---

[1] See [55] for work that covers both the theory of link graphs and the applications treated here.

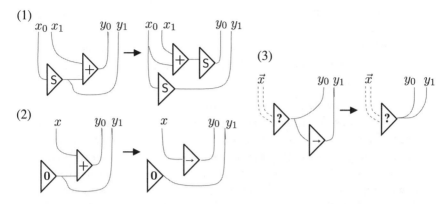

As these pictures show, link graph diagrams are simpler than those for bigraphs. Since there are no places, there is no role for dotted rectangles representing roots or sites. A node is no longer a place, so the nodes can contain nothing, therefore links never cross boundaries; this removes the need for blobs to represent ports, since their purpose in bigraphs is to distinguish ports from crossing-points.

EXERCISE 9.1 Apply the three rules as far as possible to the typical net previously shown. You should obtain a net which represents the equations $y = S0 + x$ and $z = SS0 + x$. Propose some extra rules, besides rule (3), for tidying up a net. □

If a net has cycles then our evaluation rules will not 'solve' it, in the sense that they solve the typical net by 'expressing' y and z in terms of x. However, reaction is well-behaved. To establish this, we shall first show that reaction for arithmetic nets is *strongly confluent*; that is, if $g \longrightarrow g_0$ and $g \longrightarrow g_1$ then there exists g' such that $g_0 \longrightarrow g'$ and $g_1 \longrightarrow g'$. Given g, define a *critical pair* to be a pair r_0, r_1 of distinct redexes occurring in g and sharing at least one node. For example, g may contain a critical pair, represented by f, consisting of two redexes of rule (1) sharing an S-node.

You may check that if either redex is applied first, then the other still exists; moreover, the result f' of applying both is the same, independently of the order.

Proposition 9.1 (confluence) *With the rules (1), (2) and (3) as defined, arithmetic nets are strongly confluent.*

EXERCISE 9.2 Prove this. *Hint:* First show the confluence property for disjoint redexes; then enumerate and examine every possible critical pair.   □

Let us now confine attention to what we may call *explicit nets*: those which have no cycles (as defined in the next paragraph), no inner names, and outer names all with sort s. The latter condition excludes x in the typical net shown at the start of this section, since it has sort t. It is clear that if $g \longrightarrow g'$ and g is an explicit net, then so is g'. Then our rules will evaluate every explicit net to a unique normal form – a net to which no rule applies – representing equations that express each outer name as a numeral of the form $S \cdots S0$.

To justify this claim we should define a well-founded measure of explicit nets that is decreased by every reaction. This is not so easy; it is not enough to measure a net simply by its number of nodes, because rule (1) increases this quantity. The following is helpful: Define a *path* to be a sequence $v_0, k_1, v_1, k_2, v_2, \ldots$ of nodes v_i and natural numbers k_i, where for each contiguous triple v, k, v' there is a link from the s-port of node v to the kth t-port of node v'. A path may be either infinite, or finite – of length n – ending in some v_n. A cycle is a path with $v_n = v_0$; it generates an infinite path. With the help of the notion of path one can prove

Proposition 9.2 (termination) *Every reaction sequence of an explicit net is finite.*

EXERCISE 9.3 Prove this. *Hint:* What quantity, in terms of paths, is decreased by every reaction by rule (1)? Using this, construct a well-founded linear ordering that is reduced by every reaction of an explicit net.   □

From Propositions 9.1 and 9.2 we finally deduce

Theorem 9.3 (normalisation) *Every reaction sequence for an explicit net with outer names $\vec{y}$ terminates in a unique normal form, representing the expression of each y_i as a numeral of the form $S \cdots S0$.*

We leave the theory of arithmetic nets at this point. It can be extended to the derivation of transition systems, but our main aim has been to show that the graphical representation is at least convenient, and even helpful, in analysing a reactive system other than a process calculus.

9.2 Condition–event nets

In Example 6.13 we introduced a class of Petri nets called *condition–event* nets, or c/e nets. We defined a many–one sorting discipline Σ_{petri} for them, and we now recall that such sortings are always safe. Here again is our example, with sorts, of a typical c/e net:

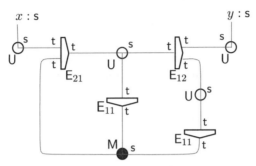

These nets form a link-graphical s-category `$LG(\Sigma_{\text{petri}})$, where names have two roles. First, they provide the interfaces through which nets are composed; second, they provide a means to observe the behaviour of nets. So we now proceed to define what an observation is, and when two nets are behaviourally equivalent. Since c/e nets are modelled in link graphs, our results depend on a behavioural theory for link graphs analogous to the theory for bigraphs. We shall not give details of this theory, which is fully developed elsewhere. The reader can rest assured that all the relevant concepts and properties are analogous to, though often simpler than, those in bigraphs.

Several ways to compose nets have been defined in the Petri-net literature, and they typically lead to a notion of behavioural equivalence. It is interesting to see how such notions compare with ours, which is based upon derived transitions. To make such a comparison we here define behaviour in two independent ways. The first is by a raw transition system, whose bisimilarity requires no link-graph theory; the second is by the derived system of engaged transitions, and on the characterisation of derived transitions in terms of RPOs.

We are able to prove that the two bisimilarites coincide. It follows that the raw bisimilarity is a congruence, since the derived one is known to be so. We omit here two important steps in the published proof:[2] first that the engaged transitions are indeed faithful to the minimal transition system, and second that the congruence of the resulting bisimilarity is transferred from concrete to abstract link graphs. The conditions for these two results in link graphs – analogous to our Theorem 8.19 and Corollary 8.20 – are simpler in link graphs than in bigraphs.

---

[2] See [55].

We shall therefore work in concrete link graphs; at the end we shall transfer our results to abstract link graphs. As a first step we define a reactive system `CE = `LG(Σ_{petri}, `$\mathcal{R}_{petri}$), by adding reaction rules `$\mathcal{R}_{petri}$ to `LG(Σ_{petri}). These rules must be based upon the usual firing rule for c/e nets, namely:

an event with all pre-conditions and no post-conditions marked may 'fire', thus unmarking its pre-conditions and marking its post-conditions.

Since we have indexed our event controls by the number of pre-conditions and post-conditions, `$\mathcal{R}_{petri}$ will contain one reaction rule for each event control E_{hk}. For $h = 1$ and $k = 2$ the rule is drawn as follows (the diagram can be interpreted either as concrete or as abstract):

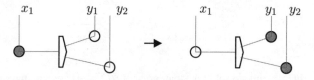

A reaction rule for condition–event nets

How may we conduct experiments, or observations, on a condition–event net? To simplify matters, let us assume that we are concerned only with the behaviour of s-*nets* – those nets whose interfaces contain only s-names. Thus every outer name is the name of a condition. We shall adopt the following form of experiment: the observer can detect and change the state (marked or unmarked) of any named condition. For example, our illustrated net can do nothing by itself (no event can 'fire'), but if the observer gives it a token at x then the E_{21} event can fire, followed by either the middle event or the E_{12} event; after the latter the observer can remove a token at y, and so on.

So we capture behaviour in the form of a raw transition system $\mathcal{L}_r$, whose agents are the ground s-nets in `CE. Its transitions are of three kinds:

$$a \xrightarrow{+x} \overline{a} \quad \text{add a token at } x$$
$$a \xrightarrow{-x} \overline{a} \quad \text{remove a token at } x$$
$$a \xrightarrow{\tau} \overline{a} \quad \text{an event within } a \text{ fires.}$$

A condition holds at most one token, so for each named condition x exactly one of the first two transitions can occur.[3] Thus the labels ℓ in $\mathcal{L}_r$ take the form $+x$, $-x$ or τ, and they are applicable to all the agents. We denote the bisimilarity of $\mathcal{L}_r$ by $\sim_r$.

---

[3] A τ-transition is not really an observation, as it occurs without the observer's participation. We have defined what is called a *strong* bisimilarity. To avoid giving τ-transitions the same status as others, it is standard practice to adopt *weak* bisimilarity instead.

We now turn to derived transitions. Because many–one sorting is safe, `CE has RPOS; hence the minimal transition system MT exists. Furthermore, the rules `$\mathcal{R}$ are such that the engaged transitions are faithful to MT; hence they generate the same bisimilarity as MT. Let us denote the engaged transition system by $\mathcal{L}_g$, and its bisimilarity – which is a congruence – by $\sim_g$. We now proceed to characterise $\mathcal{L}_g$; it corresponds to the prime engaged TS in a WRS, but that notion of prime is absent in link graphs. Thereafter we shall prove that $\sim_g$ coincides with $\sim_r$.

A label L in $\mathcal{L}_g$ takes two forms; up to isomorphism, either it is just an identity, or it is the product of an identity with an open s-net having exactly one E_{hk}-node, linked to zero or more M-nodes as pre-conditions and U-nodes as post-conditions. Since transitions are engaged, it contains strictly fewer than $h+k$ such conditions (because the agent must supply at least one). A label L applies to an agent a iff the composition $L \circ a$ exists.

For the identity labels, we note that $a \xrightarrow{\text{id}} a'$ iff $a \longrightarrow a'$; an identity label signifies a transition with no help from the context. A typical non-identity label for the case E_{21} is shown here. It lacks one pre-condition and one post-condition, to be supplied by the agent. The dashed link indicates an identity on zero or more names.

The diagram below shows the anatomy of a transition $a \xrightarrow{L} a'$ with this label. Note that a' takes the form $\overline{L} \circ \overline{a}$. In what follows we shall often write $\overline{a}$ for a s-net that differs from a only by the marking or unmarking of some conditions; we call it a *residual* of a. We see that a single transition may change the marking of several named conditions of a. Any other agent b with the same interface as a will have a similar transition, provided only that it has the same initial marking of its named conditions.

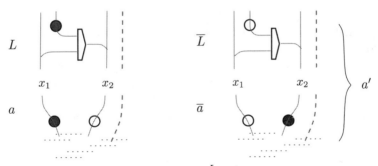

Anatomy of a transition $a \xrightarrow{L} a'$ in $\mathcal{L}_g$

The two TSs $\mathcal{L}_r$ and $\mathcal{L}_g$ are significantly different, so it is not clear that they will induce the same bisimilarity. We shall now prove that they do so. We shall first show that $\sim_g \subseteq \sim_r$ in $`CE$. This asserts that if we can distinguish two s-nets a and b by using 'experiments' that are labels in $\mathcal{L}_r$ of the form $+x$, $-x$ or τ, then we can also do so using 'experiments' that are labels in $\mathcal{L}_g$, i.e. certain link graph contexts. So among these contextual labels we look for those that can do the job of the experiments $+x$, $-x$ and τ.

It turns out that the contextual label to mimic an experiment $+x$ or $-x$ need only involve a single E_{11} event; it takes the form $P \otimes \mathrm{id}$, where P is respectively an *input* or *output probe*. The probes are denoted by in_{xz} and out_{xz}, and are shown in the first column of this diagram:

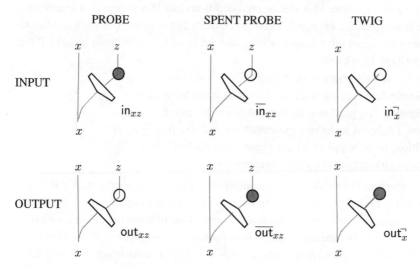

Probes for observing transitions in a s-net

The second column shows the *spent* probes $\overline{P}$, residuals of the probes that result from firing their events. The third column shows the spent probes with their post-conditions closed; they are defined by $\mathrm{in}_x^\neg \overset{\text{def}}{=} /z \circ \overline{\mathrm{in}}_{xz}$ and $\mathrm{out}_x^\neg \overset{\text{def}}{=} /z \circ \overline{\mathrm{out}}_{xz}$. In these expressions we have omitted identities; for example $/z \circ \overline{\mathrm{in}}_{xz}$ abbreviates $(/z \otimes \mathrm{id}_x) \circ \overline{\mathrm{in}}_{xz}$. We use the term 'twig' for these closed spent probes, because, up to the equivalence $\sim_g$, they can be 'broken off'. The intuition is simply that a twig occurring anywhere in a net can never fire. We express this formally as follows:

Lemma 9.4 *For any agent a with x as an outer name,* $\mathrm{in}_x^\neg \circ a \sim_g \mathrm{out}_x^\neg \circ a \sim_g a$.

Again we have abbreviated $(\mathrm{in}_x^\neg \otimes \mathrm{id}_Y) \circ a$ to $\mathrm{in}_x^\neg \circ a$, where Y are the names of a. We shall use such abbreviations in what follows, but only in a composition which determines the omitted identity id.

EXERCISE 9.4 Prove this lemma. *Hint:* Prove that $\{(a, \overline{\mathsf{in}}_x \circ a) \mid a \text{ any agent}\}$ is a bisimulation. □

Now to prove that $\sim_g \subseteq \sim_r$ it is enough to show that $\sim_g$ is an $\mathcal{L}_r$-bisimulation. For this, suppose that $a \sim_g b$, and let $a \xrightarrow{\ell} \overline{a}$ in $\mathcal{L}_r$. We must find $\overline{b}$ such that $b \xrightarrow{\ell} \overline{b}$ and $\overline{a} \sim_g \overline{b}$. If $\ell = \tau$ this is easy, because then our assumption implies the reaction $a \longrightarrow \overline{a}$, and hence $a \xrightarrow{\mathsf{id}} \overline{a}$ in $\mathcal{L}_g$; but then by bisimilarity in $\mathcal{L}_g$ we have $b \xrightarrow{\mathsf{id}} \overline{b} \sim_g \overline{a}$, and by reversing the reasoning for a we get that $b \xrightarrow{\tau} \overline{b}$ and we are done.

Now let $\ell = +x$ (the case for $-x$ is similar), so that $a \xrightarrow{+x} \overline{a}$. This means that a has an unmarked condition named x, so that in $\mathcal{L}_g$ we have

$$a \xrightarrow{\mathsf{in}_{xz} \otimes \mathsf{id}} a' = \overline{\mathsf{in}}_{xz} \circ \overline{a} \ .$$

Hence by bisimilarity in $\mathcal{L}_g$ we have

$$b \xrightarrow{\mathsf{in}_{xz} \otimes \mathsf{id}} b' = \overline{\mathsf{in}}_{xz} \circ \overline{b}$$

where $a' \sim_g b'$ and $\overline{b}$ is the residual of b under the transition. This residual $\overline{b}$ differs from b only in having a marked condition named x that was unmarked in b, and hence we also have $b \xrightarrow{+x} \overline{b}$ in $\mathcal{L}_r$. It remains only to show that $\overline{a} \sim_g \overline{b}$. We deduce this using the congruence of $\sim_g$ and Lemma 9.4:

$$\begin{aligned} \overline{a} \ &\sim_g \ \overline{\mathsf{in}}_x \circ \overline{a} = /z \circ \overline{\mathsf{in}}_{xz} \circ \overline{a} = /z \circ a' \\ &\sim_g \ /z \circ b' = /z \circ \overline{\mathsf{in}}_{xz} \circ \overline{b} = \overline{\mathsf{in}}_x \circ \overline{b} \ \sim_g \ \overline{b} \ . \end{aligned}$$

Therefore we have proved what we wished:

Lemma 9.5 $\sim_g \subseteq \sim_r$ *in* `CE`.

It remains to prove the converse, $\sim_r \subseteq \sim_g$. It will be enough to prove that

$$\mathcal{S} \stackrel{\text{def}}{=} \{ (C \circ a, C \circ b) \mid a \sim_r b \}$$

is a bisimulation up to $\asymp$. We get the required result by considering the case $C = \mathsf{id}$.[4]

So let us assume that $a \sim_r b$, and that $C \circ a \xrightarrow{M} a''$ in $\mathcal{L}_g$. (This includes the case that $M = \mathsf{id}$.) Then there is a reaction rule r and context D such that (M, D) forms an IPO for $(C \circ a, r)$, as shown in the left-hand diagram, and $a'' \asymp D \circ r'$.

We now take the IPO (L, A) for (a, r) relative to $(M \circ C, D)$, and properties of IPOs yield the right-hand diagram, in which the upper square is also an IPO:

---

[4] The proof outlined here resembles that of Theorem 7.16, the congruence theorem. The replacement of one IPO by another relies, as in that proof, on the fact that support translation preserves IPOs; here we omit that argument. The present proof is simpler; there is no notion of either width or active control in link graphs, so the location index in transitions and the argument about activity can both be omitted here.

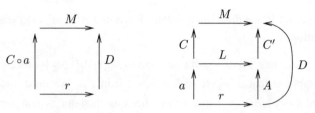

IPOs underlying transitions of $C \circ a$ and a

So there is a transition $a \xrightarrow{L} a'$, where $a' \simeq A \circ r'$; note also that $a'' \simeq C' \circ a'$. Up to isomorphism, either L is an identity or it has a single event node.

If $L = \mathrm{id}$ then $a \longrightarrow a'$, hence $a \xrightarrow{\tau} a'$ in $\mathcal{L}_r$. Since $a \sim_r a'$ we have $b \xrightarrow{\tau} b'$ with $a' \sim_r b'$. Then also $b \xrightarrow{L} b'$, with underlying IPO as in the left-hand diagram below:

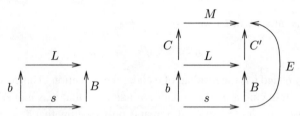

IPOs underlying transitions of b and $C \circ b$

. We then proceed, as in the non-identity case below, to construct the right-hand diagram and to find b'' with $C \circ b \xrightarrow{M} b''$ and $(a'', b'') \in \mathcal{S}^{\simeq}$.

If L has an event node then we consider the anatomy of the transition $a \xrightarrow{L} a'$, as exemplified in an earlier diagram. We know that the residual $\overline{a}$ differs from a only in the changed marking of zero or more named conditions. It follows therefore that in $\mathcal{L}_r$ there is a sequence of transitions

$$a \xrightarrow{\ell_1} a_1 \ldots \xrightarrow{\ell_n} a_n = \overline{a} \qquad (n \geq 0)$$

where $\ell_i \in \{+x_i, -x_i\}$; each transition marks or unmarks a single named condition. Moreover $a' = \overline{L} \circ \overline{a}$. Since $a \sim_r b$ there exists a similar sequence

$$b \xrightarrow{\ell_1} b_1 \ldots \xrightarrow{\ell_n} b_n = \overline{b}$$

with $\overline{a} \sim_r \overline{b}$. This implies that b has the same initial marking as a for the named conditions involved in the transitions. But we know that $L \circ b$ is defined (since we assumed $M \circ C \circ b = C' \circ L \circ b$ to be defined), so in $\mathcal{L}_g$ there is a transition $b \xrightarrow{L} b' = \overline{L} \circ \overline{b}$. Its underlying IPO is shown in the left-hand diagram above. Also it has an underlying reaction rule (s, s'), with $b' \simeq B \circ s'$. Now we form the right-hand diagram by replacing this IPO for the lower square in the previous right-hand diagram. Since both small squares are IPOs, so is the large square; therefore it underlies an $\mathcal{L}_g$-transition

$$C \circ b \xrightarrow{M} b'' \overset{\text{def}}{=} E \circ s' \,.$$

To complete our proof we need only show that the pair (a'', b'') lies in $\mathcal{S}^\simeq$. We already know that $a'' \simeq C' \circ a' = C' \circ \overline{L} \circ \overline{a}$. We can now compute

$$b'' = E \circ s' = C' \circ B \circ s' \simeq C' \circ b' = C' \circ \overline{L} \circ \overline{b} \,,$$

and hence $(a'', b'') \in \mathcal{S}^\simeq$ since $\overline{a} \sim_r \overline{b}$. It follows that $\sim_r \,\subseteq\, \sim_g$.

So we have proved the coincidence of our two bisimilarities:

Theorem 9.6 (coincidence of concrete bisimilarities) *In* ˋ**CE** *the two bisimilarities $\sim_g$ and $\sim_r$ for concrete s-nets coincide. Hence, since $\sim_g$ a congruence, so also is $\sim_r$ a congruence.*

We now transfer this result to abstract s-nets. We may regard the creation of an abstract contextual TS $\mathcal{L}_r$ as an instance of the three-step procedure defined at the end of Chapter 7. The starting point is an abstract reactive system $\mathbf{CE} = \text{LG}(\mathcal{R}_{\text{petri}})$, where $\mathcal{R}_{\text{petri}}$ are the reaction rules depicted earlier, regarded as abstract rules. The three steps are

(A) Create the concrete reactive system ˋ**CE**, whose reaction rules ˋ$\mathcal{R}_{\text{petri}}$ are lean preimages of $\mathcal{R}_{\text{petri}}$ under the lean-support quotient functor $[\![\cdot]\!]$.

(B) Derive the minimal transition system $\mathcal{L}_r = \text{MT}$ in ˋ**CE**, and use the analogue of Proposition 8.9 to ensure that it respects lean-support equivalence $\simeq$.

(C) Transfer $\mathcal{L}_r$ to **CE** by Definition 7.22, which applies the functor $[\![\cdot]\!]$ to every link graph in every concrete transition.

At the conclusion of the process, Theorem 7.23 ensures that $\sim_r$ is a congruence in **CE**, and characterised by $a \sim_r b$ in ˋ**CE** iff $[\![a]\!] \sim_r [\![b]\!]$ in **CE**.

Finally, it is clear that the raw transition system $\mathcal{L}_g$ also respects $\simeq$, so Theorem 7.23 also ensures that $a \sim_g b$ in ˋ**CE** iff $[\![a]\!] \sim_g [\![b]\!]$ in **CE**. Putting these facts together with Theorem 9.6 we arrive at

Corollary 9.7 (coincidence of abstract bisimilarities) *In* **CE** *the two bisimilarities $\sim_g$ and $\sim_r$ for abstract s-nets coincide, and are congruences.*

This result provides evidence that the general notion of behavioural theory in bigraphs and link graphs is compatible with a notion specific to a particular model: condition–event nets. Further evidence is provided by our study of CCS in Chapter 10.

This concludes our study of behaviour in link graphs.

10

Behavioural theory for CCS

In this chapter we shall see how our dynamic theory for a nice BRS can be applied to recover the standard dynamic theory of CCS.

Section 10.1 deals mainly with the translation of finite CCS into bigraphs, covering both syntactic structure and the basic features of reaction. It begins with a summary of all work done on CCS in previous chapters, in order to gather the whole application of bigraphs to CCS in one chapter. It then presents the translation into bigraphs, which encodes each structural congruence class of CCS into a single bigraph. It ends with the simple result that reaction as defined in CCS terms correponds exactly to reaction as defined by bigraphical rules.

Based upon this summary, Section 10.2 lays out the contextual transition system derived for finite CCS by the method of Chapter 8, recalling that its bisimilarity is guaranteed to be a congruence. This congruence is finer than the original bisimilarity of CCS. This is because the original is not preserved by substitution; on the other hand, our derived contextual TS contains transitions that observe the effect of substitution on an agent, and this yields a finer bisimilarity that is indeed a congruence. By omitting the substitutional transitions from the contextual TS, we then obtain a bisimilarity that coincides with the original.

This contextual TS is more complex than the original raw one, since its labels are parametric. But we are able to reduce it to a smaller faithful contextual TS whose labels are no longer parametric, and this corresponds almost exactly with the original raw TS for CCS.

Section 10.2 ends with a brief analysis of the strength of the congruence for the derived system, including its substitutional transitions.

10.1 Syntax and reactions for CCS in bigraphs

We begin this section with a summary of what has been done on finite CCS in previous chapters. The summary takes us as far as reaction for CCS. The sorting discipline Σ_{ccs} was given in Definition 6.5, and the rule-set $\mathcal{R}_{ccs}$ consists of the single rule given in Example 8.1. Together, these define the abstract BRS

$$\mathrm{BG}_{ccs} \overset{\text{def}}{=} \mathrm{BG}(\Sigma_{ccs}, \mathcal{R}_{ccs}) \ .$$

We then amplify the summary, by proving that the translation of CCS into bigraphs is completely accurate; in particular, that it respects structural congruence.

Syntax for finite CCS (Definition 6.3)

P, Q range over *processes* and A, B over *alternations* (sums).

$$
\begin{array}{rrcl}
\text{processes} & P & ::= & A \mid \nu x P \mid P \,|\, P \\
\text{alternations} & A & ::= & \mathbf{0} \mid \mu.P \mid A + A \\
\text{actions} & \mu & ::= & \overline{x} \mid x \ .
\end{array}
$$

Structural congruence (Definition 6.4)

Structural congruence is the largest equivalence $\equiv$ preserved by all term constructions, and such that

(1) $P \equiv_\alpha Q$ implies $P \equiv Q$, and $A \equiv_\alpha B$ implies $A \equiv B$;
(2) $|$ and $+$ are associative and commutative under $\equiv$, and $A + \mathbf{0} \equiv A$;
(3) $\nu x \nu y P \equiv \nu y \nu x P$;
(4) $\nu x P \equiv P$ and $\nu x\, (P \,|\, Q) \equiv P \,|\, \nu x Q$ for any x not free in P;
(5) $\nu x\, (A + \mu.P) \equiv A + \mu.\nu x P$ for any x not free in A or μ.

Sorting discipline (Definition 6.5)

The CCS place sorting Σ_{ccs} has sorts $\Theta_{ccs} = \{\mathsf{p}, \mathsf{a}\}$ and signature

$$\mathcal{K}_{ccs} = \{\mathsf{alt} : (\mathsf{p}, 0),\ \mathsf{send} : (\mathsf{a}, 1),\ \mathsf{get} : (\mathsf{a}, 1)\} \ .$$

Σ_{ccs} is hard for sort p (Definition 6.2), and also requires that

> all children of a root $r : \theta$ have sort θ, and
> all children of a node $v : \theta$ have sort opposite to θ.

Translation to bigraphs (Definition 6.6)

The translation of finite CCS into BG_{ccs} maps processes and alternations respectively into ground homsets with unary interfaces of the form $\langle \mathsf{p}, X \rangle$ and $\langle \mathsf{a}, X \rangle$. The maps $\mathcal{P}_X[\cdot]$ and $\mathcal{A}_X[\cdot]$ are defined for arguments whose free names are included in X:

$$
\begin{array}{rcl}
\mathcal{P}_X[A] & = & \mathsf{alt}.\mathcal{A}_X[A] \\
\mathcal{P}_X[\nu x P] & = & /y \circ \mathcal{P}_{y \uplus X}[\{y/x\}P] \\
\mathcal{P}_X[P \,|\, Q] & = & \mathcal{P}_X[P] \mid \mathcal{P}_X[Q]
\end{array}
\qquad
\begin{array}{rcl}
\mathcal{A}_X[\mathbf{0}] & = & X \mid 1 \\
\mathcal{A}_X[\overline{x}.P] & = & \mathsf{send}_x.\mathcal{P}_X[P] \quad (x \in X) \\
\mathcal{A}_X[x.P] & = & \mathsf{get}_x.\mathcal{P}_X[P] \quad (x \in X) \\
\mathcal{A}_X[A + B] & = & \mathcal{A}_X[A] \mid \mathcal{A}_X[B] \ .
\end{array}
$$

Bijection of the translation (Theorem 6.7)

(1) The translations $\mathcal{P}_X[\cdot]$ and $\mathcal{A}_X[\cdot]$ are surjective on prime ground homsets.
(2) $P \equiv Q$ iff $\mathcal{P}_X[P] = \mathcal{P}_X[Q]$, and $A \equiv B$ iff $\mathcal{A}_X[A] = \mathcal{A}_X[B]$.

Safeness of CCS sorting (Proposition 6.9)
Σ_{ccs} is a safe sorting.

Parametric reaction for CCS (Example 8.1)

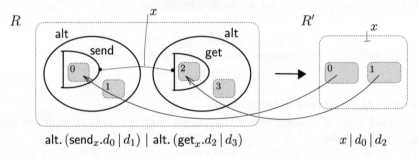

$$\text{alt.}\,(\text{send}_x.d_0 \mid d_1) \mid \text{alt.}\,(\text{get}_x.d_2 \mid d_3) \qquad\qquad x \mid d_0 \mid d_2$$

This parametric reaction rule (R, R', η) is the only reaction rule for CCS in bigraphs. The controls 'alt', 'send' and 'get' are all declared to be passive. The parametric redex $R = \text{alt.}\,(\text{send}_x \mid \text{id}) \mid \text{alt.}\,(\text{get}_x \mid \text{id})$ has four sites, to be filled by arbitrary parameters $d_0, \ldots, d_3$. Sites 0 and 2 are for processes, and sites 1 and 3 are for alternations (summations). The reactum $R' = x \mid \text{id} \mid \text{id}$ has two sites, to be filled by parameters as dictated by the instantiation map η, represented by back-pointing arrows. The placing of parameters is also shown by the algebraic expression. Parameters 1 and 3 of R are discarded by the rule.

This concludes our summary of work from previous chapters. We now amplify it by proving the structural accuracy of the CCS translation, claimed in Theorem 6.7.

Let us first give more detail of the proof of the theorem. Concerning the structural congruence laws note that clauses 4 and 5, taken in reverse, allow a restriction νx to be pulled outwards from any parallel component and any summand respectively. This gives rise to the following:

Proposition 10.1 (CCS normal form) *Every CCS process is structurally congruent to a normal form $\nu x_1 \cdots \nu x_k\, P\ (k \geq 0)$, where P is an open process form containing each name x_i free. Open process forms are defined recursively as follows:*

(i) *An open process form is a process term $P_1 \mid \cdots \mid P_m\ (m > 0)$, where each P_j is an open sum form.*
(ii) *An open sum form is a summation term $A_1 + \cdots + A_n\ (n \geq 0)$, where each A_k takes the form $\mu.P$ for some open process form P.*

Normal forms are helpful in the following:

EXERCISE 10.1 (not needed for what follows) Prove Theorem 6.7. Here is an outline, with suggestions on how to complete it.

(1) We must prove that the translation $\mathcal{P}_X[\cdot]$ is surjective on the homset $\epsilon \to \langle p, X \rangle$, and that $\mathcal{A}_X[\cdot]$ is surjective on $\epsilon \to \langle a, X \rangle$. Every well-sorted agent in these homsets can be built from smaller ones. (For example, a non-basic agent of sort a is built either from two others by merge product, or from an agent of sort p by nesting.) This allows one to prove, by induction on the size (number of nodes) of an agent, that there is always a CCS process or alternation that translates into it. More specifically, one first proves the following for all *open* agents, by induction:

for all open agents $g : \epsilon \to \langle p, X \rangle$ there exists P for which $\mathcal{P}_X[P] = g$, and
for all open agents $f : \epsilon \to \langle a, X \rangle$ there exists A for which $\mathcal{A}_X[A] = f$.

The basis of the inductive proof is that there exists a CCS alternation (which one?) that translates into the unit $1 : \epsilon \to \langle a, X \rangle$. The inductive step is that, as you make a bigger agent (of sort p or a) either by adding a single node or by forming a merge product, you can each time find a CCS process or alternation that translates into it.

Having done this proof for open agents, finish by showing that every agent with *closed* links (formed by closure, of course) is also the translation of a CCS agent.

(2) The forward implication needs a lemma which can be proved by induction on the structure of process normal forms:

Lemma $P \equiv_\alpha Q$ implies $\mathcal{P}_X[P] = \mathcal{P}_X[Q]$, and
$M \equiv_\alpha N$ implies $\mathcal{A}_X[M] = \mathcal{A}_X[N]$.

Then the main property can be proved by a similar induction. You may wish to prove the main property first, assuming the Lemma (which is harder).

For the reverse implication the task can be reduced to proving the property by induction on the structure of ground bigraphs. An important step is to show in bigraphs that if a_i ($i \in m$) and b_j ($j \in n$) are ground molecules such that $a_1 \mid \cdots \mid a_m = b_1 \mid \cdots \mid b_n$, then $m = n$, and $a_i = b_{\pi(i)}$ for some permutation π on m. $\square$

Having established the structural accuracy of the translation, we turn to dynamics. Finite CCS has the single reaction rule

$$(\overline{x}.P + A) \mid (x.Q + B) \longrightarrow P \mid Q ,$$

which may be applied anywhere not under an action prefix. On the other hand in BG_{ccs} we have the single reaction rule from Example 8.1. It is easy to demonstrate that there is an exact match between the reaction relations generated in CCS and in $\mathrm{BG_{ccs}}$, in the following sense:

Proposition 10.2 (comparing reaction) $P \longrightarrow P'$ *iff* $\mathcal{P}_X[P] \longrightarrow \mathcal{P}_X[P']$.

10.2 Transitions for CCS in bigraphs

So far all our work has been done in the abstract BRS $\mathrm{BG_{ccs}}$, especially in characterising its reactions. We are now ready to conduct the three-step procedure defined
at the end of Chapter 7, in order to develop the behavioural theory of $\mathrm{BG_{ccs}}$.

For step (A) we define the concrete BRS

$$`\mathrm{BG_{ccs}} \stackrel{\mathrm{def}}{=} `\mathrm{BG}(\Sigma_{ccs}, `\mathcal{R}_{ccs}) ;$$

this is just the s-category $`\mathrm{BG}(\Sigma_{ccs})$ equipped with the reaction rules $`\mathcal{R}_{ccs}$, which
are all lean preimages of the single abstract rule of $\mathcal{R}_{ccs}$ under the lean-support
quotient functor $[\![\cdot]\!]$.

As step (B) of the procedure we define PE the prime engaged contextual transition
system (Definition 8.15), and assert that:

Corollary 10.3 (concrete bigraphical bisimilarity for CCS) *The bisimilarity* $\sim_{\mathrm{PE}}$
in $`\mathrm{BG_{ccs}}$ *is a congruence.*

Proof   The result depends on the proof that the CCS redex is tight; see Exercise 3.4. After that it is straightforward to check that $`\mathrm{BG_{ccs}}$ is nice (Definition 8.18),
and that the agents of PE are hard; Σ_{ccs} ensures the latter. The result then follows
from the faithfulness theorem, Theorem 8.19.   □

This completes step (B). For the final step (C) we transfer the transition system PE to the abstract BRS $\mathrm{BG_{ccs}}$, as dictated by Definition 7.22. We would like
to know that this yields a transition system whose bisimilarity is again a congruence. Let us use the term PE both for the concrete transition system and for its
abstract image under the quotient by $[\![\cdot]\!]$, and let $\sim_{\mathrm{PE}}$ denote the bisimilarity in both
cases. Then, because of niceness, finally by Corollary 8.20 we deduce congruential
bisimilarity in our bigraphical representation of CCS:

Corollary 10.4 (abstract bigraphical congruence for CCS)

(1) Two processes are bisimilar ($\sim_{\mathrm{PE}}$) in $\mathrm{BG_{ccs}}$ *iff their concrete preimages are
bisimilar in* $`\mathrm{BG_{ccs}}$.

(2) $\sim_{\mathrm{PE}}$ is a congruence in $\mathrm{BG_{ccs}}$.

This completes our procedure for deriving a transition system and behavioural congruence for CCS. We devote the rest of the chapter to an analysis of this congruence. This is necessary partly because the original bisimilarity for CCS was a congruence in a weaker sense than ours, and partly because we wish to refine our derived transition system, to make it more economical without losing its bisimilarity.

We begin with a structural analysis of the transitions in PE, recalling that – in their concrete form in `BG$_{ccs}$ – they are engaged.

Notation Hitherto we have written $\lambda \circ G$ in applying a linking to a bigraph, thus emphasising that linkings are bigraphs in their own right. From now on in this chapter we shall abbreviate this composition to λG. For example, the reactum in case 4 of Figure 10.1 is $/Z \circ {}^y/x \circ \cdots$. To save parentheses we also assume such compositions bind more tightly than a product; thus $\lambda G \mid F$ means $(\lambda \circ G) \mid F$. □

The transitions of PE are tabulated in Figure 10.1, and we now explain them. The algebraic expressions can be interpreted either in the abstract BRS or (with support understood) in the concrete one. Every prime transition $p \xrightarrow{L} p'$ arises from a ground rule (r, r') with redex

$$r = \mathsf{alt}.(\mathsf{send}_x.d \ \cdot\cdot) \mid \mathsf{alt}.(\mathsf{get}_x.e \ \cdot\cdot)$$

where ‘$\cdot\cdot$’ stands for any further factors in a discrete merge product, and the pair (p, r) has (L, D) as an IPO, with D active. Also p shares at least one of the nodes of the underlying parametric redex R – the two alt-nodes, the send-node and the get-node. Since p has sort p, if it shares the send-node then it must also share the parent alt-node; similarly if it shares the get-node. So there are two sharing possibilities:

(i) p shares both nodes in one factor of R but none in the other;
(ii) p shares all four nodes of R.

The former divides clearly into two symmetric cases. The latter also divides into two cases; either the send- and get-ports are joined by a closed link x, or they belong to different open links. This explains why the figure has four cases.

We show the structure of p, L and p' in each case, taking account of the fact that any alt-node shared with R must occur actively in p. In Table 10.1, $a, b, c, \ldots$ stand for any processes (c discrete), and ‘$\cdot\cdot$’ stands for zero or more factors in a merge product; in the labels of cases 1 and 2 this product must be discrete. In each rule, the factor $\mid b$ may also be absent. According to our convention for substitutions, ${}^y/x$ here is in the homset $\langle \mathsf{p}, X \rangle \to \langle \mathsf{p}, Y \rangle$, where $Y = (X \setminus x) \cup y$; its link map sends x to y and is otherwise the identity.

The reader will note that the expressions for labels in our table are *parametric*.

	$p:I$	$L:I\to J$	$p':J$	condition
1	$/Z(\mathsf{alt}.(\mathsf{send}_x.a\;\cdot\cdot)\,|\,b)$	$\mathsf{id}_I\,|\,\mathsf{alt}.(\mathsf{get}_x.c\;\cdot\cdot)$	$/Z(a\,|\,b)\,|\,c$	$x\notin Z$
2	$/Z(\mathsf{alt}.(\mathsf{get}_x.a\;\cdot\cdot)\,|\,b)$	$\mathsf{id}_I\,|\,\mathsf{alt}.(\mathsf{send}_x.c\;\cdot\cdot)$	$/Z(a\,|\,b)\,|\,c$	$x\notin Z$
3	$/Z(\mathsf{alt}.(\mathsf{send}_x.a_0\;\cdot\cdot)$ $|\,\mathsf{alt}.(\mathsf{get}_x.a_1\;\cdot\cdot)\,|\,b)$	id_I	$/Z(a_0\,|\,a_1\,|\,b)$	none
4	$/Z(\mathsf{alt}.(\mathsf{send}_x.a_0\;\cdot\cdot)$ $|\,\mathsf{alt}.(\mathsf{get}_y.a_1\;\cdot\cdot)\,|\,b)$	y/x	$/Z\,y/x$ $(a_0\,|\,a_1\,|\,b)$	$x\neq y;$ $x,y\notin Z$

Fig. 10.1. The four forms for a transition $p\overset{L}{\dashrightarrow}p'$ in PE

For example in case 1, even for fixed p, there is a family of labels L, according as c and the unspecified factors '$\cdot\cdot$' vary. Moreover c reappears in the reactum p', whereas the factors '$\cdot\cdot$' are discarded. Parametric labels arise naturally when labels are contexts. But as we shall see shortly, in this case the transition system PE can be further reduced to a faithful one whose labels are not parametric.

We now embark on an analysis of these transitions. We shall need to establish a promised property. Recall from Definition 6.5 that $\mathsf{nil}\overset{\text{def}}{=}\mathsf{alt}.1$.

Proposition 10.5 (unit for merge product) $p\sim_{\mathrm{PE}}p\,|\,\mathsf{nil}$.

Proof   We shall prove the following relation to be a bisimulation:

$$S\overset{\text{def}}{=}\{(p,\,p\,|\,\mathsf{nil})\mid p\text{ an agent}\}\;.$$

Assume the transition $p\overset{L}{\dashrightarrow}p'$. Then the pair (p,p') matches the forms in one of the four cases of the figure. In each case, if we replace b by $b\,|\,\mathsf{nil}$ then we obtain a transition $p\,|\,\mathsf{nil}\longrightarrow p'\,|\,\mathsf{nil}$, and we also have $(p',p'\,|\,\mathsf{nil})\in S$ so we have matched the assumed transition while remaining in S.

In the other direction, assume the transition $p\,|\,\mathsf{nil}\overset{L}{\dashrightarrow}p''$. Then, in all four cases of the figure, we find that b takes the form $b'\,|\,\mathsf{nil}$ and p'' takes the form $p'\,|\,\mathsf{nil}$. Then by replacing b by b' we find that $p\overset{L}{\dashrightarrow}p'$; again we have matched the assumed transition while remaining in S. This completes the proof.   □

We are now ready to compare our derived transition system with the original CCS transitions. They are *raw* transitions, using the non-contextual labels

$$\ell\quad::=\quad\overline{x}\mid x\mid\tau$$

where the first two represent sending and receiving a message, and τ represents a communication within the agent. Rather than reverting to CCS syntax, we set up the transitions $p \xrightarrow{\ell} p'$ of this raw system directly in $\mathrm{BG}_{\mathrm{ccs}}$; this will ease our comparison. The agents and label of each transition are characterised in Figure 10.2. This raw system determines a bisimilarity which we shall denote by $\sim_{\mathrm{ccs}}$.

	p	ℓ	p'	condition
1	$/Z(\mathsf{alt}.(\mathsf{send}_x.a \; \cdot\cdot) \mid b)$	$\overline{x}$	$/Z(a \mid b)$	$x \notin Z$
2	$/Z(\mathsf{alt}.(\mathsf{get}_x.a \; \cdot\cdot) \mid b)$	x	$/Z(a \mid b)$	$x \notin Z$
3	$/Z(\mathsf{alt}.(\mathsf{send}_x.a_0 \; \cdot\cdot) \\ \mid \mathsf{alt}.(\mathsf{get}_x.a_1 \; \cdot\cdot) \mid b)$	τ	$/Z(a_0 \mid a_1 \mid b)$	none

Fig. 10.2. The three forms for a raw CCS transition $p \xrightarrow{\ell} p'$

EXERCISE 10.2 Prove that $p \sim_{\mathrm{ccs}} p \mid \mathsf{nil}$. *Hint:* As in Proposition 10.5, show that $\mathcal{S} \overset{\text{def}}{=} \{(p, p \mid \mathsf{nil}) \mid p \text{ an agent}\}$ is a bisimulation for the raw transition system.   □

It can be seen that the raw transitions of Figure 10.2 correspond closely to the first three forms shown in Figure 10.1; the notable difference is that, in the first two forms, the contextual label L is composed with the agent p, and the result p' of the transition is therefore larger than for the raw transitions.

However, no raw transition corresponds to the fourth (substitution) form of Figure 10.1. This relates to the fact that the original CCS bisimilarity is not preserved by substitution. Let us define $\mathrm{PE_m}$ to be PE (Figure 10.1) without the substitution labels. The subscript m stands for 'mono', because all the labels except the substitution label are mono. Call the weaker bisimilarity for $\mathrm{PE_m}$ *mono bisimilarity*, and denote it by $\sim_{\mathrm{m}}$. The above remarks suggest that $\sim_{\mathrm{m}}$ should coincide with the original CCS bisimilarity. We now verify this claim; the proof is in Appendix A.7.

Theorem 10.6 (recovering CCS) *Mono bisimilarity recovers CCS, i.e.* $\sim_{\mathrm{m}} = \sim_{\mathrm{ccs}}$.

The proof of this theorem can be interpreted either in the concrete $\grave{}\mathrm{BG}_{\mathrm{ccs}}$ or in the abstract $\mathrm{BG}_{\mathrm{ccs}}$. This is natural in view of Theorem 7.23, which relates the concrete and abstract bisimilarities closely. The same holds for Theorem 10.7 below, which asserts another coincidence of bisimilarities. In general, we have worked in a concrete BRS to establish behavioural equivalence as a congruence, which we have transferred to the abstract BRS by Theorem 7.23 under the stated conditions.

Let us examine the contextual transition system PE more closely. The raw CCS transition system is simple by comparison; a raw label such as $\overline{x}$ is much less cumbersome than the corresponding contextual label $\mathrm{id}_I \mid \mathrm{alt}.(\mathrm{get}_x.c\cdot\cdot)$. The latter involves categorical notation, but more seriously it is doubly parametric – both c and $\cdot\cdot$ are parameters. Can this parametric family of labels be replaced by a single contextual label, while remaining faithful to PE?

	$p : I$	$L : I \rightarrow J$	$p' : J$	condition
1	$/Z(\mathrm{alt}.(\mathrm{send}_x.a \,\cdot\cdot) \mid b)$	$\mathrm{id}_I \mid \mathrm{alt}.\mathrm{get}_x.\mathrm{nil}$	$/Z(a \mid b \mid \mathrm{nil})$	$x \notin Z$
2	$/Z(\mathrm{alt}.(\mathrm{get}_x.a \,\cdot\cdot) \mid b)$	$\mathrm{id}_I \mid \mathrm{alt}.\mathrm{send}_x.\mathrm{nil}$	$/Z(a \mid b \mid \mathrm{nil})$	$x \notin Z$
3	$/Z(\mathrm{alt}.(\mathrm{send}_x.a_0 \,\cdot\cdot) \\ \mid \mathrm{alt}.(\mathrm{get}_x.a_1 \,\cdot\cdot) \mid b)$	id_I	$/Z(a_0 \mid a_1 \mid b)$	none
4	$/Z(\mathrm{alt}.(\mathrm{send}_x.a_0 \,\cdot\cdot) \\ \mid \mathrm{alt}.(\mathrm{get}_y.a_1 \,\cdot\cdot) \mid b)$	y/x	$/Z\, y/x \\ (a_0 \mid a_1 \mid b)$	$x \neq y; \\ x, y \notin Z$

Fig. 10.3. The four forms for a transition $p \xrightarrow{L} p'$ in PE

This is indeed possible. We define the contextual transition system PE as shown in Figure 10.3. The only differences from Figure 10.1 are the simpler labels in cases 1 and 2, and the corresponding omission of c from p'. The corresponding system without the fourth case is $\mathrm{PE_m}$. Let us denote the bisimilarities for PE and $\mathrm{PE_m}$ by $\simeq$ and $\simeq_\mathrm{m}$ respectively.

We shall now show that $\mathrm{PE_m}$ is faithful to PE, i.e. that $\simeq_\mathrm{m} = \sim_\mathrm{m}$. (The proof can easily be extended to show $\mathrm{PE_m}$ faithful to PE.) Although PE is faithful to MT, the reduction of transitions in the two cases is different. In moving from MT to PE we omit certain transitions (the disengaged ones) each of which is redundant in itself; in moving from PE to PE we replace a uniformly defined *family* of transitions by a single one.

Theorem 10.7 (non-parametric transitions are faithful) $\simeq_\mathrm{m} = \sim_\mathrm{m}$.

Proof   (outline) We know that $\sim_\mathrm{m} = \sim_\mathrm{ccs}$, so it is enough (and simplest) to prove that $\simeq_\mathrm{m} = \sim_\mathrm{ccs}$. We leave this as an exercise.   □

EXERCISE 10.3 Prove the theorem. As $\mathrm{PE_m}$ is almost identical with the raw CCS system, the proof is simpler than the proof of Theorem 10.6. *Hint:* It may help to prove first that $p \simeq_\mathrm{m} p \mid \mathrm{nil}$.   □

Having successfully matched mono bisimilarity $\sim_\mathrm{m}$ to original CCS, we naturally ask the question: how well does our derived congruence agree with congruences previously proposed for CCS? The original proposed congruence, which we shall call $\sim_{ccs}^c$, was defined simply as the largest congruence included in $\sim_{ccs}$. Since $\sim_{ccs}$ is preserved by all CCS operations, $\sim_{ccs}^c$ was characterised as follows:

$$P \sim_{ccs}^c Q \stackrel{\mathrm{def}}{\Longleftrightarrow} \text{ for all substitutions } \sigma, \sigma P \sim_{ccs} \sigma Q .$$

Another candidate is *open bisimilarity*, which is the smallest relation $\sim_{ccs}^o$ such that, for all substitutions σ,

if $P \sim_{ccs}^o Q$ and $\sigma P \stackrel{\ell}{\longrightarrow} P'$, then $\sigma Q \stackrel{\ell}{\longrightarrow} Q'$ and $P' \sim_{ccs}^o Q'$ for some Q'.

This is known to be strictly finer than $\sim_{ccs}^c$. How does it compare with $\sim$, our derived congruence? Both are coinductively defined, so it is easy to prove that $\sim$ is at least as fine as $\sim_{ccs}^o$, i.e. $\sim \subseteq \sim_{ccs}^o$. In fact this inclusion is again strict. A counter-example to equality is provided by the pair

$$P = \nu z((\overline{x} + \overline{z}) \mid (y + z)) \qquad Q = \nu z((\overline{x}.y + y.\overline{x} + \overline{z}) \mid z)$$

where we abbreviate $\mu.0$ to μ. This pair illustrates an interesting point. When translated into $\mathrm{BG_{ccs}}$, P has a transition labelled x/y; this can be seen as an 'observation' by the environment of P that, by connecting the x-link with the y-link, it enables a transition of P that was previously impossible. On the other hand, Q has no such transition; so $P \not\sim Q$. But the raw transition system lacks such precise 'observations', and indeed $P \sim_{ccs}^o Q$.

This concludes our study of bigraphs applied to CCS, which has revealed considerable agreement with its original theory.

Part III : Development

11

Further topics

In this chapter we suggest some natural lines of development for bigraphs. These lines have usually been explored to some extent, without reaching a uniquely best treatment.

11.1 Tracking

S-categories, with their notion of support, allow us to identify the elements occurring in a bigraph. This has enabled us to derive labelled transitions, and thence to define congruential behavioural relations. Hitherto we have used support only to identify elements statically, not to track them through reaction. By closing the reaction relation $g \longrightarrow g'$, and similarly $g \longrightarrow_i g'$, under independent support translations of g and g', we forget the history of the elements of g', e.g. its nodes; they could be inherited from g or they could be newly created.

Let us now see how to track support along a sequence $g_1 \longrightarrow g_2 \longrightarrow \cdots$ of reactions. Such *tracking*[1] allows us to express historical properties of behaviour. For example, consider a reaction sequence $g \longrightarrow^* g'$; if a support element of g' can be tracked back to g this may have significance. It means that an individual component (a node or edge) of g still exists in g', and may be said to be part of the cause of a further reaction $g' \longrightarrow g''$. Let us look at two reaction rules that might employ tracking.

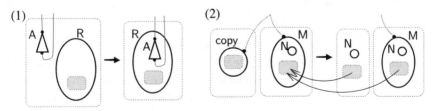

(1)　　　　　　　　　　　　　　(2)

---

[1] The word 'trace' may be preferred to 'track', but it is already overloaded. In process theory, 'trace' means something like a sequence of elementary observations, while in category theory it refers to a kind of loop-formation in spm categories.

In rule (1), which appeared in Chapter 1, we may wish to track the identity (i.e. support node) of both the agent A and the room R. This is necessary if we wish to express a historical statement like '*this* agent has visited *this* room'. We would also like to track the parameter of the rule – i.e. whatever occupies the shaded square in any particular application of the rule.

In the redex of rule (2), a 'copy' command refers to a memory register M. Provided that the register contains an N-atom, the effect of the command is to replace itself and its current contents by a copy of the contents of the register. In this case we 'lose track' of the copy command and all its contents (they vanish), but we may wish to track the register, and also both copies of all its contents. This is a case where two later support elements are tracked back to a single earlier one; this phenomenon is called *residuation* in the λ-calculus and more generally in term-rewriting systems.

In these examples, the support of a node was always tracked to a node with the same control. But this is not always what we want. A simple example is in Petri nets, as modelled in Example 6.13; to express a historical property such as reachability, e.g. '*this* marking is reachable from *that* one', we have to track the support of each condition node, whose control varies between M (marked) and U (unmarked). Of course every reaction in a Petri net leaves the net unchanged, ignoring marking; so in that case we expect the reaction rules to track each node in the reactum to the corresponding node in the redex.

We propose a revision of the definition of reaction to express tracking. First we adapt Definition 7.1 to admit ground tracking reaction rules over an s-category:

Definition 11.1 (ground tracking) A *basic tracking reactive system* $`C(`R)$ is an s-category $`C$ equipped with a set $`R$ of ground reaction rules of the form $(r : I, \; r' : I, \; \tau)$, where the *tracking map* $\tau : |r'| \rightharpoonup |r|$ is a partial map of supports. $`R$ is closed under support translations on the supports of a redex and reactum, in the following sense: For any rule of the given form, and any support relations ρ and ρ' on r and r' respectively, there is also a rule $(\rho \cdot r, \; \rho' \cdot r', \; \rho \circ \tau \circ (\rho')^{-1})$.

We define the *tracking reaction relation* $a \longmapsto^{\sigma} a'$ to mean that $a = D \circ r$ and $a' = D' \circ r'$ for some tracking rule (r, r', τ), where $D = \rho \cdot D'$ and $\sigma = \tau \uplus \rho$. If $\sigma(s)$ exists for a support element $s \in |a'|$, then we call s a *residual* of $\sigma(s)$.   □

Note that the tracking map τ in a rule is many–one; this allows for the possibility that factors of a redex r may be replicated by the rule and other factors discarded. Also, although we still allow arbitrary support translation of r and r', as in Chapter 7, the definition takes care to vary the tracking map accordingly. Finally, in defining the tracking relation, we ensure that support in the context is tracked by a support translation from D to D'.

We now adapt Definition 8.5 to *parametric* tracking reaction rules:

Definition 11.2 (parametric tracking) A *parametric tracking reaction rule* for bigraphs is a quadruple of the form

$$R = (R : m \to J, \ R' : m' \to J, \ \eta, \ \tau),$$

as in Definition 8.5 but with fourth component a *tracking map* $\tau : |R'| \rightharpoonup |R|$, a partial map of supports. The rule generates all ground tracking rules of the form

$$(R.d, \ R'.d', \ \tau \uplus \sigma)$$

where $d = d_0 \otimes \cdots \otimes d_{m-1}$ is a discrete parameter, $d' = d'_0 \parallel \cdots \parallel d'_{m'-1}$ is the instance of d defined by $\rho_j \cdot d'_j = d_{\eta(j)}$ for each $j \in m'$, and $\sigma = \rho_0 \uplus \cdots \uplus \rho_{m'-1}$.

A *tracking BRS* $`\mathrm{BG}(\Sigma, `\mathcal{R})$ has a set $`\mathcal{R}$ of tracking rules closed under support translation as in Definition 11.1. □

In connection with tracking, let us briefly examine a refinement of reaction rules that has been studied for many years in the graph-rewriting community, but has so far been ignored in bigraphs. It consists in identifying a part of a parametric redex that remains unchanged in the passage from the redex to the reactum. Let us call it a *contextual* reaction rule, and represent the unchanged part by a context C. Ignoring tracking, a simple form of contextual rule is

$$(C : J \to K, \ R : m \to J, \ R' : m' \to J, \ \eta).$$

In generating ground reaction rules the pair $(C \circ R, C \circ R')$ is treated just as previously the pair (R, R') was treated. Such explicit contexts allow a finer analysis of the possible conflict between two rule applications within an agent g. Hitherto, two redexes that overlap would be regarded as conflicting; but if the rules are contextual, and only their contextual parts overlap, then they need not be regarded as conflicting, since one of the reactions will not preclude the other.

Now, taking tracking into account, in a reaction by a rule with context C we would naturally track the support of C by a bijective tracking map, i.e. by a support translation. We leave the details as an exercise.

EXERCISE 11.1 Adapt Definition 11.2 to contextual rules, ensuring that the context is tracked through reaction. Express rule (1) in the preceding diagram so that the room R is treated as context. □

11.2 Growth

So far all sets of elements in a bigraph – its nodes, edges, names, roots and sites – are assumed to be finite. In some cases there is good reason; for example, RPOs do not exist if an interface may have an infinity of names or places. There is less reason for the node-set or edge-set to be finite; but also, there is advantage in having it finitely generated in some sense.

Consider structural congruence in CCS. A standard way to represent recursive definition in CCS has been to introduce a set – even infinite – of process identifiers $A, B, \ldots$, and to define their meaning by structural congruence axioms of the form

$$A(x, y, \ldots) \equiv P_A$$

where $x, y, \ldots$ are name parameters and P_A a process with free names among $x, y, \ldots$. P_A may also contain 'recursive calls' of the processes $A, B, \ldots$. Thus process definitions are treated as rules of structural congruence, and understood as defining the way a process expression may *grow*, or unfold, ad infinitum.

In Chapter 10 we presented all the rules for structural congruence in CCS, apart from process definitions; under translation of finite CCS into bigraphs, these rules turn into equalities. Taking the hint from CCS, can we then treat process definitions by imposing structural congruence upon bigraphs themselves? And are there other uses for the infinite bigraphs defined by unfolding these definitions? We now begin to investigate this question. The theory appears elegant and convincing, enough to conjecture that it will help to integrate the treatment of process calculi.

Definition 11.3 (germination) A *germination rule* is a pair $(\mathsf{K}_{\vec{x}}, g_\mathsf{K})$ where $\mathsf{K}_{\vec{x}}$ is a discrete atom and $g_\mathsf{K} : \langle 1, \{\vec{x}\} \rangle$ a lean epi ground bigraph. We call K a *seed*.

Given a concrete BRS `$\mathbf{C}$, let $\Delta$ be a set of germination rules each with a distinct seed not in the signature of `$\mathbf{C}$. We assume Δ to be closed under support equivalence. Extend the signature of `$\mathbf{C}$ by the seeds, declaring them atomic. Denote the result by `$\mathbf{C}(\Delta)$; call it a *growing* BRS. The same applies to an abstract BRS, omitting closure under $\rightleftharpoons$.

The *germination relation* $\hookrightarrow_\Delta$ on bigraphs is determined as follows: $G \hookrightarrow_\Delta \widehat{G}$ if $G = C \circ (\mathrm{id} \otimes \mathsf{K}_{\vec{x}})$ and $\widehat{G} \rightleftharpoons C \circ (\mathrm{id} \otimes g_\mathsf{K})$ for some $(\mathsf{K}_{\vec{x}}, g_\mathsf{K}) \in \Delta$ and context C. □

Thus germination replaces a seed K occurring in G by g_K to form $\widehat{G}$. We shall drop the subscript Δ from $\hookrightarrow$ when it is understood. The following depends on the fact that two germinations in G either arise from the same rule or occur disjointly:

Lemma 11.4 *If $G \hookrightarrow G_0$ and $G \hookrightarrow G_1$, then either $G_0 \rightleftharpoons G_1$ or there exists $\widehat{G}$ such that $G_0 \hookrightarrow \widehat{G}$ and $G_1 \hookrightarrow \widehat{G}$.*

We now define an ordering and equivalence based upon germination:

Definition 11.5 (growth order, equivalence) The *growth order* $\leq_\Delta$ and *growth* *equivalence* $\equiv_\Delta$ are essentially the transitive reflexive closure, and the symmetric transitive reflexive closure, of germination. To be precise:

(1) $\leq_\Delta \overset{\text{def}}{=} (\hookrightarrow \cup \eqsim)^*$

(2) $\equiv_\Delta \overset{\text{def}}{=} (\hookrightarrow \cup \hookleftarrow \cup \eqsim)^*$. $\qquad\qquad\qquad\qquad\qquad$ □

Again, we shall drop the subscript Δ when understood.

In what follows a hat – as in $\widehat{A}$ – will always mean a growth, while a prime as in A' will always mean the result of a reaction or transition. $(F_0, F_1, \dots) \leq (G_0, G_1, \dots)$ means $F_i \leq G_i$ for all i, and $F \leq G, H$ means $F \leq G$ and $F \leq H$.

The following properties of $\leq$ are essential:

Proposition 11.6 (congruence, confluence, independence)

(1) *Growth* $\leq$ *is congruential: if* $F \leq G$ *then* $F \circ H \leq G \circ H$, $H \circ F \leq H \circ G$ *and* $F \otimes H \leq G \otimes H$. *Similarly for the equivalence* $\equiv$.

(2) *Growth is confluent: if* $G \leq G_0, G_1$ *then there exists* $\widehat{G}$ *such that* $G_0, G_1 \leq \widehat{G}$.

(3) *The parts of a composition or product grow independently: if* $E \circ F \leq G$, *then* $G = \widehat{E} \circ \widehat{F}$ *for some* $\widehat{E}, \widehat{F}$ *such that* $(E, F) \leq (\widehat{E}, \widehat{F})$. *Similarly for product.*

We now begin to justify the claim that growth respects dynamics. We shall therefore be concerned mainly with ground bigraphs.

Assumptions In this development we shall relax the assumption adopted in Definition 8.5 that the parameter d of a parametric reaction is discrete. For in a ground redex $r = R.d$, although R cannot contain seeds, d may contain them; when one of them is germinated we have $d \hookrightarrow e$ which may be non-discrete. Then $r \hookrightarrow R.e$, and we may wish $R.e$ to be a ground redex underlying a transition.

Instead, we make the weaker assumption that a parameter d should be lean and epi; if $d \hookrightarrow e$ then e will also be lean and epi, by our assumption on germination rules. Since discreteness of parameters was useful in Chapter 8 for our dynamic theory, we leave it open how far that theory needs revision in the presence of growth.

We also assume that reaction rules are affine; this allows us to prove Proposition 11.7, on which later results depend.[2]

We now assert that, under our assumptions, growth does not prevent reaction. This is because no seed occurs in a parametric redex. Formally:

---

[2] An alternative assumption would be that the result g_K of a generation is open, i.e. contains no closed links. In binding bigraphs, where *bound* links are possible in an open bigraph, this assumption will be less of a constraint.

Proposition 11.7 (growth preserves reaction) *In a growing BRS with affine rules, if $f \longrightarrow f'$ and $f \le g$, then $g \longrightarrow g'$ for some g' such that $f' \le g'$.*

Moreover growth can enable reaction, since it can create a redex. To reflect this we define a more permissive reaction relation:

Definition 11.8 (growing reaction) Let us use $\longrightarrow\!\!\!\!\!\twoheadrightarrow$, with a double arrow head, to denote *growing reaction*, which we define as follows:

$$f \longrightarrow\!\!\!\!\!\twoheadrightarrow f' \text{ iff } g \longrightarrow g' \text{ for some } g, g' \text{ such that } (f, f') \le (g, g') . \qquad \square$$

The idea is to allow f to grow in order to enable a reaction. Clearly $\longrightarrow\!\!\!\!\!\twoheadrightarrow \supseteq \longrightarrow$. Growing reaction behaves well:

Proposition 11.9 (growing affine reaction)

(1) If $f \longrightarrow\!\!\!\!\!\twoheadrightarrow f'$ and D is active then $D \circ f \longrightarrow\!\!\!\!\!\twoheadrightarrow D \circ f'$ whenever defined.

(2) If $f \longrightarrow\!\!\!\!\!\twoheadrightarrow f'$ and $f \le g$, then $g \longrightarrow\!\!\!\!\!\twoheadrightarrow g'$ for some g' such that $f' \le g'$.

EXERCISE 11.2 Prove this. *Hint:* For (2) use confluence with Proposition 11.7.

$\square$

A good way to think of growing reaction ($\longrightarrow\!\!\!\!\!\twoheadrightarrow$) is that it represents the ordinary reaction relation but executed on fully grown bigraphs (possibly infinite), which contain no generators. Essentially, these represent the equivalence classes of $\equiv_\Delta$.

An obvious question is whether *growing transitions* behave well. We shall answer this by showing that, when defined in a natural way, the minimal ones do indeed induce a congruential bisimilarity.

Definition 11.10 (growing transition) A quadruple $(f, (L, \tilde{\imath}), f')$, which we write as $f \xrightarrow{L}\!\!\!\!\!\twoheadrightarrow_{\tilde{\imath}} f'$, is a *growing* transition if there exists a transition $g \xrightarrow{M}\!\!\!\!\!\twoheadrightarrow_{\tilde{\imath}} g'$ with $(f, L, f') \le (g, M, g')$. It is *minimal* if the transition of g is minimal.

Denote by $\simeq$ the bisimilarity induced by the minimal growing transitions.

How does growth relate to IPOs? It is rather easy to see that if $\vec{A} \le \vec{B}$ then there may be no IPO for $\vec{A}$ even if $\vec{B}$ has an IPO; indeed, $\vec{A}$ may not even have a bound. However, crucially, IPOs are preserved by growth. We now make this precise.

Lemma 11.11 *In concrete bigraphs, assume that $\vec{B}$ is an IPO for $\vec{A}$, and that an open atom $a : I$ occurs in A_0. Replace this atom in both $\vec{A}$ and $\vec{B}$ with an epi ground bigraph $g : I$ whose support is fresh. Then the result is an IPO $(B_0, \widehat{B}_1)$ for $(\widehat{A}_0, \widehat{A}_1)$, such that $(A_0, A_1, B_1) \le (\widehat{A}_0, \widehat{A}_1, \widehat{B}_1)$.*

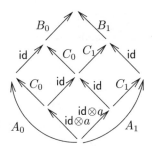 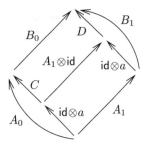

Proof   Under the assumption there are two possibilities: either a occurs in A_0 and A_1, or it occurs in A_0 and B_1. (Note that it cannot occur in B_0.)

In the first case we have $A_0 = C_0 \circ (\text{id} \otimes a)$ and $A_1 = C_1 \circ (\text{id} \otimes a)$; in the second case $A_0 = C \circ (\text{id} \otimes a)$ and $B_1 = D \circ (\text{id} \otimes a)$. Since a is epi, and hence $\text{id} \otimes a$ is epi, these decompositions are uniquely determined. Since a is also open, by Proposition 5.19 and Corollary 5.21 the main IPO can be resolved into four and two IPOs respectively, as in the diagrams.

Now, replace a by g in these diagrams, forming $\widehat{A}_0$, $\widehat{A}_1$ and $\widehat{B}_1$. Since g is epi, the squares containing a remain IPOs when g replaces a; so in each case the new full diagram represents an IPO satisfying the required condition.   □

EXERCISE 11.3 State where the assumption that a is open and epi is needed, in building these IPO diagrams.   □

Proposition 11.12 (growth preserves idem-pushouts)   *Let $\vec{A}$ have an IPO $\vec{B}$. Let $A_0 \leq \widehat{A}_0$ and $|\widehat{A}_0|\#|B_0|$. Then there exist $\widehat{A}_1$, $\widehat{B}_1$ such that $(A_1, B_1) \leq (\widehat{A}_1, \widehat{B}_1)$ such that $(\widehat{A}_0, \widehat{A}_1)$ has IPO $(B_0, \widehat{B}_1)$.*

Proof   We know this holds when $\leq$ is replaced by $\stackrel{\frown}{=}$. So since $\leq = (\hookrightarrow \cup \stackrel{\frown}{=})^*$, we need only prove it for $\hookrightarrow$. This is immediate by Lemma 11.11, since in applying the lemma we take a to be a seed, i.e. a discrete atom, which is both open and epi.   □

We now apply these results. The following is immediate from Proposition 11.12:

Corollary 11.13 (growth preserves transition)   *If $f \xrightarrow{L}_{\vec{\imath}} f'$ and if $f \leq g$ with $|g|\#|L|$, then $g \xrightarrow{L}_{\vec{\imath}} g'$ for some g' such that $f' \leq g'$.*

Let us now turn to the 'growing bisimilarity' $\simeq$. It turns out that the two bisimilarities are incomparable, as the following shows:

Example 11.14 (incomparable bisimilarities)   We consider an example in place graphs. Let K and L be distinct atomic controls, and M a passive control. Let $(K, M.K)$ be a germination rule and (M, id) a reaction rule; thus we have

$$K \hookrightarrow M.K \quad \text{and} \quad M.e \longrightarrow e$$

for all parameters e. Then $\sim$ and $\simeq$ are incomparable. For on the one hand we have $K \sim L$ but $K \not\simeq L$; on the other hand we have $K \not\sim M.K$ but $K \simeq M.K$.

This can be understood as follows. In the first case $\sim$ allows no growth so K and L are indistinguishable, while $\simeq$ allows growth of K, enabling a distinction. In the second case, the lack of growth in $\sim$ means that the reaction rule can apply to M.K but not to K, while $\simeq$ allows growth and thus removes the distinction.   □

EXERCISE 11.4 Prove these assertions, at least in terms of engaged transitions. You may assume that non-engaged transitions play no part in the argument.   □

Despite this disagreement, bisimilarity for growing transitions seems the natural way to represent the behavioural equivalence of infinite bigraphs. To reinforce the intuition, we now show that this bisimilarity is preserved by all contexts.

Theorem 11.15 (congruence of growing bisimilarity) *Let $a_0 \simeq a_1$. Then $C \circ a_0 \simeq C \circ a_1$ for all contexts C with the compositions defined.*

EXERCISE 11.5 Prove the theorem. *Hint:* Follow the proof of Theorem 7.16 as closely as possible, but move back and forth between growing transitions and standard ones. For this purpose you need Definition 11.10 and also Proposition 11.12.
                                                                              □

It is worth noting that the proof of this theorem, just as the proof of Theorem 7.16, uses no special features of bigraphs; it therefore holds for wide reactive systems in general.[3]

A next step is to investigate parametric germination; that is, when the seed $K_{\vec{x}}$ is an ion, and germination takes the form $K_{\vec{x}}.e \hookrightarrow g$ where g may contain the parameter e. If so, it can represent not only recursive definition (e.g. in CCS), but also replication in the π-calculus, which is often expressed as a structural congruence $!P \equiv P \mid !P$.

At this point we leave the study of growth for future work.

11.3 Binding

Hitherto we have studied only *pure* bigraphs, in which placing and linking are independent structures over a set of nodes. We have exploited this independence in

---

[3] Certain assumptions are needed; for example, that growth in a composition $C \circ a$ occurs independently in C and in a.

formal definitions and in the development of theory. But we wish also to accommodate useful dependencies between placing and linking. In particular we may wish
to assume, or to enforce, that certain links are confined to certain places. This is
exactly what is meant by the scope of a name in programming or process calculi.
Thus

we may wish to confine the use of a link to within a place.

This corresponds to what is usually called the *binding* of names. Binding has indeed been successfully treated in various ways for bigraphs, and has been applied to
recover the behaviour of the π-calculus, just as the behaviour of CCS is recovered
in Chapter 10 of this book, and also to encode a version of the λ-calculus. These
experiments have revealed what appears to be a unified treatment, which we now
propose.

Binding In the current notion of signature we define node controls, each with an
arity and an attribute in the set $\{$active, passive, atomic$\}$. Let us now define a fourth
value, 'binding', for this attribute. Controls with this attribute will be called *binding
controls*. This enriches a signature to become a *binding signature*.

For nodes, 'binding' implies 'atomic with arity 0'. For any binding control β we
shall call a β-node a *binding*. But we shall also treat a binding node as a kind of
link; so it is a hybrid between a node and a link. To give it this status we extend the
range of a link map to include bindings. Thus, points can be bound.

For this purpose, we assume that bindings are drawn from an infinite set $\mathcal{B}$,
disjoint from names $\mathcal{X}$, nodes $\mathcal{V}$ and edges $\mathcal{E}$. A *quasi-binding bigraph* over a
binding signature $\mathcal{K}$ takes the form

$$G = (V, B, E, ctrl, prnt, link) : I \to J$$

in which the extra component $B \subset \mathcal{B}$ is a finite set of bindings. The control map
is extended to $ctrl : V \uplus B \to \mathcal{K}$, assigning controls both to nodes and to bindings.
Further, let m, X and n, Y be the widths and names of I and J, and let P be the
ports of G. Then the parent map and link map of G take the form

$$prnt : \quad m \uplus V \uplus B \to V \uplus n$$
$$link : \quad X \uplus P \to B \uplus E \uplus Y .$$

In diagrams we shall draw bindings as little hollow circles. If q is a point – i.e.
an inner name or port – and $link(q) = b$, with $\beta = ctrl(b)$, then we say that β
or b *binds* q. We can already distinguish bindings from closed links (edges), as
illustrated here:

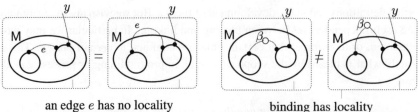

an edge e has no locality   binding has locality

In the left-hand diagram e is an edge linking two ports. It makes no difference
how we draw an edge, as long as it abuts on its ports, because an edge itself has no
location. But the right-hand diagram shows a binding control β binding the same
two ports, and the location of β matters. For if the β-binding lies inside the M-node
then it can only link ports that lie within that node. This will be enforced by our
binding discipline.

EXERCISE 11.6 Adapt the definitions of place graphs and link graphs, Definitions 2.1 and 2.2, to admit the addition of a binding-set B. Then adapt Definition 2.5
which defines composition for both place graphs and link graphs, paying particular
attention to the equations defining the *prnt* and *link* maps for composite bigraphs.
                                                                                                  □

We now turn our attention to the binding discipline. For any bigraph G (pure
or quasi-binding), let us write $w\ in_G\ w'$ to mean $w' = prnt_G^k(w)$ for some $k \geq 0$,
i.e. the place w is a *descendant* of the place w' in G. We write $w\ in\ w'$, omitting
the subscript G, when there is no ambiguity. Then for quasi-binding bigraphs we
define *localities* for ports and bindings as follows.

Definition 11.16 (locality) Let G be quasi-binding, with nodes V and bindings B.
Recall that the ports P_v of a node $v \in V$ take the form $p = (v, i)$ for $i \in ar(v)$.
Then the *localities* of ports and bindings are defined as follows:

$$
\begin{aligned}
locport &\stackrel{\text{def}}{=} \{(prnt(v), p) \mid v \in V,\, p \in P_v\} \\
locbind &\stackrel{\text{def}}{=} \{(prnt(b), b) \mid b \in B\}\,.
\end{aligned}
$$
                                                                                                  □

Thus within G each port and binding has a unique place – a node or a root. The
scope discipline for binding controls will dictate that if b binds p then the place of
p must be a descendant of the place of b. But this is not all we need for our scope
discipline; it must also be preserved by composition and product. This implies that
our present notion of interface is too weak, as shown by the following example.

Example 11.17 (bad binding) Let F be a quasi-binding bigraph, whose inner face
is $\langle 1, x \rangle$ with x bound by a binding control β. Let G have outer face $\langle 2, x \rangle$, with

x linked to a port in each of the two regions of G. Then the bigraph $(F \otimes \mathrm{id}_1) \circ G$ breaks our discipline, as shown in the diagram. □

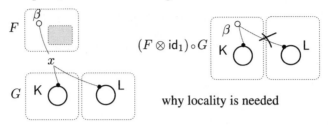

why locality is needed

To exclude such cases we enrich interfaces as follows.

Definition 11.18 (binding interface) A *binding interface* takes the form

$$I = \langle m, loc, X \rangle$$

where $loc \subseteq m \times X$ is a binary relation between places and names. If $(i, x) \in loc$ we say that x is *local (to i in I)*. Otherwise x is *non-local* (in I). □

It is sometimes easier to write $\langle m, loc, X \rangle$ in the form $\langle (X_0), \ldots, (X_{m-1}), X \rangle$, where X_i are the names local to the region i; thus $\bigcup_i X_i \subseteq X$.

Before we define the scope discipline, let us describe the effect it will have on Example 11.17. Since the β-binding binds the inner name x, it will require x to be local to the inner face of F, so this inner face must be $\langle (x), x \rangle$ (where we omit curly brackets around singleton sets). In diagrams, we shall write a local name in parentheses at each interface, so F will be drawn as follows:

Thus the inner face of $F \otimes \mathrm{id}_1$ will be $\langle (x), (\emptyset), x \rangle$, locating x at only one site. But the scope discipline will require the outer face of G to be $\langle (x), (x), x \rangle$, since x is used in both regions of G. This difference of interfaces prevents the composition of $F \otimes \mathrm{id}_1$ with G, so it destroys our example.

We now state the *scope discipline* which a quasi-binding bigraph must satisfy to qualify as a binding bigraph. Given a bigraph, let us use w to range over its places, q over its points and ℓ over its links. Roughly, the scope discipline demands that descendance and linking are compatible with binding. This means that if a link is local to a place w, then every point in the link is local to a place below w. More formally:

Definition 11.19 (binding bigraph)   Given a quasi-binding bigraph $G : I \to J$, define the localities of its points and links as follows:

$$locpoint \overset{\text{def}}{=} loc_I \uplus locport , \quad loclink \overset{\text{def}}{=} locbind \uplus loc_J .$$

We say that the points in *locpoint*, and the links in *loclink*, are *local (in G)*. Then G is a *binding bigraph* if it obeys the following *scope discipline*:

- Whenever $\ell = link(q)$ and $(w, \ell) \in loclink$, there exists w' such that w' in w and $(w', q) \in locpoint$.   □

Composition for binding bigraphs is just as we defined it for quasi-binding bigraphs, and the definitions of identities, unit, product and symmetries are obvious. It can then be proved that

Theorem 11.20 (binding bigraph categories) *The concrete binding bigraphs over any binding signature form an s-category, and the abstract ones form an spm category.*

EXERCISE 11.7 Prove that in binding bigraphs the identities obey the scope discipline, and that both composition and tensor product preserve the discipline. *Hint:* Pay attention to your adapted definition of composition in Exercise 11.6.   □

It has also been shown that if every name in an interface $I = \langle m, loc, X \rangle$ has at most one location, i.e. *loc* is a map from X to $m \uplus \{\bot\}$ (where $loc(x) = \bot$ means that x is non-local), then RPOs exist in these s-categories; hence labelled transition systems can be derived. By this means, for example, theory for the pi calculus has been recovered.

Inward binding   We have defined the scope of a β-binding to be its parent place; we may thus call β an *outward binding* control. But we may need binding nodes that bind *within themselves*. By a simple sorting discipline, as in Section 6.1, this *inward binding* can be achieved by nesting a number of bindings inside an ordinary node. These can be ordered by using binding controls $(1), (2), \ldots$. If K has arity k and we equip a K-node with h binding controls, then we have turned the K-node into an inward binding control with a double arity $h \to k$. The diagram shows the case $h, k = 2, 3$:

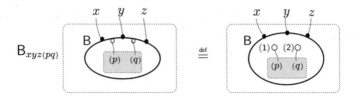

Let us now illustrate binding in the encoding of the finite π-calculus. The basic signature differs slightly from the one for encoding CCS, to cater for the passage of names as data. The 'send' and 'get' controls, previously both with arity 1, now have dual arities written send : $0 \to 2$ and get : $1 \to 1$. Thus 'get' becomes an inward binding control. Recall that the reaction rule in the π-calculus is written

$$(\overline{x}y.P + A) \mid (x(z).Q + B) \longrightarrow P \mid \{y/z\}Q .$$

The figure below represents this in binding bigraphs. Note how the meta-syntactic substitution of π-calculus is encoded by a substitution which is itself a bigraph; it substitutes a non-local name y for the local name z in parameter d_2.

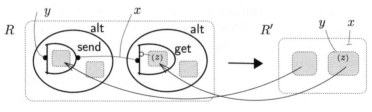

$$\mathsf{alt.}\,(\mathsf{send}_{xy}.d_0 \mid d_1) \mid \mathsf{alt.}\,(\mathsf{get}_{x(z)}.d_2 \mid d_3) \;\dashrightarrow\; x \mid d_0 \mid y/(z).d_2$$

Operations The interfaces of binding bigraphs are more complex than for pure bigraphs. This gives rise to a richer family of linkings, and we now discuss briefly a few of the new phenomena that arise. Recall that in pure bigraphs we abbreviate a prime interface $\langle 1, X \rangle$ to $\langle X \rangle$, and that we write a singleton $X = \{x\}$ as x. In binding bigraphs we also write $\langle (X) \rangle$ for the prime binding interface whose names X are all local.

Consider substitutions. The non-local substitution $y/z : z \to y$ is as before, but there are now substitutions $y/(z) : \langle (z) \rangle \to \langle y \rangle$ and $(y)/(z) : \langle (z) \rangle \to \langle (y) \rangle$. The first of these has already been used in the reactum of the π-calculus rule above, and the second may be required if a reaction rule has non-local outer names. However the fourth possibility $(y)/z : \langle z \rangle \to \langle (y) \rangle$ attempts to localise a non-local name, and this violates the scope discipline.

So there is no *bigraph* which localises a non-local name; but we can define a partial *operation* on bigraphs to do this. First, if x is non-local in the interface J, we define $(x)J$ to be the result of making the x local to every place in J. We call this the *localisation* of x in J. Now suppose that $G : I \to J$ where I is local, i.e. all its names are local. In this case to make x local in J does not violate the scope discipline, and we obtain the *localisation* of x in G:

$$(x)G : I \to (x)J \quad (I \text{ local}) .$$

Clearly one can then define multiple localisation $(X)G$, where X is a finite set of names. An especially useful case of localisation is when $I = \epsilon$, i.e. G is ground.

Substitution and localisation appear to represent the main effect of binding on the bigraphical operations.

Reactions We also have to adjust reaction rules and the reaction relation. For example, we wish to define a reaction rule whose redex binds its parameter, as in the π-calculus. This raises three points:

(i) As parametric reaction rules are defined in Definition 8.5, a parameter d has to be *discrete*, meaning that there are no closed links and the link map is bijective. But this notion must be qualified so that it does not constrain the local names of d, which are to be bound by the parametric redex R. The non-local names Y of d can still be exported in a ground reaction whose redex is given by $r \simeq (\mathrm{id}_Y \otimes R) \circ d$.

(ii) Discreteness of d should still require that it has no closed links. But it must be permitted *bound* links. Then if a prime factor of d – say d_0 – is replicated by a reaction, each copy of d_0 will have its own copy of any bound link. Thus, for example, if we encode the π-calculus with replication into bigraphs, each π-calculus restriction $\nu x P$ will be faithfully modelled by a bound link.

(iii) Some or all of the outer names of a redex R may be non-local. But we may wish to allow reactions in a context in which the links involved will be local. This can be achieved in two ways. We may simply define R with a local outer name, say (z), and use a substitution like $^z/(z)$ to make it non-local where required. Or we may define R with the outer name z non-local, and modify the way we define the reaction relation $\longrightarrow$ in Definition 7.1; define it now to be the smallest such that $a \longrightarrow a'$ whenever $a \simeq D \circ (X)r$ and $a' \simeq D \circ (X)r'$ for some ground reaction rule (r, r') and context D, where X are the non-local names of r. This use of localisation respects the scope discipline because r is ground.

Some of the points raised above, concerning both operations and reactions, have already been addressed in existing work. But a definitive treatment of binding is still lacking, and is an important topic for future research.

11.4 Stochastics

As mentioned in the Prologue to this book, it is important to deploy bigraphs in experimental applications in order to assess their modelling power. Many applications, such as ubiquitous computing, are inherently non-deterministic, at least in the sense that in modelling them we are ignorant of precise details of timing. But to aid experiment we must ensure that simulations are realistic; this entails somehow attaching relative probabilities to reactions. Consider, for example, our simple example in Chapter 1 of behaviour in a built environment; once we have defined enough rules to express simple behaviour of people we would like to experiment with the effect of varying the relative rates of their actions.

For this purpose we can attach a stochastic rate to each inference rule. Indeed, in biological applications this approach may be considered essential to the model; typically there is a large population of entities (e.g. of protein molecules), and if each entity can perform a certain reaction then the speed of reactions may plausibly be computed as the product of the population size and the stochastic rate assigned to that reaction rule. This approach is adopted, for example, in the κ-calculus [27] for biological modelling.

Taking a hint from this work, stochastic bigraphs have recently been defined [51]. In the context of bigraphs, what corresponds to population size is the number of distinct occurrences within an agent g of a given ground redex r; to get the reaction speed this count is multiplied by the rate attached to the given reaction rule. The count, i.e. the number of distinct occurrences of r, is easily defined in terms of support. (This use of support is quite distinct from its role in deriving contextual transition rules via RPOs.) One detailed point: one must avoid double counting in the case of support automorphisms of the redex r.

Let us give a more precise idea of the approach, omitting a few details. Assume that we have a family $\mathcal{R}$ of reaction rules, where each rule R has an associated rate ρ_R. Given agents g and g', we may wish to compute the rate of the reaction $g \longrightarrow g'$. This reaction may occur with different underlying rules, so we sum over $\mathcal{R}$:

$$rate_{\mathcal{R}}[g, g'] \stackrel{\text{def}}{=} \sum_{R \in \mathcal{R}} rate_R[g, g'] .$$

Now for a given rule R, we define $\mu_R[g, g']$ to be the number of distinct ground rules (r, r') generated by R such that, for some active context C, $C \circ r = g$ and $C \circ r' \asymp g'$. Then

$$rate_R[g, g'] \stackrel{\text{def}}{=} \rho_R \cdot \mu_R[g, g'] ,$$

and this completes our definition of the rate of the reaction $g \longrightarrow g'$.

In previous work [42, 71] associated with process calculi, rates have been attached not only to reaction rules, but also to labelled transitions. In that work, the speed of communication depends on the rate attached independently to the two or more transitions that perform the communication. However, the theory of bigraphs suggests a different approach: since labelled transitions are *derived* from reaction rules, rather than defined independently, one would expect to derive the rate of a transition from the rate of its underlying reaction rule. This indeed can be done, rather simply. It remains, however, to find criteria that determine in what circumstances to prefer one approach to the other.

Thus work on a stochastic interpretation of bigraphs is still in progress. Much will be learned by experiment, both in biology and in ubiquitous computing. But it is already clear that some such interpretation is a necessity, not a luxury; it is also encouraging that it can be done generically, not tailor-made for each application.

12

Background, development and related work

In this chapter we place the bigraph model in the broader informatic context.

The bigraph model attempts to bridge two distinct cultures. On the one hand is the adolescent culture of ubiquitous computing; on the other hand is the more mature theory of concurrent processes. The first two sections of this chapter describe the two cultures in enough detail to show how the bigraph model fits into each of them, and how together they demand the existence of some such model. In the third section I describe how bigraphs evolved as a generic model of processes. Finally I describe ongoing work to create software tools that will bring bigraphs to life as a language for programming and simulation, thus admitting experiments that will help to assess the scientific value of this model.

Background in ubiquitous computing Let us first look at the vision of ubiquitous computing. Mark Weiser [79] is generally credited with forming this vision and inspiring research that will bring it to reality; I quoted him briefly in the Prologue. The vision represents one of the most ambitious aspirations of computer science, and has been adopted as a Grand Challenge by the UK Computing Research Committee (UKCRC). The title of its manifesto [1], '*Ubiquitous computing: experience, design and science*', reflects the insight that to realise the vision demands collaboration among three distinct research communities: those concerned with the human–computer interface and human behaviour, those concerned with engineering principles and design patterns for large systems, and those concerned with theoretical models and the languages that bring them to life. These three themes cannot be addressed in isolation.

The first theme, human involvement, is well represented by a recently completed six-year research project, the Equator project [2]. On that website can be found citations of the work carried out. The role of humans in a ubiquitous system is two-fold; first as users of a massive software system, and second as entities forming part of the system, and to be modelled as such. There is a close analogy with the role of humans in an economic system. The Equator project performed extensive experiments aiming to link the human sciences with the role played in society by informatic systems. Here is a quotation from the final project report:

Equator aimed to forge a clearer understanding of what it means to live in an age when digital and physical activities not only coexist but cooperate. This is the age we are now entering, and it promises radical change in how we communicate, interact, work and play; that is, how we live. But to fulfil that promise requires more than new technology. We need equally new ways of thinking about technology, and thus also about ourselves.

One may add that, to support new thinking about how the technology relates to society, we also need accurate understanding of the technology in its own terms. This is exactly how the first of the three themes depends upon the second and third.

The second theme, engineering principles and design, is well represented by a wide range of papers, both previous to the Grand Challenge initiative and arising from it. A few examples will illustrate the breadth of the engineering challenge. Wooldridge [81] puts forward the concept of an intelligent agent as a model for building self-managing and decision-taking systems. Jennings *et al.* [45] advocate negotiation, underpinned by game theory, as a principle underlying the interaction of agents in a non-hierarchical population. Sloman *et al.* [77], in the context of health-care, propose a model of the 'self-managed cell', a generic design concept for ubiquitous systems; notably, the model offers an explanation of how two ubiquitous systems, conforming to this pattern, may combine organically into a single system. Crowcroft [25] examines structural design criteria for systems to manage driverless vehicles on the highway. Dix *et al.* [28] explore informally how space and locality may be used in a semantic model of mobile systems.

Besides their engineering significance, such papers yield insight into how models – formal or informal – of advanced software can provide systems to underpin a highly instrumented human society.

The third theme, then, is concerned with conceptual modelling. There remains a question: Given a variety of models for ubiquitous systems, how will the models fit together? Each one will deal with some concepts such as those listed in the Prologue, but a single model is unlikely to deal with all of them. So how can they provide an integrated scientific understanding of ubiquitous computing? In a recent paper [66] I proposed a *tower of models*. The idea is that, just as some models are designed to explain reality, so a model at a higher level may explain, or may be implemented by, a lower-level model. For example, in the Prologue I suggested how the complex concept of trust (between informatic agents) can be implemented at a lower level.

There is surely a precedent in natural science for this levelling of models. It is crucially significant in informatics, whose ultimate realities are extraordinarily complex artifacts, and can only be understood via many levels of abstraction.

Background in mathematical models The history of informatics is rich with such levelling of understanding, either formal or informal. We now turn to models that are formal, embodying some kind of mathematical theory. In contrast with the recent surge of interest in ubiquitous systems, over the past half-century there has been a progression of mathematical models of computation, each of which typically deals with a well-delineated range of phenomena. Without going back to basic models such as Turing machines and automata theory, let us confine attention to models of interactive processes; these are the models that I have tried to draw together in the present book.

An early theory of concurrent processes was Petri nets [70] in the 1960s; it was perhaps the first that gave a significant mathematical structure to discrete events. In 1979, with Milne, I explored certain aspects of algebraic structure for processes [59, 60]. A tradition of self-contained algebraic calculi for concurrent systems began around that time; early representatives are the Calculus of Communicating Systems (CCS) [61], Communicating Sequential Processes (CSP) by Hoare *et al.* [13, 44] and Process Algebra by Baeten, Weijland, Bergstra and Klop [3, 8].

Bigraphs have also used ideas from many other sources: the Chemical Abstract machine (Cham) of Berry and Boudol [6], the bisimilarity of Park [68], the π-calculus of Milner, Parrow and Walker [62a, 67] with extended theory by Sangiorgi and Walker [73], the interaction nets of Lafont [52], the mobile ambients of Cardelli and Gordon [18], the sharing graphs of Hasegawa [38], the distributed π-calculus of Hennessy [39], the explicit fusions of Gardner and Wischik [34] developed from the fusion calculus of Parrow and Victor [69], Nomadic Pict by Wojciechowski and Sewell [80]. In each of these cases my emphasis has been not to extend the work in its own terms, but rather to use its inspiration to find a framework that can embrace them all. Notably helpful was a wide-ranging survey by Castellani [19] of the notion of locality, and the many ways it has been defined and deployed in process models. Particularly influential was the work of Meseguer and Montanari [58] explaining Petri nets in monoidal categories. More generally, the idea of using monoidal categories for computational structure can be traced back to Benson [5]. A good textbook for basic category theory is by Barr and Wells [4].

Graphs and their transformation are often chosen as the way to model spatially-aware systems. There is a long tradition in *graph-rewriting*, based upon the *double pushout* (DPO) construction originated by Ehrig [29]. That work typically uses a category with graphs as objects and embeddings as arrows. In contrast, our s-categories have interfaces as objects and graphs as arrows. These formulations have been linked, both via cospans by Gadducci, Heckel and Llabrés [31] and via an isomorphism between the category of graph embeddings and a coslice of an s-category (over its origin) by Cattani *et al.* [20]. Ehrig [30] investigated these links further, after discussion with the author, and we believe that useful cross-fertilisation is possible. Gadducci *et al.* [31] represent graph-rewriting by 2-categories, whose 2-cells correspond to our reactions. Several other formulations of graph-rewriting employ hypergraphs. An example is by Hirsch and Montanari [43]; their hypergraphs are not nested as bigraphs are, but rewriting rules may replace a hyperedge by an arbitrary graph.

Besides graph rewriting, there is a variety of other frameworks for modelling concurrent interactive behaviour; for example[1]

(i) *Term rewriting* by a group of authors led by Klop [78], which can accommodate arbitrary equational axioms.

(ii) *Rewriting logic* led by Meseguer [22, 57] which includes MAUDE, an automated logic for rewriting.

(iii) *The tile model* led by Montanari [32], whose tiles represent rewriting rules and can be composed in two dimensions, one to yield longer rewritings and one to yield compound rules.

(iv) *X-KLAIM*, led by De Nicola [7], designed to program distributed systems through multiple tuple spaces and mobile code.

Thus we are in the early days of the search for an agreed framework for the design and analysis of spatially-aware systems. In the bigraph model most of the effort hitherto has been devoted to integrating pre-existing theories. From now on, the emphasis is likely to change towards case studies in different application topics, and in the provision of computer-assisted tools for their analysis.

Development of bigraphs The bigraph model arose from *action calculi* [62], the author's first attempt at a spatial framework unifying process calculi. In action calculi there was a technical difficulty, which was resolved by the main idea of bigraphs: that locality (placing) and connectivity (linking) should be treated independently. Gardner [33] contributed significantly to the emergence of this idea. This independence also reflects a property of real-life systems; we need only think of wireless networks.

The technical difficulty with action calculi arose as follows. One criterion for their success was that they should recover theory for existing process calculi, in particular their behavioural equivalences and pre-orders, which are often based upon labelled transition systems. This recovery depends upon treating certain contexts as labels. How to choose these contexts remained an open problem for many

---

[1] We use the term 'framework' to mean not just a single process calculus (e.g. CCS) but a method or style for defining a family of such calculi.

years. As a first step, Sewell [76] was able uniformly to derive satisfactory context-labelled transitions for parametric term-rewriting systems with parallel composition and blocking, and showed bisimilarity to be a congruence. It remained a problem to do it for reactive systems dealing with connectivity, such as the π-calculus, and to do it uniformly across bigraphical calculi.

This problem was solved by Leifer and Milner [55], who defined minimal contextual labels in terms of the categorical notion of *relative pushout* (RPO), also ensuring that behavioural equivalence is a congruence. These results were extended and refined in Leifer's PhD Dissertation [54], and applied by Cattani *et al.* [20] to action graphs with rich connectivity. Leifer and Milner [55] showed how to derive these transition systems in any categorical model possessing relative pushouts. The demonstration by Leifer [54] that action calculi possess them was hard, but in bigraphs the independence of placing and linking rendered it tractable, as expounded by Jensen and Milner [48]. This allowed those three authors [46–48, 56, 63, 65] and Bundgaard and Sassone [16] to recover a significant amount of the theory of several calculi, via their embedding in bigraphs.

S-categories appear to be well-suited to the work of this book. However, they can be recast in the context of enriched category theory [50, 53]. Technically, they are equivalent to categories enriched over the category of species of structures [49] with respect to the multiplication monoidal structure.[2] The notion of relative pushout has been generalised to groupoidal 2-categories by Sassone and Sobocinski [74, 75], thus again recasting bigraphs within a standard categorical framework.

As abstract bigraphs form a symmetric partial monoidal category, it has been important to examine their equational theory. Milner [64] provided a sound and complete axiomatisation of the structure of pure bigraphs; it is rather simple, due to the independence of placing and linking. This axiomatisation has been refined by Damgaard and Birkedal [26] for a version of the binding bigraphs outlined in Section 11.3; it remains sound and complete. I conjecture that this result can also be adapted to concrete bigraphs.

Hennessy and Milner [40] demonstrated in 1985 that process calculi are closely associated with modal logics; for example, two processes are bisimilar if and only if they satisfy the same sentences in such a logic. A first step has been taken for bigraphs in this direction by Conforti, Macedonio and Sassone [23, 24]. For a spatial model such as bigraphs, an attractive goal is a logic that expresses properties such as 'Mary has not visited this room before', which depend upon tracking the identity of individuals through time, as briefly discussed in Section 11.1.

Grohmann and Miculan have generalised bigraphs to *directed bigraphs* [37],

---

[2] I am grateful to Marcelo Fiore for making me aware of this.

whose link graphs are self-dual; that is, their link graphs have a symmetric structure with regard to composition. Importantly, RPOs still exist. The mild extra complexity of directed bigraphs adds expressive power; indeed, the authors show how to encode the fusion calculus of Parrow and Victor [69], which cannot be handled directly in bigraphs.

Implementation and application The modelling of large-scale informatic systems is still at an experimental stage. Moreover, as with programming languages, the useful experiments are those carried out with real applications, involving real users and an assessment of their experience. With this in mind, a group [9] led by Birkedal at the IT University (ITU) of Copenhagen has embarked on the design and implementation of a bigraphical language for specification and programming, and its implementation as a simulator. As with many languages, the workhorse for the implementation is a matching algorithm, in this case for bigraphs; the implemented algorithm is based upon specification by an inference system [12]. The first experiments with the language are being carried out in the (ITU) laboratory, on topics including ubiquitous computing [10], context-aware systems [11], mobile resources [15] and business processes [17, 82]; the authors include Birkedal, Bundgaard, Damgaard, Debois, Elsborg, Glenstrup, Hildebrandt, Niss and Olsen.

It is worth giving a little detail about one such experiment, involving *location-awareness*, a special case of context-awareness. A location-aware system maintains a record of the physical location of agents via input from hardware sensors; it is then able to answer queries from agents such as 'where is device X?'. This can be regarded as a refinement of the simple example of a built environment used in Example 1.2. The model used, called a *Plato-graphical model* [11], combines three BRSs into one; the first W ('world') models the built environment, the second L ('locality') models the information about location reported by sensors in W, and the third A models an application that queries L about W. A large class of real location systems and applications, such as the Lancaster tour guide [21], can be represented and simulated. Experiments are continuing.

As explained in Chapter 6, most applications of bigraphs involve not only a signature $\mathcal{K}$, but also a sorting discipline that determines the admissible bigraphs over $\mathcal{K}$. Sorting disciplines for process calculi are given in theoretical papers already cited [48, 56, 65], and have also been studied for polyadic π-calculus by Bundgaard and Sassone [16] and reactive systems by Birkedal, Debois and Hildebrandt [14].

Finally, inspired by pioneering work [72] on applying process calculi to biology, a stochastic treatment of the behaviour of bigraphs is proposed by Krivine, Milner and Troina [51], in the spirit of the stochastic κ-calculus by Danos *et al.* [27]; it associates a stochastic rate to each reaction rule. This work shows how rates for labelled transitions can be derived uniformly, and applies the model to cell behaviour (membrane budding) in biology. Many applications of bigraphs, including biology, are non-deterministic; thus the stochastic treatment has special relevance to implementation, in order to yield useful simulation.

Conclusion It can be seen from this work that the bigraph model is being developed through a combination of mathematical intuition and experiment. The experiment involves real interactive systems – both natural, as in biology, and artificial as in ubiquitous computing and business systems. The model tests the hypothesis that the simple ideas of *placing* and *linking*, both physical and metaphorical, unite the mathematical foundation of interactive systems with their applications.

Appendices

Appendix A

Technical detail

A.1 Support translation

Recall that S is an infinite repertoire of support elements. This appendix complements Definition 2.13 by axiomatising the notion of support translation introduced there.

Definition A.1 (support translation) For any arrow $f : I \to J$ in an s-category `C and any partial injective map $\rho : S \rightharpoonup S$ whose domain includes $|f|$, there is an arrow $\rho \cdot f : I \to J$ called a *support translation* of f. Support translations satisfy the following equations when both sides are defined:

$$
\begin{array}{ll}
\text{(T1)} \quad \rho \cdot \mathrm{id}_I = \mathrm{id}_I & \text{(T5)} \quad \rho \cdot f = (\rho \upharpoonright |f|) \cdot f \\
\text{(T2)} \quad \rho \cdot (g \circ f) = \rho \cdot g \circ \rho \cdot f & \text{(T6)} \quad |\rho \cdot f| = \rho(|f|) \\
\text{(T3)} \quad \mathrm{Id}_{|f|} \cdot f = f & \text{(T7)} \quad \rho \cdot (f \otimes g) = \rho \cdot f \otimes \rho \cdot g\,. \\
\text{(T4)} \quad (\rho' \circ \rho) \cdot f = \rho' \cdot (\rho \cdot f) &
\end{array}
$$

Two arrows f and g are *support-equivalent*, written $f \mathrel{\hat\simeq} g$, if $\rho \cdot f = g$ for some support translation ρ. □

Readers familiar with category theory will recognise these axioms as closely related to the conditions governing 2-cells in a 2-category. More precisely, support translations correspond to the isomorphisms between arrows. *Groupoidal* 2-categories (where all 2-cells are isomorphisms) have been proposed as an alternative basis for bigraphs, and that work continues. They differ from our s-categories, since the latter associate a support set with each arrow. At the same time, s-categories are convenient for many proofs, and support provides a direct means of tracking the history of individual agents (Section 11.1); it plays a role similar to labels and residuation in the λ-calculus.

A.2 Public versus private names

In this appendix we explain the decision to represent names alphabetically, drawn from an infinite alphabet $\mathcal{X}$, rather than by ordinals. Let us call $\mathcal{X}$ the *public names*.

The alternative to public names is to use interfaces $I = \langle k, m \rangle$ where k indexes places as before, and $m = \{0, \ldots, m-1\}$ is a finite ordinal indexing names, instead of a finite set $X \subset \mathcal{X}$ of public names. These ordinal names are no longer public. Let us call them *private names*; they are private to an interface I, and therefore private to each bigraph having I as its inner or outer face.

The immediate consequence of adopting private names is that the tensor product of two interfaces, and therefore of two abstract bigraphs, is always defined. For such a pair of $F_i : \langle k_i, m_i \rangle \to \langle \ell_i, n_i \rangle$, the tensor product becomes

$$F_0 \otimes F_1 : I \to J \, ,$$
$$\text{where } I = \langle k_0 + k_1, m_0 + m_1 \rangle \text{ and } J = \langle \ell_0 + \ell_1, n_0 + n_1 \rangle \, .$$

This alternative has two advantages. First, there is simplicity in using the same regime for indexing names as for indexing regions. But the major advantage is that, by conforming exactly to the standard notion of symmetric monoidal category, it allows the theory of the latter to be applied to bigraphs without any adaptation.

Why then should we adopt our present regime of a repertoire $\mathcal{X}$ of public names? First, the partial definedness of tensor product complicates our theory only slightly. For example the proof that our axiomatisation of bigraphical structure is sound and complete [64], as asserted in Theorem 3.6, is rendered no more complex. Second – a pragmatic advantage – the use of different indexing regimes for names and regions adds notational clarity in technical manipulations.

Third, public names yield a major advantage in deriving operations that are standard in process calculi, especially the parallel and merge products ' $\|$ ' and ' $|$ ' and the nesting operation '.' as detailed in Chapter 3. For example, to juxtapose in parallel a set $a_1, \ldots, a_n$ of agents sharing certain channels for interaction, one requires only a single derived product ' $\|$ ' that is commutative and associative, and one writes

$$a_1 \| \cdots \| a_n \, .$$

On the other hand, if names are private then such a juxtaposition must be written

$$\sigma \circ (a_1 \otimes \cdots \otimes a_n) \, ,$$

where σ is a specific substitution (a map of finite ordinals). To distribute σ over this product requires a hierarchy of smaller substitutions. One can avoid explicit mention of substitutions, but only by deriving a family of parallel products, each composing different substitutions with a tensor product.

Thus, although the embedding of process calculi in bigraphs can probably be achieved using private names, it will be less direct and may be cumbersome. It is remarkable that, though process calculi differ in other ways, they appear to agree in the efficacy of public names. Therefore, by adopting these also for bigraphs, we lower the barrier between it and the existing process theories. This serves two main purposes: first, to investigate what is fundamental to those theories, and second, to serve as a tool based upon those theories for design, analysis and programming.

For purposes closer to categorical mathematics, it should not be hard to reformulate bigraph theory in terms of private names.

A.3 RPOs for link graphs

In this appendix we prove the validity of the construction of RPOs for link graphs.

Lemma 5.7 *As defined in Construction 5.5, $(\vec{B}, B)$ is a bound for $\vec{A}$ relative to $\vec{D}$.*

Proof To prove $B_0 \circ A_0 = B_1 \circ A_1$, by symmetry it will be enough to consider cases for $p \in W \uplus P_0$, and for the value of $A_0(p)$.

Case $p \in P_0 \setminus P_2$, $A_0(p) = e \in E_0$. Then $(B_1 \circ A_1)(p) = B_1(p) = D_1(p) = (D_1 \circ A_1)(p) = (D_0 \circ A_0)(p) = A_0(p) = (B_0 \circ A_0)(p)$.

Case $p \in P_0 \setminus P_2$, $A_0(p) = x_0 \in X_0$. Then $(B_1 \circ A_1)(p) = B_1(p) = \widehat{x_0} = B_0(x_0) = (B_0 \circ A_0)(p)$.

Case $q \in W \uplus P_2$, $A_0(q) = e \in E_0 \setminus E_2$. Then $(B_0 \circ A_0)(q) = A_0(q) = e$. Also $(D_1 \circ A_1)(q) = (D_0 \circ A_0)(q) = e$, so for some $x_1 \in X_1$ we have $A_1(q) = x_1$ and $D_1(x_1) = e$, hence $x_1 \notin X_1'$. Then $(B_1 \circ A_1)(q) = B_1(x_1) = D_1(x_1) = e$.

Case $q \in W \uplus P_2$, $A_0(q) = e \in E_2$. Then $(D_1 \circ A_1)(q) = (D_0 \circ A_0)(q) = e$, so also $A_1(q) = e$. Hence $(B_1 \circ A_1)(q) = e = (B_0 \circ A_0)(q)$.

Case $q \in W \uplus P_2$, $A_0(q) = x_0 \in X_0'$. Then $D_0(x_0) \in E_3 \uplus Z$, and so $(D_1 \circ A_1)(q) = (D_0 \circ A_0)(q) \in E_3 \uplus Z$; hence for some $x_1 \in X_1'$ we have $A_1(q) = x_1$ and $D_1(x_1) = D_0(x_0)$. Hence $(B_0 \circ A_0)(q) = B_0(x_0) = D_0(x_0) = D_1(x_1) = B_1(x_1) = (B_1 \circ A_1)(q)$.

Case $q \in W \uplus P_2$, $A_0(q) = x_0 \in X_0 \setminus X_0'$. Then $D_0(x_0) = e \in E_1 \setminus E_2$; hence $(D_1 \circ A_1)(q) = (D_0 \circ A_0)(q) = e$, so $A_1(q) = e$. So $(B_1 \circ A_1)(q) = e = D_0(r_0) = B_0(x_0) = (B_0 \circ A_0)(q)$.

We now prove $B \circ B_0 = D_0$ by case analysis.

Case $x \in X_0'$. Then $(B \circ B_0)(x) = B(\widehat{0, x}) = D_0(x)$.

Case $x \in X_0 \setminus X_0'$. Then $B_0(x) = D_0(x) \in E_0 \setminus E_2$, hence $(B \circ B_0)(x) = D_0(x)$.

Case $p \in P_1 \backslash P_2, D_0(p) \in E_1 \backslash E_2$. Since $D_0 \circ A_0 = D_1 \circ A_1$ we have $A_1(p) \notin X_1$, so $B_0(p) = D_0(p) \in E_1 \setminus E_2$; hence $(B \circ B_0)(p) = B_0(p) = D_0(p)$.

Case $p \in P_1 \setminus P_2, D_0(p) \in E_3 \uplus Z$. Since $D_0 \circ A_0 = D_1 \circ A_1$ there exists $x \in X_1$ with $A_1(p) = x$; moreover we readily deduce $x \in X_1'$, so $B_0(p) = \widehat{1, x}$. Hence $(B \circ B_0)(p) = B(\widehat{1, x}) = D_1(x) = (D_1 \circ A_1)(p) = (D_0 \circ A_0)(p) = D_0(p)$.

Case $p \in P_3$. Then $(B \circ B_0)(p) = B(p) = D_0(p)$. $\square$

Theorem 5.8 (RPOs in link graphs) ``LG`(K)$ has RPOs; that is, whenever a span $\vec{A}$ of link graphs has a bound $\vec{D}$, there exists an RPO $(\vec{B}, B)$ for $\vec{A}$ to $\vec{D}$. Moreover Construction 5.5 yields such an RPO.*

Proof   We have already proved that the triple $(\vec{B}, B)$ built in Construction 5.5 is an RPO candidate. Now consider any other candidate $(\vec{C}, C)$ with intervening interface Y. C_i has nodes $V_{\overline{i}} \setminus V_2 \uplus V_4$ $(i = 0, 1)$ and C has nodes V_5, where $V_4 \uplus V_5 = V_3$. We have to construct a unique mediating arrow $\widehat{C}$, as shown in the diagram.

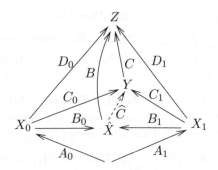

We define $\widehat{C}$ with nodes V_4 as follows:

$$\text{for } \hat{x} = \widehat{i, x} \in \hat{X} : \quad \widehat{C}(\hat{x}) \overset{\text{def}}{=} C_i(x)$$
$$\text{for } p \in P_4 : \qquad \widehat{C}(p) \overset{\text{def}}{=} C_i(p) .$$

Note that the equations $\widehat{C} \circ B_i = C_i$ $(i = 0, 1)$ determine $\widehat{C}$ uniquely, since they force the above definition. We now prove the equations (considering $i = 0$):

Case $x \in X_0'$. Then $(\widehat{C} \circ B_0)(x) = \widehat{C}(\widehat{0, x}) = C_0(x)$.

Case $x \in X_0 \setminus X_0'$. Then $D_0(x) \in E_1 \setminus E_2$, so $B_0(x) = D_0(x)$, hence $(\widehat{C} \circ B_0)(x) = D_0(x)$. Also since $C \circ C_0 = D_0 \in E_1 \backslash E_2$ we have $C_0(x) = D_0(x)$.

Case $p \in P_1 \setminus P_2, D_0(p) \in E_1 \setminus E_2$. Since $D_0 \circ A_0 = D_1 \circ A_1$ we have $A_1(p) \notin$

X_1, so $B_0(p) = D_0(p)$, hence $(\widehat{C} \circ B_0)(p) = D_0(p)$. Also $C_0(p) = (C \circ C_0)(p) = D_0(p)$.

Case $p \in P_1 \setminus P_2$, $D_0(p) \in E_3 \uplus Z$. Then $A_1(v) = x \in X_1'$ with $D_1(x) = D_0(p)$, and $B_0(p) = \widehat{1, x}$. So $(\widehat{C} \circ B_0)(p) = \widehat{C}(\widehat{1, x}) = C_1(x) = (C_0 \circ A_0)(p) = C_0(p)$.

Case $p \in P_4$. Then $(\widehat{C} \circ B_0)(p) = \widehat{C}(p) = C_0(p)$.

It remains to prove that $C \circ \widehat{C} = B$. The following cases suffice:

Case $\hat{x} = \widehat{0, x}$, $x \in X$, $B(\hat{x}) \in E_4$. Then $(C \circ \widehat{C})(\hat{x}) = \widehat{C}(\hat{x}) = C_0(x) = D_0(x) = B(\hat{x})$.

Case $\hat{x} = \widehat{0, x} \in X$, $B(\hat{x}) \in E_5 \uplus Z$. Then $D_0(x) = B(\hat{x}) \in E_5 \uplus Z$, so for some $y \in Y$ we have $C_0(x) = y$ and $C(y) = B(\hat{x})$. But by definition $\widehat{C}(\hat{x}) = y$, so $(C \circ \widehat{C})(\hat{x}) = C(y) = (C \circ C_0)(x) = D_0(x) = B(\hat{x})$.

Case $p \in P_4$, $B(v) \in E_4$. Then $(C \circ \widehat{C})(p) = \widehat{C}(p) = C_0(p) = D_0(p) = B(p)$.

Case $p \in P_4$, $B(p) \in E_5 \uplus Z$. Then $B(p) = D_0(p) = C(y)$, where $C_0(p) = y \in Y$, and by definition $\widehat{C}(p) = C_0(p)$, so $(C \circ \widehat{C})(p) = C(y) = B(p)$.

Case $p \in P_5$. Then $(C \circ \widehat{C})(p) = C(p) = D_0(p) = B(p)$.

Hence $\widehat{C}$ is the required unique mediator; so $(\vec{B}, B)$ is an RPO. $\qquad \square$

A.4 Quotient of a transition system

In this appendix we prove Theorem 7.23, justifying the transfer of a transition system and its bisimilarity from a concrete WRS to its quotient abstract WRS.

Theorem 7.23 (bisimilarity induced by quotient) *Let* $`\mathbf{C}$ *be equipped with a raw or contextual transition system* $\mathcal{L}$ *that respects a structural congruence* $\equiv$. *Denote the quotient* $`\mathbf{C}/\equiv$ *by* $\mathbf{C}$. *Then the following hold for* $[\![\mathcal{L}]\!]$:

(1) $a \sim b$ *in* $`\mathbf{C}$ *iff* $[\![a]\!] \sim [\![b]\!]$ *in* $\mathbf{C}$.

(2) *If bisimilarity is a congruence in* $`\mathbf{C}$ *then it is a congruence in* $\mathbf{C}$.

Proof We treat only the contextual case; the raw case is simpler.

$(1)\Rightarrow$ We establish in $\mathbf{C}$ the bisimulation

$$\mathcal{R} = \{([\![a]\!], [\![b]\!]) \mid a \sim b\} \,.$$

Let $a \sim b$ in $`\mathbf{C}$, and let $p = [\![a]\!]$, $q = [\![b]\!]$ and $p \xrightarrow{g}_{\tilde{\imath}} p'$ in $\mathbf{C}$. By definition of the induced transition system, the triple $(p, g, p')$ has an $[\![\cdot]\!]$-preimage $(a_1, f_1, a_1')$ such that $a_1 \xrightarrow{f_1}_{\tilde{\imath}} a_1'$ in $`\mathbf{C}$. Now, since the labels in a TS are closed under $\simeq$, there exists a label $(f, \tilde{\imath})$ with $f \simeq f_1$ and both $f \circ a$ and $f \circ b$ defined. Hence by respect, since $f \simeq f_1$ implies $f \equiv f_1$, there exists $a' \equiv a'_1$ such that $a \xrightarrow{f}_{\tilde{\imath}} a'$.

Since $a \sim b$ and $f \circ b$ is defined, there exists b' such that $b \xrightarrow{f}_{\tilde{\imath}} b'$ and $a' \sim b'$. It follows that $q \xrightarrow{g}_{\tilde{\imath}} q'$ in $\mathbf{C}$, where $q' = [\![b']\!]$ and $(p', q') \in \mathcal{R}$, so we are done.

$(1){\Leftarrow}$ We establish in $`\mathbf{C}$ the bisimulation

$$\mathcal{S} = \{(a, b) \mid [\![a]\!] \sim [\![b]\!]\} \ .$$

Let $[\![a]\!] \sim [\![b]\!]$ in $\mathbf{C}$, and let $p = [\![a]\!]$, $q = [\![b]\!]$ where $a \xrightarrow{f}_{\tilde{\imath}} a'$ in $`\mathbf{C}$ with $f \circ b$ defined. Then $p \xrightarrow{g}_{\tilde{\imath}} p'$ in $\mathbf{C}$, where $g = [\![f]\!]$ and $p' = [\![a']\!]$. So for some q' we have $q \xrightarrow{g}_{\tilde{\imath}} q'$ with $p' \sim q'$.

This transition must arise from a transition $b_1 \xrightarrow{f_1}_{\tilde{\imath}} b'_1$ in $`\mathbf{C}$, where $q = [\![b_1]\!]$, $g = [\![f_1]\!]$ and $q' = [\![b'_1]\!]$. But then $b_1 \equiv b$ and $f_1 \equiv f$; we also have $f \circ b$ defined, and $\mathcal{L}$ respects $\equiv$, so we can find b' for which $b \xrightarrow{f}_{\tilde{\imath}} b'$ and $b'_1 \equiv b'$. But $(a', b') \in \mathcal{S}$, so we are done.

(2) Assume that bisimilarity in $`\mathbf{C}$ is a congruence. In $\mathbf{C}$, let $p \sim q$ with $p, q : I$, and let $r : I \to J$ be a context with $r \circ p$ and $r \circ q$ defined. Then since $[\![\cdot]\!]$ is surjective on each homset, there exist $a, b : I$ and $c : I \to J$ in $`\mathbf{C}$ with $p = [\![a]\!]$, $q = [\![b]\!]$ and $r = [\![c]\!]$; moreover, since $c \simeq c' \Rightarrow [\![c]\!] = [\![c']\!]$, c can be chosen so that $c \circ a$ and $c \circ b$ are defined.

From $(1){\Leftarrow}$ we have $a \sim b$, hence by assumption $c \circ a \sim c \circ b$. Applying the functor $[\![\cdot]\!]$ we have from $(1){\Rightarrow}$ that $r \circ p \sim r \circ q$ in $\mathbf{C}$, as required. $\qquad \square$

A.5 Unambiguity of labels

In this appendix we prove that, under certain conditions, prime transition labels are unambiguous, i.e. a label cannot belong to both an engaged and a disengaged transition. We first need a lemma that characterises prime disengaged transitions.

Lemma A.2 *Let $a \xrightarrow{L} a'$ be a prime disengaged transition, based on a parametric redex R that is simple and unary. Let $a : \langle X \rangle$, and let $r = R.(d_0 \otimes \cdots \otimes d_{m-1})$ be the underlying ground redex. Then*

(1) The outer nodes of L are those of R.

(2) The node-set of a is non-empty and included in that of d_i for some $i \in n$.

(3) The single site of L is guarded.

(4) No $x \in X$ is linked to any port in L.

Proof For (1), use $|R| \subseteq |L| \subseteq |r|$, with R guarding. For (2), recall that if $|a| \cap |r| = \emptyset$ then the IPO would be tensorial, hence a' non-prime, contra hypothesis.

For (3), use (2) and the fact that R is guarding. For (4), appeal to the IPO construction and each d_i discrete. $\qquad\Box$

Now, using the notions of *split* and *tight redex* from Definition 3.19, we prove:

Proposition 8.14 (unambiguous label) *Let L be the label of a prime transition in* MT, *in a safe BRS where every redex is simple, unary and tight. Then the label L is unambiguous.*

Proof   Suppose to the contrary that some L-transition is disengaged, but that $b \overset{L}{\longrightarrow} b'$ is engaged with underlying ground redex $s = S.d$ such that (b, s) has IPO (L, E). We shall derive a contradiction.

Let $b : \langle X \rangle$. Because L is the label of some prime disengaged transition, it satisfies the conditions in Lemma A.2; thus its node-set is non-empty. Now each node of L is a node of s; in particular each outermost node of L must be an outermost node of S, since $L \circ b = E \circ s$ and S is guarding. So $|S| \cap |L| \neq \emptyset$. Also, $|S| \cap |b| \neq \emptyset$ since the transition is engaged.

Thus (L, b) is a unary split for S. By assumption this split is tight, hence some node of b is linked via X to some node of L. But this contradicts Lemma A.2(4), completing our proof that the transition of b is disengaged. $\qquad\Box$

A.6 Faithfulness of engaged transitions

This appendix proves Theorem 8.19, asserting the faithfulness of engaged transitions for prime agents in a nice concrete BRS `BG$(\Sigma, \mathcal{R})$. Thus, in an interface the regions and names may have place sorts and link sorts respectively. As in Chapter 8, we avoid heavy notation by leaving these implicit. Occasionally we need to pull results from the unsorted BRS to the sorted one, back along the forgetful functor $\mathcal{U} :$ `BG$(\Sigma) \to$ `BG$(\mathcal{K})$, where $\mathcal{K}$ is the basic signature underlying Σ.

We first show that, for prime a, if we apply an affine instantiation $\overline{\eta}$ to $G \circ a$ then the result has a form independent of a.

Proposition A.3 (affine instantiation) *Let $G : \langle X \rangle \to \langle m, Z \rangle$ be a context, and let $\eta : n \to m$ be an injective map. Then:*

> *either there exists $C : \langle X \rangle \to \langle n, Z \rangle$ such that $\overline{\eta}(G \circ a) \asymp C \circ a$ for all a ;*
> *or there exists a ground $c : \langle n, Z \rangle$ such that $\overline{\eta}(G \circ a) \asymp c$ for all a .*

Proof   Since G has unary inner face, by Proposition 3.9 we can express it as

$$G = \mu \circ (\mathrm{id}_X \otimes d_0 \otimes \cdots \otimes d_{k-1} \otimes D \otimes d_{k+1} \otimes \cdots \otimes d_{m-1})$$

for some $k \in m$ and some linking $\mu : X \uplus Y \to Z$, where $d_i : \langle Y_i \rangle$ ($i \neq k$) are all discrete, $D : 1 \to \langle Y_k \rangle$ is discrete and $Y = \biguplus_{i \in m} Y_i$.

Now any $a : \langle X \rangle$ can be expressed as $a = \lambda \circ d$ for some linking $\lambda : W \to X$ and discrete $d : \langle W \rangle$. Then we can express the composition $G \circ a$ as follows:

$$G \circ a = \mu \circ (\lambda \otimes \mathrm{id}_Y) \circ (d_0 \otimes \cdots \otimes d_{k-1} \otimes d_k \otimes d_{k+1} \otimes \cdots \otimes d_{m-1})$$

where $d_k \stackrel{\text{def}}{=} (\mathrm{id}_W \otimes D) \circ d$; its names are $W \uplus Y_k$. Since d_k is discrete this expression for $G \circ a$ is a DNF, and therefore by Definition 8.3 its instance by $\overline{\eta}$ is

$$\overline{\eta}(G \circ a) \simeq \mu \circ (\lambda \otimes \mathrm{id}_Y) \circ (d_{\eta(0)} \otimes \cdots \otimes d_{\eta(n-1)}) \ .$$

Since η is injective the $d_{\eta(j)}$ have disjoint name-sets, so may be combined by $\otimes$ rather than by $\parallel$ as in Definition 8.3. Since η may not be surjective there are two cases:

(1) $\eta(\ell) = k$ for some $\ell \in n$. Then we may rewrite the instance as

$$
\begin{aligned}
\overline{\eta}(G \circ a) \ &\simeq \ \mu \circ (\lambda \otimes \mathrm{id}_Y) \circ (d_{\eta(0)} \otimes \cdots \otimes d_k \otimes \cdots \otimes d_{\eta(n-1)}) \\
&= \ \mu \circ (\lambda \otimes \mathrm{id}_Y) \circ (d_{\eta(0)} \otimes \cdots \otimes ((\mathrm{id}_W \otimes D) \circ d) \otimes \cdots \otimes d_{\eta(n-1)}) \\
&= \ C \circ a
\end{aligned}
$$

where $C \stackrel{\text{def}}{=} \mu \circ (d_{\eta(0)} \otimes \cdots \otimes (\mathrm{id}_X \otimes D) \otimes \cdots \otimes d_{\eta(n-1)})$ is independent of a.

(2) $\eta(\ell) \neq k$ for all $\ell \in n$. Then the inner names W of $\lambda : W \to X$ are not among the names of $d_{\eta(0)} \otimes \cdots \otimes d_{\eta(n-1)}$. But it is easily seen that $\lambda \circ W \simeq X$; hence

$$
\begin{aligned}
\overline{\eta}(G \circ a) \ &\simeq \ \mu \circ (\lambda \otimes \mathrm{id}_Y) \circ (d_{\eta(0)} \otimes \cdots \otimes d_{\eta(n-1)}) \\
&\simeq \ c \stackrel{\text{def}}{=} \mu \circ (X \otimes \mathrm{id}_Y) \circ (d_{\eta(0)} \otimes \cdots \otimes d_{\eta(n-1)})
\end{aligned}
$$

which is independent of a as required. $\square$

We continue with a lemma that lifts an IPO property from unsorted to sorted bigraphs; it is that certain spans whose members have disjoint support have an IPO that is tensorial.

Lemma A.4 *In* `BG(Σ)*, with Σ safe, let $A : I' \to I$ and $B : J' \to J$ be both hard, with disjoint supports, and let B be open with no idle names. Let the span $(A \otimes \mathrm{id}_{J'}, \mathrm{id}_{I'} \otimes B)$ have an IPO (C, D). Then, up to an iso at their common outer face K, we have $C = \mathrm{id}_I \otimes B$ and $D = A \otimes \mathrm{id}_J$.*

Proof   We use many safety properties from Definition 4.6. Let $\mathcal{U} :$ `BG($\Sigma$) $\to$ `BG($\mathcal{K}$) be the sorting functor. Since $\mathcal{U}$ preserves RPOs and identities, it also preserves IPOs. So $\mathcal{U}(C, D)$ is an IPO for the span $\mathcal{U}(A \otimes \mathrm{id}_{J'}, \mathrm{id}_{I'} \otimes B)$. Also $\mathcal{U}$ preserves the properties assumed for A and B. Since both $\mathcal{U}(A)$ and $\mathcal{U}(B)$ are hard, no other IPO for the span can arise from place elisions, and since $\mathcal{U}(B)$ is open with no idle names, none can arise from link elisions either. Hence, up to isomorphism, the IPO is unique, and must be the tensorial IPO defined in Corollary 5.21; thus, for some iso ι' we have

$$\iota' \circ \mathcal{U}(C) = \mathrm{id} \otimes \mathcal{U}(B) \text{ and } \iota' \circ \mathcal{U}(D) = \mathcal{U}(A) \otimes \mathrm{id} \,.$$

Now ι' has inner face $\mathcal{U}(K)$, and since $\mathcal{U}$ creates isos there exists an iso ι with inner face K such that $\mathcal{U}(\iota) = \iota'$. We deduce

$$\mathcal{U}(\iota \circ C) = \mathrm{id} \otimes \mathcal{U}(B) \text{ and } \mathcal{U}(\iota \circ D) = \mathcal{U}(A) \otimes \mathrm{id} \,.$$

But $\mathcal{U}$ reflects products, so $\iota \circ C = \mathrm{id} \otimes B$ and $\iota \circ D = A \otimes \mathrm{id}$ as required. □

We next consider the IPO underlying a minimal transition $a \xrightarrow{L}_{\widetilde{\imath}} a'$ with redex R. It can be decomposed into an IPO pair, as shown in the diagram, with R simple and d discrete.

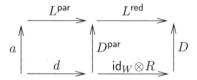

From now on we shall call a transition *simple* when its underlying redex is simple. We need three lemmas about simple minimal transitions that are disengaged.

Lemma A.5 *Let the diagram underlie a disengaged simple minimal transition. Then $D^{\mathsf{par}} = D' \otimes \mathrm{id}_m$ for some D', up to iso, where m is the inner face of R.*

Proof Since $|D^{\mathsf{par}}| \subseteq |a|$ we also have $|D^{\mathsf{par}}| \cap |R| = \emptyset$. Let K be the outer face of D^{par}. It is enough to prove, for each site $i \in m$, that (1) $D^{\mathsf{par}}(i) = k$ is a root in K, and (2) i has no siblings in D^{par}.
(1) Since R is guarding, $R(i) = v$ for some node v, hence $(L^{\mathsf{red}} \circ D^{\mathsf{par}})(i) = v$. But v is not in D^{par} by assumption, so $D^{\mathsf{par}}(i) = k$ and $L^{\mathsf{red}}(k) = v$ for some root k.
(2) Now suppose i has a sibling, i.e. $D^{\mathsf{par}}(w) = k$ for some site or node $w \neq i$. Then we have $(L^{\mathsf{red}} \circ D^{\mathsf{par}})(w) = v$, whence also $R(w) = v$. If w is a site this contradicts R inner-injective; if it is a node then it contradicts $|D^{\mathsf{par}}| \cap |R| = \emptyset$. Hence no such w can exist. This completes the proof. □

Lemma A.6 *Let the diagram underlie a disengaged simple minimal transition based upon (R, R', η), where a is prime and hard with $|a| \cap |d| \neq \emptyset$. Then D and a' take the following form up to iso, where $\lambda : W \to W'$ is a linking:*

$$L^{\mathsf{red}} = \mathrm{id}_{W'} \otimes R \,, \quad D = \lambda \otimes \mathrm{id}_J \quad \text{and} \quad a' = (\mathrm{id}_{W'} \otimes R') \circ \overline{\eta}(L^{\mathsf{par}} \circ a) \,.$$

Proof   From Lemma A.5 we find that D^{par} takes the form $D^{\text{par}} = D' \otimes \text{id}_m$ up to iso, where D' has domain W and m is the inner width of R.

First we claim that D' has no nodes. For since d is discrete there exists a node $u \in |a| \cap |d|$. If there exists also a node $v \in |D'|$ then $v \in |a|$, hence (since a is prime) u, v would be in the same region of $L^{\text{par}} \circ a$ but different regions of $D^{\text{par}} \circ d$, contra the commutation of the left-hand square.

Now any root in D' would be idle, contradicting a hard (since the left square is an IPO). Hence D' has no roots, so $D' = \lambda : W \to W'$, a linking, and $D^{\text{par}} = \lambda \otimes \text{id}_m$.

Now consider the right-hand IPO. D^{par} is hard, since a is hard, and R is hard and open since it is a parametric redex. Thus we may apply Lemma A.4, and this immediately yields the first two equations. For the third:

$$\begin{aligned}
a' &= D \circ (\text{id}_W \otimes R') \circ \overline{\eta}(d) \\
&= (\text{id}_{W'} \otimes R') \circ (\lambda \otimes \text{id}_{I'}) \circ \overline{\eta}(d) \\
(*) \quad &= (\text{id}_{W'} \otimes R') \circ \overline{\eta}((\lambda \otimes \text{id}_I) \circ d) \\
&= (\text{id}_{W'} \otimes R') \circ \overline{\eta}(L^{\text{par}} \circ a)
\end{aligned}$$

where at $(*)$ we commute an instantiation with a linking, by Proposition 8.4. $\square$

Lemma A.7 *Let the span* (a, d) *have a bound* $(D, \lambda \otimes \text{id}_m)$, *where* a *is hard and* d, D *are discrete. Then the bound is an IPO.*

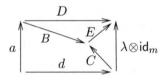

Proof   Let (B, C, E) be an RPO for (a, d) relative to $(D, \lambda \otimes \text{id}_m)$. Then (B, C) is an IPO for (a, d), so it will be enough to prove E to be an iso.

Consider place graphs: C^P has no idle roots since a is hard; also $E^P \circ C^P = \text{id}$, so E^P is a place iso. Now consider link graphs: B^L is discrete since d^L is so, and has the same nodes as D^L; hence E^L is a link iso.

It follows that E is an iso, completing the proof. $\square$

We can now prove the faithfulness theorem.

Theorem 8.19 (engaged transitions are faithful) *In a nice BRS, let* PE *be a prime engaged transition system whose agents are hard. Then*

(1) PE *is faithful to the minimal wide transition system* MT.

(2) $\sim_{\text{PE}}$ *is a congruence.*

Proof Since faithfulness means that $\sim_{PE} = \sim_{MT}$ when restricted to the agents of PE, (2) follows from (1) together with the congruence of $\sim_{MT}$. It remains to prove (1).

We know from Theorem 8.16 that PE is definite, and hence that $\sim_{MT} \subseteq \sim_{PE}$ on prime agents. For the converse, $\sim_{PE} \subseteq \sim_{MT}$, we shall show that

$$\mathcal{S} = \{(C \circ a_0, C \circ a_1) \mid a_0 \sim_{PE} a_1\} \cup \eqsim$$

is a bisimulation for MT up to support equivalence. We then obtain the main result by taking $C = \mathrm{id}$.

Suppose that $a_0 \sim_{PE} a_1$. Let $C \circ a_0 \xrightarrow{M}_{\tilde{\jmath}} b'_0$ be a transition of MT with $M \circ C \circ a_1$ defined. We must find b'_1 such that $C \circ a_1 \xrightarrow{M}_{\tilde{\jmath}} b'_1$ and $(b'_0, b'_1) \in \mathcal{S}^{\eqsim}$.

There exists a ground reaction rule (r_0, r'_0) and an IPO – the large square in diagram (a) below – underlying the given transition of $C \circ a_0$. Moreover E_0 is active, and if $\mathrm{width}(\mathrm{cod}(r_0)) = m$ then $\mathrm{width}(E_0)(m) = \tilde{\jmath}$ and $b'_0 \eqsim E_0 \circ r'_0$. By taking an RPO for (a_0, r_0) relative to $(M \circ C, E_0)$ we get two IPOs as shown in the diagram. Note that a_0 is prime, but $C \circ a_0$ and b'_0 may not be.

Now D_0 is active, so the lower IPO underlies a transition $a_0 \xrightarrow{L}_{\tilde{\imath}} a'_0 \overset{\mathrm{def}}{=} D_0 \circ r'_0$, where $\tilde{\imath} = \mathrm{width}(D_0)(m_0)$. Again, a'_0 may not be prime. Also E is active at $\tilde{\imath}$, and $b'_0 \eqsim E \circ a'_0$. Since $M \circ C \circ a_1$ is defined we deduce that $L \circ a_1$ is defined, and we proceed to show in three separate cases the existence of a transition $a_1 \xrightarrow{L}_{\tilde{\imath}} a'_1$, with underlying IPO as in diagram (b). (We cannot always infer such a transition for which $a'_0 \sim_{PE} a'_1$, even though $a_0 \sim_{PE} a_1$, since the transition of a_0 may not be engaged.) Substituting this IPO for the lower square in (a) then yields a transition

$$C \circ a_1 \xrightarrow{M}_{\tilde{\jmath}} b'_1 \overset{\mathrm{def}}{=} E \circ a'_1 \,.$$

In each case we shall verify that $(b'_0, b'_1) \in \mathcal{S}^{\eqsim}$, completing the proof of the theorem.

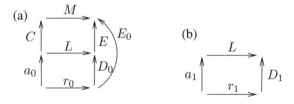

Case 1 The transition of a_0 is engaged.
Then since r_0 is prime, by considering the IPO (L, D_0) and the outer face of D_0 we find that a'_0 is prime, so the transition may be written $a_0 \xrightarrow{L} a'_0$ and lies in PE. Since $a_0 \sim_{PE} a_1$, there exists a transition $a_1 \xrightarrow{L} a'_1$ with $a'_0 \sim_{PE} a'_1$. This readily yields the required transition of $C \circ a_1$.

Case 2 $|a_0| \# |r_0|$.

Consider the lower IPO of (a). Since a_0 is hard, and r_0 both hard and open (since it is a ground redex), we may apply Lemma A.4 to obtain that up to iso

$$L = \mathrm{id} \otimes r_0 \quad \text{and} \quad D_0 = a_0 \otimes \mathrm{id} .$$

Then $a_0' \simeq (\mathrm{id} \otimes r_0') \circ a_0$. Taking $C' \overset{\text{def}}{=} E \circ (\mathrm{id} \otimes r_0')$ we have $b_0' \simeq C' \circ a_0$.

Now, since $L \circ a_1$ is defined, $|a_1| \# |r_0|$. So, taking $r_1 = r_0$ and $D_1 = a_1 \otimes \mathrm{id}$, we obtain again by Lemma A.4 that the diagram (b) is an IPO. Substitute it for the lower square in (a), yielding a transition $C \circ a_1 \xrightarrow{M}_{\tilde{j}} b_1' \overset{\text{def}}{=} E \circ a_1'$. Then $b_1' = C' \circ a_1$, so $(b_0', b_1') \in \mathcal{S}^{\simeq}$ as required.

Case 3 The transition of a_0 is not engaged, but $|a_0| \cap |r_0| \neq \emptyset$.

Then there is a rule $(R, R', \overline{\eta})$ with $|a_0| \# |R|$, and a discrete parameter d_0 such that

$$r_0 = (\mathrm{id}_{W_0} \otimes R) \circ d_0 \quad \text{and} \quad r_0' = (\mathrm{id}_{W_0} \otimes R') \circ \overline{\eta}(d_0) .$$

Assume $R : m \to J$. Since a_0 is prime, from Lemma A.6 we find that, up to isomorphism, the IPO pair underlying the transition of a_0 takes the form of diagram (c) below, and moreover that $a_0' = (\mathrm{id}_{W'} \otimes R') \circ \overline{\eta}(L^{\mathrm{par}} \circ a_0)$.

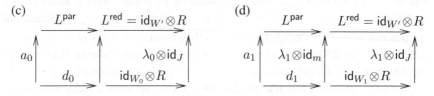

We seek a similar transition for a_1. First we claim that, since support equivalence respects transition, we may assume that $|a_1| \# |R|$. For we may translate the support of R, and hence of L, M and C, in the diagram underlying the assumed transition $C \circ a_0 \xrightarrow{M}_{\tilde{j}} b_0'$ without affecting its result b_0', since the latter is defined only up to $\simeq$. Moreover this support translation can achieve $|a_1| \# |R|$ while retaining $|a_0| \# |R|$ and $|d_0| \# |R|$.

Now consider $L^{\mathrm{par}} \circ a_1$. By Proposition 3.9 there is a linking $\lambda_1 : W_1 \to W'$ and discrete $d_1 : W_1 \otimes m$ such that $L^{\mathrm{par}} \circ a_1 = (\lambda_1 \otimes \mathrm{id}_m) \circ d_1$. Also, since d_0 is discrete, we know by Proposition 5.19 that L^{par} is discrete; hence $(L^{\mathrm{par}}, \lambda_1 \otimes \mathrm{id}_m)$ is an IPO for (a_1, d_1) by Lemma A.7. This is the left-hand square in diagram (d).

By Lemma A.4 the right-hand square of (d) is also an IPO. Since $|L^{\mathrm{par}}| \# |L^{\mathrm{red}}|$ and $|d_1| \# |R|$, we may paste the squares together to form a larger IPO. Therefore, by manipulations as in Lemma A.6,

$$
\begin{aligned}
a_1 \xrightarrow{L}_{\tilde{i}} a_1' \quad &\overset{\text{def}}{=} \quad (\lambda_1 \otimes \mathrm{id}_J) \circ (\mathrm{id}_{W_1} \otimes R') \circ \overline{\eta}(d_1) \\
&= \quad (\mathrm{id}_{W'} \otimes R') \circ \overline{\eta}(L^{\mathrm{par}} \circ a_1) .
\end{aligned}
$$

As in the previous case, this yields a transition $C \circ a_1 \xrightarrow{M}_{\tilde{j}} b_1' \overset{\text{def}}{=} E \circ a_1'$. We now have

$$(b_0', b_1') = (\, F \circ \overline{\eta}(L^{\text{par}} \circ a_0),\ F \circ \overline{\eta}(L^{\text{par}} \circ a_1)\,)$$

for a certain context F, where $a_0 \sim_{\text{PE}} a_1$ (both prime). Since $\overline{\eta}$ is affine, we can appeal to Proposition A.3 to find two cases. In the first case there is a context C such that $\overline{\eta}(L^{\text{par}} \circ a) \eqsim C \circ a$ for any a, and hence $(b_0', b_1') \in \mathcal{S}^{\eqsim}$. In the second case there is a ground arrow c such that $\overline{\eta}(L^{\text{par}} \circ a) \eqsim c$ for any a, hence $b_0' \eqsim b_1'$, so $(b_0', b_1') \in \mathcal{S}$. Thus the bisimulation up to support equivalence is established.

This completes the proof of the theorem. □

As we have seen in case 1 of the proof, when a simple transition $a \xrightarrow{L}_{\tilde{j}} a'$ is engaged, and a is prime, then so is a'. Thus, in proving the bisimilarity of prime agents, we can indeed confine attention to bisimulations containing only prime agents.

A.7 Recovering bisimilarity for CCS

Theorem 10.6 (recovering CCS) *Mono bisimilarity recovers CCS, i.e. $\sim_{\text{m}} = \sim_{\text{ccs}}$.*

Proof $(\supseteq)$ To show $\sim_{\text{m}} \supseteq \sim_{\text{ccs}}$ it will suffice to prove that

$$\mathcal{S} \overset{\text{def}}{=} \{(p_1|q, p_2|q) \mid p_1 \sim_{\text{ccs}} p_2\}$$

is a bisimulation for PE_{m}; the result follows from Proposition 10.5 by taking $q = \text{nil}$. Assume $p_1 \sim_{\text{ccs}} p_2$, and let $p_1 \mid q \xrightarrow{L} u_1$, where L is not a substitution label. We seek a transition $p_2 \mid q \xrightarrow{L} u_2$ such that $(u_1, u_2) \in \mathcal{S}$. We consider the cases for L; we need only consider cases 1 and 3 of Figure 10.1, since case 2 is like the first.

Case 1 $L = \text{id} \mid \text{alt.}(\text{get}_x c \cdots)$. Then, from Figure 10.1, $p_1 \mid q$ contains an unguarded molecule $\text{alt.}(\text{send}_x a \cdots)$, in which x is free. There are two subcases:

If the molecule lies in q, then from Figure 10.1

$$\begin{aligned} q &= /Z(\text{alt.}(\text{send}_x a \cdots) \mid b) \\ u_1 &= p_1 \mid /Z(a \mid b) \mid c \end{aligned}$$

where $x \notin Z$ and we can assume no free name of p_2 lies in Z. Then, from Figure 10.1, $p_2 \mid q \xrightarrow{L} u_2 \overset{\text{def}}{=} p_2 \mid /Z(a \mid b) \mid c$. But $(u_1, u_2) \in \mathcal{S}$, so we are done.

On the other hand, if the molecule lies in p_1 then

$$p_1 = /Z_1(\mathsf{alt}.(\mathsf{send}_x a_1 \cdot\cdot) \,|\, b_1)$$
$$u_1 = /Z_1(a_1 \,|\, b_1) \,|\, q \,|\, c$$

where $x \notin Z_1$ and we can assume no free name of q lies in Z_1. Then from Figure 10.2 there is a raw transition $p_1 \xrightarrow{\overline{x}} p_1' \stackrel{\text{def}}{=} /Z_1(a_1 \,|\, b_1)$, so $u_1 = p_1' \,|\, q \,|\, c$. But $p_1 \sim_{\text{ccs}} p_2$, so for some p_2' we have $p_2 \xrightarrow{\overline{x}} p_2' \sim_{\text{ccs}} p_1'$, and from Figure 10.2 we find

$$p_2 = /Z_2(\mathsf{alt}.(\mathsf{send}_x a_2 \cdot\cdot) \,|\, b_2)$$
$$p_2' = /Z_2(a_2 \,|\, b_2)$$

where $x \notin Z_2$, and we can assume no free name of q or c lies in Z_2. Then from Figure 10.1 we find $p_2 \,|\, q \xrightarrow{L} u_2 \stackrel{\text{def}}{=} p_2' \,|\, q \,|\, c$. But $(u_1, u_2) \in \mathcal{S}$, so we are done.

Case 3 $L = \mathsf{id}$. Then $p_1 \,|\, q$ has an unguarded pair of molecules, together corresponding to a redex. There are four cases, depending on whether each molecule lies in p_1 or in q. If both lie in p_1 or both in q the argument is easy; we therefore consider just one of the remaining (symmetric) pair of cases.

Suppose then, consulting Figure 10.1, that

$$p_1 = /Z_1(\mathsf{alt}.(\mathsf{send}_x.a_1 \cdot\cdot) \,|\, b_1)$$
$$q = /Z(\mathsf{alt}.(\mathsf{get}_x.a \cdot\cdot) \,|\, b)$$
$$u_1 = /Z_1(a_1 \,|\, b_1) \,|\, /Z(a \,|\, b)$$

where we can assume that no free name of one is closed in the other, and $x \notin Z_1 \uplus Z$. Then we have a raw transition $p_1 \xrightarrow{\overline{x}} p_1' \stackrel{\text{def}}{=} /Z_1(a_1 \,|\, b_1)$. But $p_1 \sim_{\text{ccs}} p_2$, so there exists p_2' with $p_2 \xrightarrow{\overline{x}} p_2' \sim_{\text{ccs}} p_1'$, and by Figure 10.2 this takes the form

$$p_2 = /Z_2(\mathsf{alt}.(\mathsf{send}_x.a_2 \cdot\cdot) \,|\, b_2)$$
$$p_2' = /Z_2(a_2 \,|\, b_2) \,.$$

Then from Figure 10.1 we deduce $p_2 \,|\, q \xrightarrow{\mathsf{id}} u_2 \stackrel{\text{def}}{=} p_2' \,|\, /Z(a \,|\, b)$, and $(u_1, u_2) \in \mathcal{S}$, so we are done.

($\subseteq$) To show $\sim_{\text{m}} \subseteq \sim_{\text{ccs}}$ we shall prove that $\sim_{\text{m}}$ is a bisimulation for $\sim_{\text{ccs}}$. Assume $p \sim_{\text{m}} q$ and $p \xrightarrow{\alpha} p'$; we seek a matching transition $q \xrightarrow{\alpha} q'$ such that $p' \sim_{\text{m}} q'$.

If $\alpha = \overline{x}$ then the structure of p and p' is dictated by case 1 of Figure 10.2. Now, choosing $L = \mathsf{alt}.(\mathsf{get}_x.\mathsf{nil})$, we find from case 1 of Figure 10.1 that $p \xrightarrow{L} p' \,|\, \mathsf{nil}$. Since $p \sim_{\text{m}} q$ we have $q \xrightarrow{L} q''$ with $p' \,|\, \mathsf{nil} \sim_{\text{m}} q''$. By case 1 of both Figures 10.1 and 10.2 there exists q' such that $q'' = q' \,|\, \mathsf{nil}$ and $q \xrightarrow{\overline{x}} q'$. Appealing to Proposition 10.5, we then find $p' \sim_{\text{m}} q'$ as required.

The argument for $\alpha = x$ is similar. The argument for $\alpha = \tau$ is even simpler, using case 3 of both Figures 10.1 and 10.2. This completes the proof of the theorem.

$\square$

Appendix B
Solutions to exercises

Solutions for Chapter 1

1.1

(1)

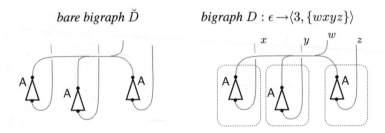

bare bigraph $\check{D}$ *bigraph $D : \epsilon \rightarrow \langle 3, \{wxyz\} \rangle$*

(2)   Choose interface $\langle 2, \emptyset \rangle$; the diagram for E is similar to that for E_3.

bigraph $C : \langle 3, \{xyzw\} \rangle \rightarrow \langle 2, \emptyset \rangle$

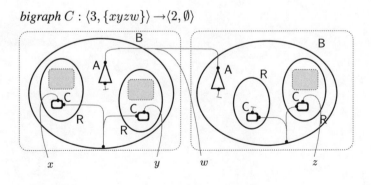

1.2

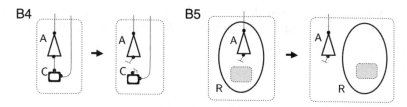

(1)   With **B1**–**B5** there are at least the following invariants:

the structure of buildings and rooms is unchanged;

each room contains a single computer, linked to the infrastructure of its building;

each computer is linked to at most one agent, who is in the same room; there are exactly five agents;

there is at most one conference call in progress;

an agent who leaves a conference call never rejoins it.

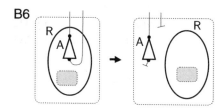

(2)   When **B4** and **B5** are replaced by **B6** all the above hold, and also:

an agent cannot unlink from a computer without leaving the room.

When you have read Definition 8.5 and the remarks following it, you will see that some of these invariants make sense only when the identity of an agent (i.e. its support) can be tracked through a reaction.

1.3

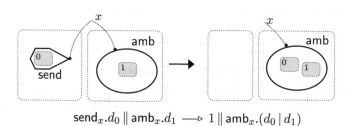

$$\mathsf{send}_x.d_0 \parallel \mathsf{amb}_x.d_1 \longrightarrow 1 \parallel \mathsf{amb}_x.(d_0 \mid d_1)$$

Solutions for Chapter 2

2.1 For link graphs, suppose that $A : X \to Y$, $B : Y \to Z$, $C : Z \to W$. Let $link_0$, $link_1$ be the link graphs of $C \circ (B \circ A)$ and $(C \circ B) \circ A$ respectively. They both take points $p \in X \uplus P_A \uplus P_B \uplus P_C$ to links in $E_A \uplus E_B \uplus E_C \uplus Z$.

Consider the six possible cases.

(i) $p \in X \uplus P_A$. Then $link_0(p)$ lies in E_A, or in E_B, or in $E_C \uplus W$.

(ii) $p \in P_B$. Then $link_0(p)$ lies in E_B or in $E_C \uplus W$.

(iii) $p \in P_C$. Then $link_0(p)$ lies in $E_C \uplus W$.

In each case prove $link_1(p) = link_0(p)$. It is just a matter of unpacking the definition of composition.

The argument for place graphs is similar.

2.2 For the inductive basis, with $\mathcal{C} = [\cdot]$, take $f = \mathrm{id}$.

For the inductive step, first suppose $\mathcal{C}' = g \otimes \mathcal{C}$ (the case $\mathcal{C}' = \mathcal{C} \otimes g$ is similar), and assume there exists f such that $f \circ a = \mathcal{C}[a]$ for all ground a. Then take $f' = g \otimes f$, and prove $f' \circ a = \mathcal{C}'[a]$ as follows:

$$
\begin{aligned}
f' \circ a &= (g \otimes f) \circ a \\
&= (g \otimes f) \circ (\mathrm{id}_\epsilon \otimes a) && \text{by M2} \\
&= (g \circ \mathrm{id}_\epsilon) \otimes (f \circ a) && \text{by M3} \\
&= g \otimes (f \circ a) && \text{by C3} \\
&= g \otimes \mathcal{C}[a] \\
&= \mathcal{C}'[a] \,.
\end{aligned}
$$

Now suppose $\mathcal{C}' = h \circ \mathcal{C}$; then take $f' = h \circ f$, and justify it as follows:

$$
\begin{aligned}
f' \circ a &= (h \circ f) \circ a \\
&= h \circ (f \circ a) && \text{by C2} \\
&= h \circ \mathcal{C}[a] \\
&= \mathcal{C}'[a] \,.
\end{aligned}
$$

2.3 Any bigraph $G : I \to \epsilon$ has an empty place graph, since a non-empty place graph implies at least one root. Also, in the link graph $G^{\mathsf{L}} : X \to \emptyset$ of G, every link is an edge. But if G has empty support then it has no edges, so $X = \emptyset$, $I = \epsilon$ and $G = \mathrm{id}_\epsilon$.

Solutions for Chapter 3

3.1 A linking is just a map from inner names to outer names and edges. So a substitution σ from X to Y is just a tensor product of elementary substitutions

$$
\sigma \stackrel{\text{def}}{=} y_0/X_0 \otimes \cdots \otimes y_{n-1}/X_{n-1}, \text{ where } X = X_0 \uplus \cdots \uplus X_{n-1} \text{ and } Y = \{\vec{y}\} \,.
$$

Now partition Y into $Z = \{y_0 \cdots y_{k-1}\}$ and $W = \{y_k \cdots y_{n-1}\}$. We get any link map λ by setting $/W \overset{\text{def}}{=} /y_k \otimes \cdots \otimes /y_{n-1}$, and forming $\lambda \overset{\text{def}}{=} (\text{id}_Z \otimes /W) \circ \sigma$. This use of composition is the only way to close a substitution.

3.2 The expression G can be specialised to the four quoted cases by setting (1) $C_1 = \text{id}$ and $I = \epsilon$, (2) $I = \epsilon$ and $C_0 = \text{id}$, (3) $C_1 = \text{id}$ and $C_0 = \text{id}_J \otimes C$ (for $F : J \to K$), and (4) $C_1 = \gamma_{K,I}$ and $C_0 = (\text{id}_J \otimes C) \circ \gamma_{I,J}$.

To show that $g = C \circ a$ implies that a occurs in g, take $F = a$, $I = \epsilon$, $C_0 = \text{id}_\epsilon$. For the converse, assume that $g = C \circ (a \otimes \text{id}_I) \circ C'$; we must find D such that $g = D \circ a$. Indeed, since a is ground we have $g = C \circ (a \otimes C')$; the result follows by taking $D = C \circ (\text{id} \otimes C')$.

If E occurs in F and F occurs in G then we have

$$
\begin{aligned}
F &= C_1 \circ (E \otimes \text{id}_I) \circ C_0 \text{ and} \\
G &= D_1 \circ (F \otimes \text{id}_J) \circ D_0 \, .
\end{aligned}
$$

So one can deduce 'E occurs in G', i.e. $G = B_1 \circ (E \otimes \text{id}_K) \circ B_0$, by setting $K = I \otimes J$, $B_1 = D_1 \circ (C_1 \otimes \text{id}_J)$ and $B_0 = (C_0 \otimes \text{id}_J) \circ D_0$.

3.3

$$
\begin{aligned}
H.(G.F) &= (\text{id}_{X \cup Y} \parallel H) \circ (\text{id}_X \parallel G) \circ F \\
&= (\text{id}_X \parallel \text{id}_Y \parallel H) \circ (\text{id}_X \parallel G) \circ F \\
&= ((\text{id}_X \circ \text{id}_X) \parallel (\text{id}_Y \parallel H) \circ G) \circ F \\
&= (\text{id}_X \parallel (H.G)) \circ F \\
&= (H.G).F \, .
\end{aligned}
$$

3.4 Recall that R is open, so has no edges. Consider any split A, B for R. Let (u_0, u_1) be the send-node and get-node of R, and let v_0, v_1 be their respective parents, the alt-nodes. Since A must have at least one node of R, at least one of (u_0, u_1) must be in A.

If both (u_0, u_1) are in A then, since B must have at least one node of R, A can contain at most one of (v_0, v_1). If it contains neither, then the A-parents of (u_0, u_1) must be distinct roots of A, since their parents (v_0, v_1) in $B \circ A$ are distinct. If A contains exactly one of (v_0, v_1), say v_0, then by a similar argument the parents of (v_0, u_1) must be distinct roots of A. In both these cases the split is non-unary.

Therefore A contains exactly one of (u_0, u_1) and B contains the other. So the split is tight, since these two nodes are linked.

The redexes of A1–A3 and B1 are tight (in the case of B1 there is no split); those of B2 and B3 are not tight.

Solutions for Chapter 4

4.1 Assume that $(\vec{h}, h)$ is an RPO for $\vec{f}$ relative to $\vec{g}$. We have to prove that $\vec{h}$ is an IPO. So, for an arbitrary bound $(\vec{\ell}, \ell)$ for $\vec{f}$ relative to $\vec{g}$, we seek a unique y such that

$$y \circ \vec{h} = \vec{\ell} \text{ and } \ell \circ y = \text{id} .$$

First, we know that $\ell \circ \vec{\ell} = \vec{h}$, and also that $(\vec{\ell}, h \circ \ell)$ is a bound for $\vec{f}$ relative to g, whence there exists unique x such that

$$x \circ \vec{h} = \vec{\ell} \text{ and } h \circ \ell \circ x = h .$$

Now, as in the proof of Proposition 4.5(1), we can show that $\ell \circ x = \text{id}$; thus $y = x$ satisfies the required equations for y. But any y satisfying these equations also satisfies the equations for x. This assures unicity for y, and we are done.

4.2 Assume that $(\vec{k}, k)$ is an RPO. Since $\vec{h}$ is an IPO, $(\vec{h}, h)$ is a bound for $\vec{f}$ relative to $(h \circ h_0, h \circ h_1)$; so there exists unique x such that

$$x \circ \vec{k} = \vec{h} \text{ and } h \circ x = k .$$

Hence $(\vec{k}, x)$ is a bound for $\vec{f}$ relative to $\vec{h}$, which is an IPO, so if H is the codomain of $\vec{h}$ there exists unique y such that

$$y \circ \vec{h} = \vec{k} \text{ and } x \circ y = \text{id}_H .$$

Now since $(\vec{k}, k)$ is an RPO, it follows from Proposition 4.5(2) that $\vec{k}$ is an IPO. Since $(\vec{h}, y)$ is a bound for $\vec{f}$ relative to $\vec{k}$, we deduce that there exists unique z such that

$$z \circ \vec{k} = \vec{h} \text{ and } y \circ z = \text{id}_K .$$

From $x \circ y = \text{id}_H$ and $y \circ z = \text{id}_K$ we deduce $x = z$. It follows that $x : K \to H$ is an iso with inverse y. So since $(\vec{k}, k)$ is an RPO, from the equations for x and Proposition 4.5(1) we deduce that $(\vec{h}, h)$ is also an RPO, as required.

4.3 Let $\mathcal{F} : \mathbf{`A} \to \mathbf{`B}$, and assume $\vec{g}$ bounds $\vec{f}$ in $\mathbf{`A}$. So, denoting $\mathcal{F}$-images by a prime, $\vec{g}'$ bounds $\vec{f}'$ in $\mathbf{`B}$. Assume that this is a pushout; then we want to prove that $\vec{g}$ is a pushout for $\vec{f}$ in $\mathbf{`A}$.

Let $\vec{h}$ bound $\vec{f}$ in $\mathbf{`A}$. Denote the arrow $g_0 \circ f_0 = g_1 \circ f_1$ by g, and the arrow $h_0 \circ f_0 = h_1 \circ f_1$ by h. We require unique k such that $k \circ \vec{g} = \vec{h}$. It is enough to find some k satisfying these equations; uniqueness follows from two facts:

   (i) k' will be the unique arrow in $\mathbf{`B}$ such that $k' \circ \vec{g}' = \vec{h}'$, and
   (ii) g is op-cartesian, so k is the unique preimage of k' such that $k \circ g = h$.

Now, for each $i \in \{0, 1\}$, since g_i is op-cartesian there exists a preimage k_i of k' such that $k_i \circ g_i = h_i$. But these equations imply that $k_i \circ g = h$, so $k_0 = k_1$ since g is op-cartesian, and our required arrow is $k \overset{\text{def}}{=} k_0 = k_1$. This completes the proof.

Solutions for Chapter 5

5.1 We prove the epi case for link graphs. (The other cases are similar.)

Assume $F : X \to Y$ is epi; we prove that it has no idle names. Suppose $Y = y \uplus Z$ where y is idle in F. Pick $G = \overline{G} \otimes \text{id}_Z$ and $H = \overline{H} \otimes \text{id}_Z$ as shown. Then $G \neq H$ but $G \circ F = H \circ F$, contradicting F epi.

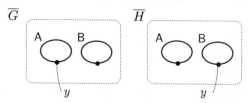

Now assume F has no idle names; we prove it to be epi. Let $G \circ F = H \circ F$. Then G and H have the same nodes, edges and control map; so to prove $G = H$ it remains to prove that $link_G = link_H$. For this, let q be any point of G (and hence of H). If q is a port, then it is a port of $G \circ F$, and we have

$$link_G(q) = link_{G \circ F}(q) = link_{H \circ F}(q) = link_H(q) .$$

On the other hand, if q is an inner name, say $q = y \in Y$, then y is not idle in F so $y = link_F(p)$ for some point p of F. But then

$$link_G(y) = link_{G \circ F}(p) = link_{H \circ F}(p) = link_H(y) .$$

This completes the proof that F is epi.

5.2 The name y should not be merged with x_0 in B_0; instead we add y to the outer face of B_0, defining $link_{B_0}(y) = y$ and $link_B(y) = x$. Then also y_1 should not be merged with x_1 in B_1; instead, define $link_{B_1}(y_1) = y$ (thus keeping the outer faces of B_0 and B_1 equal).

5.3 CL0: If $v \in V_2$ then it is a node of $B_0 \circ A_0 = B_1 \circ A_1$, hence $ctrl_0(v) = ctrl_{B_0 \circ A_0}(v) = ctrl_{B_1 \circ A_1}(v) = ctrl_1(v)$.

CL1: Take $i = 0$. Since $A_0(p) = e \in E_0$ we have $p \in W \uplus P_0$. Also $(B_0 \circ A_0)(p) = e$, so $(B_1 \circ A_1)(p) = e$. But $e \in E_1$ by assumption, hence $A_1(p) = e = A_0(p)$ as required, hence also $p \in W \uplus P_1$, hence $p \in W \uplus P_2$ as required.

CL2: Take $i = 0$. Since $A_0(p_2) = e \in E_0$ we have $(B_0 \circ A_0)(p_2) = e$, hence $(B_1 \circ A_1)(p_2) = e$. But $p_2 \notin E_1$, so for some $x \in X_1$ we have $A_1(p_2) = x$ as required, and $B_1(x) = e$. If also $A_1(p) = x$ then $p \in W \uplus P_1$; so $(B_0 \circ A_0)(p) = (B_1 \circ A_1)(p) = B_1(x) = e$. But then p is a point of A_0, so $A_0(p) = e$ as required.

5.4 In Construction 5.15 the edges of C_1 are defined to be $E_0 \setminus E_2$. This holds for all IPOs, since elisions change no edges. But $E_0 = \emptyset$, hence C_1 has no edges.

5.5 The distinguished IPO $(\mathrm{id}, \mathrm{id})$ is the unique IPO for (A, A) up to iso, because id has no nodes or edges, hence permits no elisions. But if A is not epi it has an idle name or idle root; this gives rise to an idle name or root in the IPO cospan.

5.6 (1) We have shown that there can be no K-node in B_0; so to achieve $\widehat{C} \circ B_0 = C_0$ we need $\widehat{C}$ to contain a K-node linked to z. But then $\widehat{C} \circ B_1 = C_1$ fails, since C_1 contains no such K-node.

(2) In concrete link graphs, nodes have support. There are two cases for the K nodes in A_0 and A_1. If they have the same support, i.e. A_0 and A_1 share a K-node, then the RPO construction would require $\vec{C}$ to have no nodes; hence $(\vec{C}, C)$ would not be an RPO. On the other hand if they have different supports, then $\vec{D}$ would not even be a bound for $\vec{A}$; hence $(\vec{D}, D)$ would not be an RPO. In either case exactly one of $(\vec{C}, C)$ and $(\vec{D}, D)$ would be a relative bound – and it would be the required RPO.

Solutions for Chapter 6

6.1 The formation rule Φ for stratified sorting constrains only place graphs, so we can ignore link graphs when checking it. And since a place graph is a forest of trees, if it is augmented with sorts then the forest satisfies Φ iff each tree does.

A place interface m augmented with sorts is a sequence $\theta_0 \cdots \theta_{m-1}$ of sorts. So in an identity id_I augmented with sorts, each tree whose root has sort θ has just one child with sort θ. This clearly satisfies Φ.

Now suppose that each of F and G, augmented with sorts, satisfies Φ. Each tree of a tensor product $F \otimes G$ is just a tree of either F or G, so clearly $F \otimes G$ satisfies Φ. Each tree of a composition $G \circ F$ is a tree of G in which each site $i : \theta$ is replaced by some tree of F whose root (with sort θ) is removed. Now every place in $G \circ F$ is either a root of G or a node of G or a node of F; the appropriate condition of Φ can be checked for each case separately.

6.2 $\Theta = \{a, b, c, r, \widehat{ac}, \widehat{ar}\}$, $\mathcal{K} = \{A : a, \ B : b, \ C : c, \ R : r\}$. Φ requires:

an a-node or c-node has no children (i.e. A and C are atomic);
all children of an r-node or $\widehat{ac}$-root have sort a, c or $\widehat{ac}$;
all children of a b-node or $\widehat{ar}$-root have sort a, r or $\widehat{ar}$;
all children of a θ-root have sort θ, where $\theta \in \{a, b, c, r\}$.
The interfaces are

$E : \epsilon \to J$ where $J = \langle b\,b,\ \emptyset \rangle$;
$D : \epsilon \to I$ where $I = \langle a\,a\,a, \{xyzw\} \rangle$;
$C : I \to J$.

Alternatively, replace a by $\widehat{ac}$ in I.
The redex of rule **B1** can have sort a or $\widehat{ac}$; the redex of **B2** must have sort $\widehat{ac}$; the redex of **B3** must have sort $\widehat{ar}$.

6.3 (1) If $x : \theta$, it may be that in $link_{g'}(x) = e$ (say) where $e : \theta'$ in h; then $link_g(x) : \theta'$ is forced, preventing the well-sorting of g.
(2) Let $\vec{A}$ be bounded by $\vec{B}$ in a plain-sorted s-category, and let the unsorted $\mathcal{U}$-image $(\vec{A}', \vec{B}')$ of this diagram be a pushout. We argue that $(\vec{A}, \vec{B})$ is also a pushout.

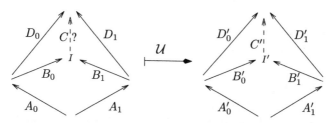

Let $\vec{D}$ bound $\vec{A}$; then its image $\vec{D}'$ bounds $\vec{A}'$. We require a unique mediating arrow C in the left-hand diagram. A unique such arrow C' exists in the right-hand diagram; so define its preimage C by ascribing to all its ports and edges the sorts that they have in D_0 and in D_1. If this makes C well-sorted, then it is the unique arrow required.

If a link of C contains no inner name in I then the link and its points are sorted as in D_0 and D_1, so they obey the plain-sorting formation rule. Thus, to conclude that C is well-sorted, we need only show that if $x : \theta$ is an arbitrary name in I then $link_C(x) : \theta$.

Now $\vec{B}'$ is a pushout, hence an IPO, so x is not idle in both B_0' and B_1'. Without loss of generality, x has a point p in B_0', and hence in B_0. Since B_0 is well-sorted, $p : \theta$ in B_0 and also in D_0. Since D_0 is well-sorted, $link_{D_0}(p)$ has sort θ. But this link (outer name or edge) is in C too; hence, by our construction, $link_C(x) : \theta$ as required.

A similar argument shows that the functor creates RPOs.

Solutions for Chapter 7

7.1 In bigraphs, to say '$G \circ F$ is active at i' means that all ancestor nodes of i in $G \circ F$ are active. This is true iff all ancestor nodes of i in F are active, and all ancestor nodes of j in G are active, where j is the ancestor root of i in F. But this is the same statement as 'F is active at i and G is active at $\mathrm{width}(F)(i)$'.

Recall that $1:0 \to 1$ is the place graph with no sites and one root. Take $F = A \otimes 1:1 \to 2$ and $G = join \circ (A \otimes B):2 \to 1$. Then $G \circ F$ is active, but G is not active at its second site.

7.2 Trivially both $\eqsim$ and $\asymp$ include support equivalence ($\simeq$). To see that $\eqsim$ is preserved by $\circ$ (for example), suppose $F \eqsim G$ and $F' \eqsim G'$. Then G, G' are obtained from F, F' by support translations ρ, ρ' respectively. But if $F \circ F'$ and $G \circ G'$ are both defined then $\rho \uplus \rho'$ is also a support translation, and takes $F \circ F'$ to $G \circ G'$; hence $F \circ F' \eqsim G \circ G'$.

Now let F^- mean F with idle edges removed. To check $\asymp$ is preserved by $\circ$ (for example), note that $F \asymp G$ means that $F^- \eqsim G^-$. The rest follows from the fact that $(F \circ F')^- = (F^- \circ (F')^-)^-$.

7.3 From the commutation of the second diagram, prove that the first diagram commutes when a is replaced by $f \circ a$.

7.4 For the first part, let $a \xrightarrow{f}_{\tilde{\imath}} a'$ and $a \eqsim b$ with $f \circ b$ defined. Then there is a reaction rule (r, r') and an IPO (f, d) for (a, r), such that $a' \eqsim d \circ r'$. Let ρ be the support translation such that $\rho \cdot a = b$. Apply ρ, extended by the identity map, to the whole IPO; then Proposition 4.5 yields an IPO (f, e) for (b, s), with $e \eqsim d$ and $s \eqsim r$. Pick $s' \eqsim r'$ so that $e \circ s'$ is defined; then (s, s') is also a reaction rule (since these are closed under $\eqsim$), so if $b' \overset{\mathrm{def}}{=} e \circ s'$ then $b \xrightarrow{f}_{\tilde{\imath}} b'$ with $a' \eqsim b'$, as required.

For the second part, we must show that if $\mathcal{S}$ is a bisimulation up to $\eqsim$ then $\mathcal{S} \subseteq \sim$. For this, we show that $\mathcal{S}^{\eqsim}$ is a bisimulation, for then $\mathcal{S}^{\eqsim} \subseteq \sim$, which implies $\mathcal{S} \subseteq \sim$.

For this purpose, suppose that $a\mathcal{S}^{\eqsim}b$, i.e. that $a \eqsim a_1 \mathcal{S} b_1 \eqsim b$, and let $a \xrightarrow{f}_{\tilde{\imath}} a'$. Then, since $\eqsim$ is a bisimulation, there exist a'_1, b'_1 and b' such that $b \xrightarrow{f}_{\tilde{\imath}} b'$ and $a' \eqsim a'_1 \mathcal{S}^{\eqsim} b'_1 \eqsim b'$. But $\mathcal{S}$ is closed under $\eqsim$, so $a'\mathcal{S}^{\eqsim}b'$. This completes the proof that $\mathcal{S}^{\eqsim}$ is a bisimulation, and hence that $\mathcal{S} \subseteq \sim$, as required.

7.5 (1) $\overline{G \circ F}$ can differ from $\overline{G} \circ \overline{F}$; in the latter, a B-node in $\overline{G}$ can still be linked to an A-node in $\overline{F}$. But the equivalence is a structural congruence: this can be proved by showing that if $F_0 \equiv F_1$ then they have the same normal form, the result of removing every B-node linked to an A-node. It is not an abstraction; we may have $F \eqsim G$, but $F \neq G$; if neither has a B-node linked to an A-node then $F \not\equiv G$.

The equivalence does not necessarily respect MT; for the redex of a reaction rule may contain a B-node; then if we drop a B-node from an agent a we may lose a transition.

(2) As in (1) the equivalence is a structural congruence, but not an abstraction. It may not respect MT, even if no redex contains a B- or A-node. For we may have A passive and B active; then replacing B by A may prevent a reaction – and hence a transition – by turning an active context into a passive one.

7.6 By the definition of induced transitions there exist a, f and a' in **C** such that $p = [\![a]\!]$, $g = [\![f]\!]$, $p' = [\![a']\!]$, with $a \xrightarrow{f}_{\tilde{\imath}} a'$. By Exercise 7.3 it follows that $f \circ a \longrightarrow_{\tilde{\imath}} a'$. So from Theorem 7.7 we deduce that $[\![f \circ a]\!] \longrightarrow_{\tilde{\imath}} [\![a']\!]$. Since $[\![\cdot]\!]$ is a functor, we immediately deduce $g \circ p \longrightarrow \tilde{\imath} p'$.

Solutions for Chapter 8

8.1 For the CCS rule:

$R : \langle \mathsf{p\,a\,p\,a}, \emptyset \rangle \rightarrow \langle \mathsf{p}, x \rangle \qquad R' : \langle \mathsf{p\,p}, \emptyset \rangle \rightarrow \langle \mathsf{p}, x \rangle$
$r, r' : \langle \mathsf{p}, x \uplus Y \rangle$
$d : \langle \mathsf{p\,a\,p\,a}, Y \rangle \qquad d_i : \langle \theta_i, Y_i \rangle$ where $\theta_0, \theta_1, \theta_2, \theta_3 = \mathsf{p}, \mathsf{a}, \mathsf{p}, \mathsf{a}$.

8.2 For an engaged transition take $R = \mathsf{A}^w \circ (\mathsf{id}_1 \,|\, \mathsf{B}^v)$, $d = \mathsf{B}^u$; for a disengaged transition take $R = \mathsf{A}^w \circ (\mathsf{id}_1 \,|\, \mathsf{B}^u)$, $d = \mathsf{B}^v$.

Solutions for Chapter 9

9.1 The final net should be as on the left below. A clean-up rule is shown on the right, where '?' may be any control.

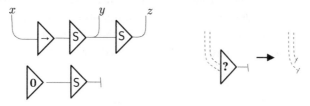

9.2 If two redexes are disjoint then one reaction cannot destroy either the nodes or the linkage of the other. No critical pair can be formed from an instance of (1) with an instance of (2). A critical pair of instances of (1) must share the S-node; a critical pair of instances of (2) must share the 0-node; in both cases – as already seen for (1) – confluence holds. A critical pair of (3) with any of (1)–(3) can only share the ?-node and is clearly confluent.

9.3 Let the S-*measure* of any net be the number of distinct finite paths leading from an S-node to a +-node. For explicit nets this measure is finite. For each explicit net, let its *measure* be the triple $m = (m_S, m_+, m_\to)$ of its S-measure, its number of +-nodes, and its number of $\to$-nodes. Prove the following (the first being crucial):

   (i) Rule (1) decreases m_S, while rules (2) and (3) do not increase it.
  (ii) Rule (2) decreases m_+, while rule (3) does not increase it.
 (iii) Rule (3) decreases $m_\to$.

So the lexicographic ordering on measure is well-founded and decreased by reaction.

Solutions for Chapter 10

10.1 For (1), following the hint, in the inductive step we assume the property for agents with less than n nodes and prove it for any agent with n nodes.

One such agent has the form $a = \mathsf{send}_x.p : \langle \mathsf{p}, X \rangle$, where p has $n - 1$ nodes. So by inductive assumption there is a CCS process P such that $\mathcal{P}_X[P] = p$; hence for the CCS alternation $\overline{x}.P$ we have $\mathcal{A}_X[\overline{x}.P] = a$.

To complete the inductive proof, apply a similar argument for all ways (there are four or five ways) of building larger agents from smaller ones.

For (2) follow the hint. We omit the proof of the Lemma here; it is not very instructive.

10.2 For example, suppose that $p \,|\, \mathsf{nil} \stackrel{x}{\longrightarrow} p''$. Then the pair $(p \,|\, \mathsf{nil}, p'')$ matches the forms in case 2 of the figure. It follows that b takes the form $b' \,|\, \mathsf{nil}$, so that p'' takes the form $p' \,|\, \mathsf{nil}$, where p and p' also match that case with b' in place of b.

We have therefore shown that the assumed transition is matched by $p \stackrel{x}{\longrightarrow} p'$ such that $(p, p') \in \mathcal{S}$. The same can be done for the other labels α in place of x.

In the other direction, starting with an assumed transition $p \stackrel{\alpha}{\longrightarrow} p'$, it is even easier to deduce $p \,|\, \mathsf{nil} \stackrel{\alpha}{\longrightarrow} p' \,|\, \mathsf{nil}$.

10.3 Having proved $p \simeq_m p \,|\, \mathsf{nil}$, use this together with Exercise 10.2 to prove that each of $\simeq_m$ and $\sim_{\mathsf{ccs}}$ is a bisimulation for the other.

Solutions for Chapter 11

11.1 The contextual rule is

$$(C : J \to K, \; S : m \to J, \; S' : m' \to J, \; \eta, \; \tau)$$

where $\tau : |S|' \rightharpoonup |S|$ is a tracking map. (We use S, S' in place of R, R' to avoid confusion with the room control R.) Given a parameter d, define d' and σ as before. Then the ground rules generated take the form

$$((C \circ S).d \, , \, (C' \circ S').d' \, , \, \rho \uplus \tau \uplus \sigma)$$

where $C = \rho \cdot C'$.

For rule (1) we construct the contextual rule (with the above notation) as follows. Let $K = \langle 1, xy \rangle$ and $J = 1 \otimes K = \langle 2, xy \rangle$. Then the agent is the atom $a \overset{\text{def}}{=} A_{xy}.1 : \epsilon \to K$, and the room ion is R $: 1 \to 1$. Then for the contextual rule we take

$$C = \mathsf{id}_I \mid \mathsf{R}, \quad S = a \otimes \mathsf{id}_1 \text{ and } S' = 1 \otimes (a \mid \mathsf{id}_1)$$

where $C : J \to K$ and $S, S' : 1 \to J$. Also $\eta = \{1 \mapsto 1\}$, and $\tau = \{u \mapsto u\}$ if we assume a has support $\{u\}$ in both S and S'.

11.2 (1) Since $f \relbar\joinrel\twoheadrightarrow f'$ there exist g, g' with $g \relbar\joinrel\rightarrow g'$ and $(f, f') \leq (g, g')$. Hence by congruence $(C \circ f, C \circ f') \leq (C \circ g, C \circ g')$. But $C \circ g \relbar\joinrel\rightarrow C \circ g'$; hence by definition $C \circ f \relbar\joinrel\twoheadrightarrow C \circ f'$. Similarly for tensor product.

(2) Since $f \relbar\joinrel\twoheadrightarrow f'$, we have $h \relbar\joinrel\rightarrow h'$ where $(f, f') \leq (h, h')$. By confluence, there exists k with $g, h \leq k$. By Proposition 11.7 there exists g' such that $k \relbar\joinrel\rightarrow g'$ and $h' \leq g'$. Therefore by definition $g \relbar\joinrel\twoheadrightarrow g'$; also $f' \leq h' \leq g'$, so we are done.

11.3 The first step in creating the left-hand diagram is to take the RPO for (id $\otimes$ a, id $\otimes$ a) relative to $(B_0 \circ C_0, B_1 \circ C_1)$. The bottom square is then an IPO, and its upper members are identities (up to iso) because a is epi (see Exercise 5.5). The second step is to take an RPO for (C_0, id) relative to $(B_0, B_0 \circ C_0)$, and a matching IPO on the other side. (The resulting IPOs are unique up to iso since an identity is both epi and open.)

The right-hand diagram results from taking the RPO for (id $\otimes$ a, A_1) relative to $(B_0 \circ C, B_1)$. Since the lower square is an IPO, we know it is unique (up to iso) because a is epi and open; hence it takes the form of the IPO defined in Corollary 5.21.

11.4 On the one hand K $\sim$ L since $\sim$ does not allow growth, but K $\not\simeq$ L since K $\relbar\joinrel\twoheadrightarrow$ K and L $\not\relbar\joinrel\twoheadrightarrow$. On the other hand K $\not\sim$ M.K since M.K $\relbar\joinrel\rightarrow$ K and K $\not\relbar\joinrel\twoheadrightarrow$, but K $\simeq$ M.K since K $\hookrightarrow$ M.K.

11.5 As in the proof of Theorem 7.16, we establish the following as a bisimulation for $\simeq$, up to $\dot\simeq$:

$$\mathcal{S} \overset{\text{def}}{=} \{(C \circ a_0, C \circ a_1) \mid a_0 \simeq a_1, C \text{ any context}\} .$$

(Here we omit mention of activeness; it is handled just as in the cited theorem.)

Let $a_0 \simeq a_1$, and suppose there is a grown transition $C \circ a_0 \xrightarrow{M}_{\hat{\jmath}} b_0'$. We have to find b_1' such that $C \circ a_1 \xrightarrow{M}_{\hat{\jmath}} b_1'$ and $(b_0', b_1') \in \mathcal{S}^{\hat{=}}$.

STAGE 1: By definition there is a standard transition $\widehat{C} \circ \widehat{a}_0 \xrightarrow{\widehat{M}}_{\hat{\jmath}} \widehat{b}_0'$, where

$$(C, a_0, M, b_0') \leq (\widehat{C}, \widehat{a}_0, \widehat{M}, \widehat{b}_0') .$$

This depends on Proposition 11.6(3), ensuring independent growth in $C \circ a_0$. The transition is based on an underlying IPO, and on a ground rule (r_0, r_0') such that $\widehat{b}_0' \simeq E_0 \circ r_0'$. Take an RPO, yielding a pair of IPOs as shown in diagram (a).

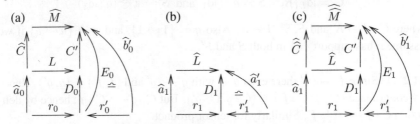

(a) $\widehat{M}$ (b) (c) $\widehat{\widehat{M}}$

STAGE 2: The lower IPO underlies a standard transition $\widehat{a}_0 \xrightarrow{L}_{\hat{\imath}} a_0' \stackrel{\text{def}}{=} D_0 \circ r_0'$. Note that $\widehat{b}_0' \simeq C' \circ a_0'$. By definition, we then have a grown transition $a_0 \xrightarrow{L}_{\hat{\imath}} a_0'$. Since $a_0 \simeq a_1$, there is a grown transition $a_1 \xrightarrow{L}_{\hat{\imath}} a_1'$ with $a_0' \simeq a_1'$. Then, by definition, there exists a standard transition $\widehat{a}_1 \xrightarrow{\widehat{L}}_{\hat{\imath}} \widehat{a}_1'$ such that

$$(a_1, L, a_1') \leq (\widehat{a}_1, \widehat{L}, \widehat{a}_1') ,$$

where the transition is based on a ground rule (r_1, r_1') and an IPO as shown in diagram (b), with $a' \simeq D_1 \circ r_1'$. Moreover, since reaction rules and growth are closed under $\simeq$, this triple may be chosen with support disjoint from C'.

STAGE 3: We now turn attention to the upper IPO in diagram (a). Since $L \leq \widehat{L}$ and $|\widehat{L}| \cap |C'| = \emptyset$, by Proposition 11.12 there exist $\widehat{\widehat{C}}, \widehat{\widehat{M}}$ such that

$$(\widehat{C}, \widehat{M}) \leq (\widehat{\widehat{C}}, \widehat{\widehat{M}})$$

and $(\widehat{\widehat{M}}, C')$ is an IPO for $(\widehat{\widehat{C}}, \widehat{L})$. We may paste this IPO onto diagram (b), and define $\widehat{b}_1' \stackrel{\text{def}}{=} E_1 \circ r_1'$, where $E_1 = C' \circ D_1$. Thus diagram (c) represents the standard transition $\widehat{\widehat{C}} \circ \widehat{a}_1 \xrightarrow{\widehat{\widehat{M}}}_{\hat{\jmath}} \widehat{b}_1'$. Also $\widehat{b}_1' \simeq C' \circ \widehat{a}_1'$, so we define $b_1' \stackrel{\text{def}}{=} C' \circ a_1'$. So finally, since

$$(C \circ a_1, M, b_1') \leq (\widehat{\widehat{C}} \circ \widehat{a}_1, \widehat{\widehat{M}}, \widehat{b}_1')$$

we have a grown transition $C \circ a_1 \xrightarrow{M} \gg_{\widetilde{\jmath}} b_1'$. Recalling that $b_0' \simeq C' \circ a_0'$, we have that $(b_0', b_1') \in \mathcal{S}^{\simeq}$, and the proof is complete.

11.6 In the definitions of both place graphs and link graphs, Definitions 2.1 and 2.2: (1) add to the tuple representing F an extra component B_F, a finite set of bindings; (2) extend $ctrl_F : V_F \to \mathcal{K}$ to $ctrl_F : V_F \uplus B_F \to \mathcal{K}$; (3) in forming $G \circ F$ give it bindings $B = B_F \uplus B_G$. In Definition 2.5, adapt the defining equations as follows:

  (i) Let w range over $k \uplus V_F \uplus V_G \uplus B_F \uplus B_G$, and replace the conditions $w \in k \uplus V_F$ and $w \in V_G$ by the conditions $w \in k \uplus V_F \uplus B_F$ and $w \in V_G \uplus B_G$.
  (ii) Replace the condition $link_F(q) \in E_F$ by the condition $link_F(q) \in E_F \uplus B_F$.

11.7 It is easy to prove that the identities satisfy the scoping discipline, and that tensor product preserves it. Here we confine ourselves to proving that composition preserves the scoping discipline.

Let $F : I \to J$ and $G : J \to K$ satisfy the scope discipline, and define $H : I \to K \overset{\text{def}}{=} G \circ F$. Let $\ell = link_H(q)$ in H, with $(w, \ell) \in loclink_H$. We must find w' such that $w' \, in_H \, w$ and $(w', q) \in locpoint_H$. Since ℓ is local it cannot be an edge in E_H, so it is either a name in K or a binding $b \in B_H$. We divide the argument into two cases:

Case 1 $\ell = b \in B_F$. Then $q \in X \uplus P_F$ where X are the names of I. We easily verify that $(w, b) \in loclink_F$. Since $b = link_H(q)$ in H and b is in F, it follows that $b = link_F(q)$ in F, hence by the scope discipline for F we deduce that there exists $w' \, in_F \, w$ with $(w', q) \in locpoint_F$. Composition with G preserves these properties, i.e. $w' \, in_H \, w$ with $(w', q) \in locpoint_H$, and we are done.

Case 2 $\ell \in B_G \uplus Z$, where Z are the names of K. Now since $(w, \ell) \in loclink_H$, we also have $(w, \ell) \in loclink_G$. Furthermore $q \in X \uplus P_F \uplus P_G$, so we treat the two possible subcases for q:

  (a) $q \in X \uplus P_F$. Then for some name y in J we have $\ell = link_G(y)$ and $y = link_F(q)$. Now by the scope discipline for G there exists a site s in J with $s \, in_G \, w$ and $(s, y) \in loc_J$. But then $(s, y) \in loclink_F$, so by the scope discipline for F there exists $w' \, in_F \, s$ with $(w', q) \in locpoint_F$. It readily follows that $w' \, in_H \, w$ with $(w', q) \in locpoint_H$, and we are done.
  (b) $q \in P_G$. Then by the scope discipline for G we have $w' \, in_G \, w$ with $(w', q) \in locpoint_G$. It follows immediately that $w' \, in_H \, w$ with $(w', q) \in locpoint_H$, and we are done.

Glossary of terms and symbols

Each entry refers to the definition or construction $n.m$ which introduces it, except that § refers to Chapter n or Section $n.m$.

BIGRAPHS						
$\breve{F}, \breve{G}$	bare bigraph	§ 1		β	binding control	§ 11.3
$A, B, \ldots$	bigraph	§ 1		$\mathcal{K}$	signature	1.1
$I, J, \ldots$	interface	§ 1		ar	arity (of control)	1.1
$m, n, \ldots$	finite ordinal	§ 1		$ctrl$	control map	2.1
$x, y, \ldots$	name	§ 1		$prnt$	parent map	2.1
v	node	§ 1		in	descendance relation	§ 11.3
e	edge	§ 1		$link$	link map	2.2
$X, Y, \ldots$	name-set	§ 1		Σ	sorting discipline	6.1
$\langle m, X \rangle$	interface	§ 1		θ, Θ	sort, set of sorts	6.1
$A^{\mathsf{P}}, \ldots$	place constituent	§ 1		Φ	sorting formation rule	6.1
$A^{\mathsf{L}}, \ldots$	link constituent	§ 1		$`\mathrm{BG}(\Sigma)$	concrete Σ-bigraphs	6.1
$\langle A^{\mathsf{P}}, A^{\mathsf{L}} \rangle$	combination	§ 1		$\mathrm{BG}(\Sigma)$	abstract Σ-bigraphs	6.1
$\mathcal{X}$	all names	§ 2.1		$\mathcal{U}$	functor forgets sorts	§ 6.1
$\mathcal{V}$	all nodes	§ 2.1		s, t	many–one sorts	6.12
$\mathcal{E}$	all edges	§ 2.1				
$\mathcal{B}$	all bindings	§ 11.3		CATEGORIES, SETS		
V	node-set	2.1		$\mathbf{A}, \mathbf{B}, \ldots$	category	2.8
E	edge-set	2.2		$`\mathbf{A}, `\mathbf{B}, \ldots$	precategory	2.12
B	binding-set	§ 11.3		$\mathcal{F}$	functor	2.8
w	place	2.1		$\mathrm{dom}(I)$	domain	2.8
p	port	2.2		$\mathrm{cod}(I)$	codomain	2.8
q	point	2.2		$(I \to J)$	homset	2.8
ℓ	link	2.2		$I, J, \ldots$	object	2.8
$\mathsf{K}, \mathsf{L}, \mathsf{M}$	control	1.1		$f, g, \ldots$	arrow	2.8
				id	identity (arrow)	2.8

177

References

[1] Ubiquitous computing: experience, design and science. A Grand Challenge of UKCRC, the UK Computing Research Committee. http://www-dse.doc.ic.ac.uk/Projects/UbiNet/GC/Manifesto/manifesto.pdf.

[2] Equator. A 6-year Interdisciplinary Research Collaboration funded by the UK Engineering and Physical Sciences Research Council. http://www.equator.ac.uk.

[3] Baeten, J. and Weijland, W. (1990), *Process Algebra*. Cambridge Tracts in Theoretical Computer Science 18, Cambridge University Press.

[4] Barr, C. and Wells, M. (1990), *Category Theory for Computing Science*. Prentice Hall.

[5] Benson, D. (1975), The basic algebraic structures in categories of derivations. *Information and Control* **28**, 1–29.

[6] Berry, G. and Boudol, G. (1992), The chemical abstract machine. *Journal of Theoretical Computer Science* **96**, 217–248.

[7] Bettini, L. and De Nicola, R. (2005), Mobile distributed programming in X-Klaim. In: *SFM-05:Moby, 5th International School on Formal Methods for the Design of Computer, Communication and Software Systems: Mobile Computing*, Lecture Notes in Computer Science 3465, Springer-Verlag, 29–68.

[8] Bergstra, J. and Klop, J.-W. (1985), Algebra of communicating processes with abstraction. *Theoretical Computer Science* **37**, 77–121.

[9] Birkedal, L. and Hildebrandt, T. (2004), Bigraphical programming languages. Laboratory for Context-Dependent Mobile Communication, IT University, Denmark. http://www.itu.dk/research/bpl/.

[10] Birkedal, L., Bundgaard, M., Damgaard, T., Debois, S., Elsborg, E., Glenstrup, A., Hildebrandt, T., Milner, R. and Niss, H. (2006), Bigraphical programming languages for pervasive computing. In: *Proc. International Workshop on Combining Theory and Systems Building in Pervasive Computing*, 653–658.

[11] Birkedal, L., Debois, S., Elsborg, E., Hildebrandt, T. and Niss, H. (2006), Bigraphical models of context-aware systems. In: *Proc. 9th International Conference on Foundations of Software Science and Computation Structure*, Lecture Notes in Computer Science 3921, 187–201.

[12] Birkedal, L., Damgaard, T., Glenstrup, A. and Milner, R. (2007), Matching of bigraphs. In: *Proc. Workshop on Graph Transformation for Verification and Concurrency*, Electronic Notes in Theoretical Computer Science 175, Elsevier, 3–19.

[13] Brookes, S., Hoare, C. and Roscoe, W. (1984), A theory of communicating sequential processes. *J. ACM* **31**, 560–599.

[14] Birkedal, L., Debois, S. and Hildebrandt, T. (2008), On the construction of sorted reactive systems. In: *Proc. 19th International Conference on Concurrency Theory (CONCUR)*, Lecture Notes in Computer Science 5201, 218–232.

[15] Bundgaard, M. and Hildebrandt, T. (2006), Bigraphical semantics of higher-order mobile embedded resources with local names. In: *Proc. Workshop on Graph Transformation for Verification and Concurrency*, Electronic Notes in Theoretical Computer Science 154, Elsevier, 7–29.

[16] Bundgaard, M. and Sassone, V. (2006), Typed polyadic pi-calculus in bigraphs. In: *Proc. 8th ACM SIGPLAN International Conference on Principles and Practice of Declarative Programming*, 1–12.

[17] Bundgaard, M., Glenstrup, A., Hildebrandt, T., Højsgaard, E. and Niss, H. (2008), Formalising higher-order mobile embedded business processes with binding bigraphs. In: *Proc. 10th International Conference on Coordination Languages*, Lecture Notes in Computer Science 5052, 83–99.

[18] Cardelli, L. and Gordon, A. D. (2000), Mobile ambients. *Theoretical Computer Science* **240**, 177–213.

[19] Castellani, I. (2001), Process algebras with localities. In: *Handbook of Process Algebra*, eds Bergstra, J., Ponse, A. and Smolka, S., Elsevier, 945–1045.

[20] Cattani, G. L., Leifer, J. J. and Milner, R. (2000), Contexts and embeddings for closed shallow action graphs. University of Cambridge Computer Laboratory, Technical Report 496.

[21] Cheverst, K., Davies, N., Mitchell, K. and Friday, A. (2000), Experiences of developing and deploying a context-aware tourist guide: the GUIDE project. In: *Proc. Mobicom*, Boston, Massachusetts, 20–31.

[22] Clavel, M., Eker, S., Lincoln, P. and Meseguer, J. (1996), Priniciples of Maude. In: J. Meseguer (ed.) *Proc. First International Workshop on Rewriting Logic and its Applications*, Electronic Notes in Theoretical Computer Science 4, Elsevier, 1–25.

[23] Conforti, G., Macedonio, D. and Sassone, V. (2005), Spatial logics for bigraphs. In: *International Conference on Automata, Languages and Programming*, Lecture Notes in Computer Science 3580, Springer-Verlag, 766–778.

[24] Conforti, G., Macedonio, D. and Sassone, V. (2005), Bigraphical Logics for XML. In: *Proc. 13th Italian Symposium on Advanced Datebase Systems (SEBD)*, 392–399.

[25] Crowcroft, J. (2006), The privacy and safety impact of technology choices for command, communications and control of the public highway. *SIGCOMM Comput. Commun. Rev.* **36**(1), 53–58.

[26] Damgaard, T. and Birkedal, L. (2006), Axiomatizing binding bigraphs. *Nordic Journal of Computing* **13**(1–2), 58–77.

[27] Danos, V., Feret, J., Fontana, W. and Krivine, J. (2007), Scalable modelling of biological pathways. In: Z. Shao (ed.), *Proceedings of APLAS*, 4807, 139–157.

[28] Dix, A. *et al.* (2000), Exploiting space and location as a design framework for interactive mobile systems. *ACM Trans. Comput. Human Interact* **7**(3), 285–321.

[29] Ehrig, H. (1979), Introduction to the algebraic theory of graph grammars. In: *Graph Grammars and their Application to Computer Science and Biology*, Lecture Notes in Computer Science 73, Springer-Verlag, 1–69.

[30] Ehrig, H. (2002), Bigraphs meet double pushouts. EATCS Bulletin 78, October 2002, 72–85.

[31] Gadducci, F., Heckel, R. and Llabrés, M. (1999), A bi-categorical axiomatisation of concurrent graph rewriting. In: *Proc. 8th Conference on Category Theory in Computer Science (CTCS)*, Electronic Notes in Theoretical Computer Science 29, Elsevier Science.

[32] Gadducci, F. and Montanari, U. (2000), The tile model. In: Plotkin, G., Stirling, C. and Tofte, M. (eds) *Proof, Language and Interaction*, MIT Press, 133–166.

[33] Gardner, P. (2000), From process calculi to process frameworks. In: *Proc. 11th International Conference on Concurrency Theory (CONCUR)*, Lecture Notes in Computer Science 1877, Springer-Verlag, 69–88.

[34] Gardner, P. and Wischik, L. (2000), Explicit fusions. In: *Proc. Mathematical Foundations of Computer Science*, Lecture Notes in Computer Science 1893, Springer-Verlag, 373–382.

[35] Grohmann, D. and Miculan, M. (2007), Directed bigraphs. In: *Proceedings of 23rd MFPS Conference*, Electronic Notes in Computer Science 173, Elsevier, 121–137.

[36] Grohmann, D. and Miculan, M. (2007), Reactive systems over directed bigraphs. In: *Proceedings of 18th Conference on Concurrency Theory (CONCUR)*, Lecture Notes in Computer Science 4703, Springer-Verlag, 380–394.

[37] Grohmann, D. and Miculan, M. (2008), An algebra for directed bigraphs. In: *Proc. 4th International Workshop in Computing with Terms and Graphs*, Electronic Notes in Theoretical Computer Science **203**(1), 49–63.

[38] Hasegawa, M. (1999), Models of sharing graphs. PhD Dissertation, Division of Informatics, University of Ednburgh. Available as Technical Report ECS–LFCS–97–360. Also in Springer Series of Distinguished Dissertations in Computer Science.

[39] Hennessy, M. (2007), *A Distributed Pi Calculus*. Cambridge University Press.

[40] Hennessy, M. and Milner, R. (1985), Algebraic laws for non-determinism and concurrency. *Journal of ACM* **32**, 137–161.

[41] Hildebrandt, T., Niss, H. and Olsen M. (2006), Formalising business process execution with bigraphs and Reactive XML. In: *Proc. 8th International Conference on Coordination Models and Languages*, Lecture Notes in Computer Science 4038, Springer Verlag, 113–129.

[42] Hillston, J. (1996), *A Compositional Approach to Performance Modelling*. Cambridge University Press.

[43] Hirsch, D. and Montanari, U. (2001), Synchronised hyperedge replacement with name mobility. In: *Proc. 12th International Conference on Concurrency Theory (CONCUR)*, Lecture Notes in Computer Science 2154, Springer-Verlag, 121–136.

[44] Hoare, C.A.R. (1985), *Communicating Sequential Processes*. Prentice Hall.

[45] Dash, R., Parkes, D. and Jennings, N. (2003), Computational mechanism design: a call to arms. *IEEE Intell. Syst.* **18**(6), 40–47.

[46] Jensen, O. H. (2006), *Mobile Processes in Bigraphs*. Monograph available at http://www.cl.cam.ac.uk/~rm135/Jensen-monograph.html.

[47] Jensen, O. H. and Milner, R. (2003), Bigraphs and transitions. In: *30th SIGPLAN-SIGACT Symposium on Principles of Programming Languages*, ACM Press, 38–49.

[48] Jensen, O. H. and Milner, R. (2004), Bigraphs and mobile processes (revised). Technical Report UCAM-CL-TR-580, University of Cambridge Computer Laboratory.

[49] Joyal, A. (1986), Foncteurs analytiques et espèces de structures. In: *Proc. Colloque de combinatoire énumérative*, Lecture Notes in Mathematics 1234, Springer-Verlag, 126–159.

[50] Kelly, G. M. (1982), *Basic Concepts of Enriched Category Theory*. Lecture Notes in Mathematics 64, Cambridge University Press. Republished (2005) in *Theory and Applications of Categories* **10**, 1–136.

[51] Krivine, J., Milner, R. and Troina, A. (2008), Stochastic bigraphs. In: *Proc. 24th International Conference on Mathematical Foundations of Programming Systems*, to appear in Electronic Notes in Theoretical Computer Science.

[52] Lafont, Y. (1990), Interaction nets. In: *Proc. 17th ACM Symposium on Principles of Programming Languages*, ACM Press, 95–108.

[53] Lawvere, F. W. (1973), Metric spaces, generalized logic, and closed categories. Rendiconti del Seminario Matematico e Fisico di Milano XLII, 135–166. Republished (2002) in *Reprints in Theory and Applications of Categories*, 1, 1–37.

[54] Leifer, J. J. (2001), Operational congruences for reactive systems. PhD Dissertation, University of Cambridge Computer Laboratory. Distributed in revised form as Technical Report 521. Available from http://pauillac.inria.fr/~leifer.

[55] Leifer, J. J. and Milner, R. (2000), Deriving bisimulation congruences for reactive systems. In: *Proc. CONCUR 2000, 11th International Conference on Concurrency Theory*, Lecture Notes in Computer Science 1877, Springer-Verlag, 243–258. Available at http://pauillac.inria.fr/~leifer.

[56] Leifer, J. J. and Milner, R. (2006), Transition systems, link graphs and Petri nets. *Mathematical Structures in Computer Science* **16**, 989–1047.

[57] Meseguer, J. (1992), Conditional rewriting logic as a unified model of concurrency. *Theoretical Computer Science* **96**, 73–155.

[58] Meseguer, J. and Montanari, U. (1990), Petri nets are monoids. *Information and Computation* **88**, 105–155.

[59] Milne, G. and Milner, R. (1979), Concurrent processes and their syntax. *J. ACM* **26**, 302–321.

[60] Milner, R. (1979), Flow graphs and flow algebras. *J. ACM* **26**, 794–818.

[61] Milner, R. (1980), *A Calculus of Communicating Systems*. Lecture Notes in Computer Science 92, Springer-Verlag.

[62] Milner, R. (1996), Calculi for interaction. *Acta Informatica* **33**, 707–737.

[62a] Milner, R. (1999), *Communicating and Mobile Systems: The π-calculus*. Cambridge University Press.

[63] Milner, R. (2001), Bigraphical reactive systems. In: *Proc. 12th International Conference on Concurrency Theory*, Lecture Notes in Computer Science 2154, Springer-Verlag, 16–35.

[64] Milner, R. (2005), Axioms for bigraphical structure. *Mathematical Structures in Computer Science* **15**, 1005–1032.

[65] Milner, R. (2006), Pure bigraphs: Structure and dynamics. *Information and Computation* **204**, 60–122.

[66] Milner, R. (2006), Ubiquitous computing: Shall we understand it? *The Computer Journal* **49**, 383–389. (The first *Computer Journal Lecture*.)

[67] Milner, R., Parrow, J. and Walker D. (1992), A calculus of mobile processes, Parts I and II. *Journal of Information and Computation* **100**, 1–40 and 41–77.

[68] Park, D. (1981), Concurrency and automata on infinite sequences. In: *Proc. 5th GI-Conference Conference on Theoretical Computer Science*, Lecture Notes in Computer Science 104, Springer-Verlag, 167–183.

[69] Parrow, J. and Victor, B. (1998), The fusion calculus: expressiveness and symmetry in mobile processes. In: *Proceedings of Logics in Computer Science 1998*, IEEE Computer Society Press, 176–185.

[70] Petri, C. (1962), *Kommunikation mit Automaten*. Institut für Instrumentelle Informatik, Schriften des IIM 2, 1962.

[71] Priami, C. (1995), Stochastic π-calculus. *The Computer Journal* **38**(6), 578–589.

[72] Regev, A., Silverman, W. and Shapiro, E. (2001), Representation and simulation of biochemical processes using the π-calculus process algebra. In: *Proc. Pacific Symposium of Biocomputing 2001 (PSB2001)*, Vol. 6, 459–470.

[73] Sangiorgi, D. and Walker, D. (2001), *The π-calculus: A Theory of Mobile Processes*. Cambridge University Press.

[74] Sassone, V. and Sobocinski, P. (2002), Deriving bisimulation congruences: a 2-categorical approach. *Electronic Notes in Theoretical Computer Science* **68**(2), 105–123.

[75] Sassone, V. and Sobocinski, P. (2005), Locating reaction with 2-categories. *Theoretical Computer Science* **333**, 297–327.

[76] Sewell, P. (2002), From rewrite rules to bisimulation congruences. *Theoretical Computer Science* **274**, 183–230.

[77] Sloman, M. *et al.* (2007), AMUSE: Autonomic management of ubiquitous e-health systems. In: *Concurrency and Computation: Practice and Experience*, John Wiley & Sons.

[78] Terese (Bezem, M., Klop, J.-W. and de Vrijer, R. *et al.*) (2003) *Term Rewriting Systems*. Cambridge University Press.

[79] Weiser, M. (1991), The computer for the 21st century. *Sci. Am.* **265**(3), 94–104.

[80] Wojciechowski, P. T. and Sewell, P. (1999), Nomadic Pict: Language and infrastructure design for mobile agents. In: *Proc. ASA/MA*, Palm Springs, California.

[81] Wooldridge, M. (1999), Intelligent agents. In: *Multi-Agent Systems*, MIT Press.

[82] Zhang, M., Shi, L., Zhu, L., Wang, Y., Feng, L. and Pu, F. (2008), A bigraphical model of WSBPEL. In: *2nd Joint IEEE/IFIP Symposium on Theoretical Aspects of Software Engineering*, IEEE Computer Society, 117–120.

Index